Empowering Play in Primary Education

The education system does not always promote or give primacy to play within the curriculum, yet research and policy alike acknowledge the importance of play for children and young people. *Empowering Play in Primary Education* addresses this issue, contributing innovative ideas about how teachers, teaching assistants and children may incorporate play within the classroom while also advocating for its use as a powerful tool for ensuring successful learning outcomes.

Packed with imaginative ideas and practical suggestions, this essential book combines theory with tried and tested practice to encourage and inspire teachers to make use of the pedagogy of play and enhance their children's learning experience. Topics explored within the book include but are not limited to:

- Playful enquiry exploring the relationship between academic research and practitioner wisdom;
- Practices of play within different settings;
- Inclusive practice for play in the primary school;
- Designing a high-quality, low-cost model for play in the Early Years;
- Play within the wider school community, e.g., playful leadership and pedagogy as play.

This is an essential read for any teacher, teaching assistant, headteacher, senior leader or policy maker who wishes to embed more opportunities for play within their curriculum and school.

Aimee Durning is the Director of Inclusion & Community at the University of Cambridge Primary School, the first University Primary School in the country, which has a principled, research-informed approach to education.

Sara Baker is a Professor in Developmental Psychology and Education at the University of Cambridge and a principal investigator in the Centre for Research on Play in Education, Development and Learning and has worked with teachers and early years educators throughout the UK.

Paul Ramchandani is the LEGO Professor of Play in Education, Development and Learning at the University of Cambridge. He also works as a Consultant Child and Adolescent Psychiatrist in the NHS.

Unlocking Research
Series Editors: James Biddulph and Julia Flutter

Unlocking Research offers support and ideas for students and practising teachers, enriching their knowledge of research and its application in primary school contexts. Packed with imaginative ideas and practical suggestions, the series aims to empower teachers, teaching assistants and school leaders to take research-informed and principled approaches to making necessary changes in schools so that teaching and learning ignites the social imagination for 21st century educators and learners.

Expanding Possibilities for Inclusive Learning
Edited by Kristine Black-Hawkins and Ashley Grinham-Smith

Unleashing Children's Voices in New Democratic Primary Education
Edited by James Biddulph, Luke Rolls and Julia Flutter

Sculpting New Creativities in Primary Education
Edited by Pam Burnard and Michelle Loughrey

Reimagining Professional Development in Schools
Edited by Eleanore Hargreaves and Luke Rolls

Inspiring Primary Curriculum Design
Edited by James Biddulph and Julia Flutter

Empowering Play in Primary Education
Edited by Aimee Durning, Sara Baker and Paul Ramchandani

For more information about this series, please visit: https://www.routledge.com/Unlocking-Research/book-series/URS

Empowering Play in Primary Education

Edited by Aimee Durning, Sara Baker
and Paul Ramchandani

LONDON AND NEW YORK

Designed cover image: Art by the Children of University of Cambridge Primary School and Linda Culverwell of Artbash www.artbash.co.uk

First published 2025
by Routledge
4 Park Square, Milton Park, Abingdon, Oxon OX14 4RN

and by Routledge
605 Third Avenue, New York, NY 10158

Routledge is an imprint of the Taylor & Francis Group, an informa business

© 2025 selection and editorial matter, Aimee Durning, Sara Baker and Paul Ramchandani; individual chapters, the contributors

The right of Aimee Durning, Sara Baker and Paul Ramchandani to be identified as the authors of the editorial material, and of the authors for their individual chapters, has been asserted in accordance with sections 77 and 78 of the Copyright, Designs and Patents Act 1988.

All rights reserved. No part of this book may be reprinted or reproduced or utilised in any form or by any electronic, mechanical, or other means, now known or hereafter invented, including photocopying and recording, or in any information storage or retrieval system, without permission in writing from the publishers.

Trademark notice: Product or corporate names may be trademarks or registered trademarks, and are used only for identification and explanation without intent to infringe.

British Library Cataloguing-in-Publication Data
A catalogue record for this book is available from the British Library

Library of Congress Cataloging-in-Publication Data
Names: Durning, Aimee, editor. | Baker, Sara, editor. | Ramchandani, Paul, editor.
Title: Empowering play in primary education / edited by Aimee Durning, Sara Baker and Paul Ramchandani.
Description: New York : Routledge, 2024. | Series: Unlocking research | Includes bibliographical references and index.
Identifiers: LCCN 2023055916 (print) | LCCN 2023055917 (ebook) | ISBN 9781032342726 (hbk) | ISBN 9781032342733 (pbk) | ISBN 9781003321279 (ebk)
Subjects: LCSH: Play. | Early childhood education. | Education, Primary. | Child development.
Classification: LCC LB1139.35.P55 E66 2024 (print) | LCC LB1139.35.P55 (ebook) | DDC 372.21--dc23/eng/20240206
LC record available at https://lccn.loc.gov/2023055916
LC ebook record available at https://lccn.loc.gov/2023055917

ISBN: 978-1-032-34272-6 (hbk)
ISBN: 978-1-032-34273-3 (pbk)
ISBN: 978-1-003-32127-9 (ebk)

DOI: 10.4324/9781003321279

Typeset in Bembo and Helvetica
by KnowledgeWorks Global Ltd.

Contents

The state of play: (primary education) introduction 1
Sara Baker, Aimee Durning and Paul Ramchandani

1 Playful enquiry: between academic research and practitioner wisdom 4
Paul Ramchandani, Aimee Durning and Sara Baker

2 Play instead of learning, or play as learning? Reconceptualising play for a new generation of children 17
Sarah Seleznyov

3 Practices of play in education: play at home, school readiness, and a positive transition to school 27
Beth Barker and Christine O'Farrelly

4 Inclusive practice and play in primary education 48
Lenka Janik-Blaskova and Stephen Kilgour

5 Designing opportunities for play in primary education: A no-trade off approach to play and learning 66
Luke Rolls, Rachel Lownsbrough and Liam Connolly

6 Risky play in primary schools 86
Helen Dodd, Rachel Nesbit, and Matt Robinson

7 BRAC Play Labs: designing a high-quality, low-cost model for early years 101
Erum Mariam, Jahanara Ahmad, and Sarah Tabassum

8 Developing playful mathematical thinking in Ghanaian
   early primary classrooms through the use of the game "Achi" 121
   Esinam Ami Avornyo and Edith Afari Mensah

9 Becoming a playful school 134
   Idah Khan O'Neill and Bo Stjerne Thomsen

10 Playful school leadership: being serious about leadership playfully 147
   James Biddulph and Neil Gibrid

11 Fostering playful learning in school through a Pedagogy of Play 167
   Mara Krechevsky

   Play is for children not for school 185
   James Biddulph

Appendix *188*
Index *200*

1
The state of play: (primary education) introduction

Sara Baker, Aimee Durning and Paul Ramchandani

It is our privilege to have developed a book on play as part of this series of Unlocking Research. The chapters and the overall focus of the book reflect our attempt to bring together research and practice to try to support and inform teaching and learning in primary education. The overall endeavour represents a collaboration between the University of Cambridge Primary School (UCPS) and the Research Centre for Play in Education, Development and Learning (PEDAL) at the University of Cambridge.

We have been fortunate to work together with teachers and researchers in developing the chapters that you see here, and we are grateful to all of them for their contributions, covering different facets of play and learning. What we hope to add through the publication of this book is an up-to-date look at research and practice to share ideas that teachers, teaching assistants and school leaders can use to make every child's experience of school as positive as it can be.

For many, the first thing that comes to mind when we say 'play' is a game, like hopscotch. However, play has many meanings and can take a variety of forms, as illustrated in the variety of chapters in this book. Play is everywhere. While play is vital according to the UN Convention on the rights of the child (1989), global education systems and forms of accountability, assessment, pedagogy, knowledge and curricula do not always promote or give primacy to play. There are many misconceptions about play which can limit its use. For example in their chapter in this book, Rolls, Lownsbrough and Connolly describe the 'play as discovery only' misconception. Instead of this radical view, the authors explain how discovery and experiential learning can be combined with teacher-directed and curriculum-linked experiences to generate the most effective learning opportunities. For instance, an awareness of travelling from one physical place to another, how long it takes, observing changes in the environment … these are all child-centred experiences that lay the foundation for more abstract teacher-led geography work with maps.

In some cases play is curtailed in schools because of a mindset that would place play and learning in separate spaces. To play, then, would be to relax or entertain, but not in any 'useful' way and so why should schools think about it? More recently, the case has gained momentum for considering play as an integral part of learning and development. One needs only to look at how engaged learners are when their work is meaningful to them, when they can have some say as to the direction it takes, and when they are given opportunities to approach their learning in a variety of ways. These features of learning through play promote learners' agency in their learning, and their desire to keep coming back for more. Instead of feeling like school is being imposed on them, they feel like active members of the learning community, with space and support to grow and learn.

Creative schools and teachers are incorporating innovation into their pedagogy in the UK and internationally as part of a play-rich diet because they can see the benefits. Children learn through play, not only to communicate, problem-solve, be creative and move their bodies, but they also develop their understanding of maths, language and so many subject areas traditionally seen as the remit of 'chalk and talk'.

In the Seleznyov chapter (Chapter 2), we hear about School 360 in Stratford, London, where educators have been on a journey of reflection and innovation, putting play to work in a variety of ways for both the children and the adults to realise their full potential. Additional inspiring examples of the 'Pedagogy of Play' can be seen in Krechevsky's chapter (Chapter 11) which includes tools for teachers on taking responsible risks and sharing decision-making with learners. Both of these chapters illustrate the possibilities of evidence-informed pedagogy that puts children at the centre, carried along by adults' thoughtful consideration at each step.

At its core, play develops children's agency and, by extension, educators' agency too. Excellent pedagogy can promote learning intentions set by the teacher while at the same time allowing space for the teachers and learners to explore, enact, reflect, adapt … in short, to play. O'Neill and Stjerne Thomsen's chapter explains how a group of teachers in Denmark host their own reflective study group to 'see-think-wonder' about what is happening in their classrooms, giving each other the space to explore ideas and collectively think through their pedagogical decisions.

These beacons of innovative educational practice give hope to others, who may feel confined by the habitual way of doing things. In other countries, too, educators are working with researchers to develop teaching techniques based on playful learning. Avornyo and Mensah's chapter brings us a case study from Ghana, where a familiar game is adapted for teaching maths. The range of examples brought to life in this book shows how play can be incorporated into teaching and learning by evolution, without requiring a whole-school revolution. It is achievable!

One of the known factors in achieving a playful approach to teaching and learning is the tone that is set by senior leaders. Gilbride and Biddulph dedicate their chapter to playful leadership, which involves creating enabling environments that support play for staff as well as for children. This can involve playing by example, showing colleagues it is ok to take risks and experiment and go outside of the classroom walls to create collective, joyful experiences so the playful ethos includes learners of all ages.

In addition to the examples of play being used in mainstream school settings, this book showcases innovations in the ways educators and children can learn through play, in play and with play in unusually challenging circumstances. For example, in the Marium, Ahmad and Tabassum chapter, we learn about the power of Play Labs for children in low-resource settings in Bangladesh. By design, these spaces provide excellent examples of building a sense of ownership of children's learning in the wider community.

The richness of play, the many forms it can take and the variety of benefits it can offer to both children and adults, means that play can easily be adapted to include all learners. Blaskova and Kilgour's chapter reminds us how, in play, children can be themselves and they have the chance to build positive relationships with others. The value of play for well-being is also seen in schools that have a policy supporting risky play, as described in the Dodd, Nesbit and Robinson's chapter (Chapter 6). These authors suggest that risky play builds learners' sense of adventure and can be foundational to developing children's self-confidence. Schools need policies to support a variety of types of play, with inclusion in mind, and to ensure that staff are confident in themselves with a shared vision for the school.

The importance of what children do in the here and now, their individuality, their motivations and their needs for a fulfilling life in the present sometimes takes a back seat when it comes to schools' duty to prepare children for later learning. Barker and O'Farrelly use their chapter to highlight the lived experiences of young children who are just starting school. When asked what matters to them, children talk about their excitement about learning, and also their need for security, for friendships and for play.

We wish to dedicate this collection of work to our colleague, Dr David Whitebread, who was a constant advocate for children's right to play. We know he would be delighted to read each and every one of the chapters in this book, especially as he worked so hard throughout his career to get teachers and researchers working together to 'unlock research' and co-create solutions to education's challenges.

The invitation is open: let's get serious about play and the benefits of learning through play in all its forms, for children and adults, in schools and beyond.

CHAPTER 1

Playful enquiry: between academic research and practitioner wisdom

Paul Ramchandani, Aimee Durning and Sara Baker

Play is what humans do. If you live near a school or walk past a playground, the sounds of children at play remind us of the social, creative and emotional experiences of playing. We can assume that as children grow to adolescence and then to adulthood, they stop playing (or reduce types of play significantly) and become serious members of society. And yet, the most innovative ideas arise from playful creativities (Biddulph and Burnard, 2021) and within communities of practice where people are excited about problems, are enthusiastic about engaging with diversities and, through this intercultural playful lens, look for solutions to questions, perhaps not yet asked.

In this chapter we introduce the choreography between academic research and practitioner wisdom in relation to play. We provide a brief introduction to the work at the Play in Education, Development and Learning (PEDAL) Research Centre and also the University of Cambridge Primary School where we, the editors of this book, work. Both education spaces have play as a core part of their focus and approach. We journey from the PEDAL Research Centre through whole school playful enquiry and to the personal reflections of Aimee, whose engagement with playful enquiry brought new ideas and insights into the life of children with whom she works.

Centre for Research on Play in Education, Development and Learning (PEDAL), University of Cambridge

The Centre for Research on PEDAL was established at the University of Cambridge in 2015. It was initially funded by a donation from the LEGO Foundation, following several years of collaborative work on projects between staff at the University of Cambridge and the LEGO Group. The donation also funded a permanent professorial position at the University (the LEGO Professor of PEDAL).

The LEGO Foundation has continued to fund much of the work (now alongside other research funders) and is also focused on play, and the role that play has in children's education. The PEDAL Centre has grown from these early beginnings and now has a large team of staff and students from a wide range of disciplinary, geographical and cultural backgrounds. A large component of the Centre's research work has focused on children's learning in the early years and primary school and the factors that facilitate this. This includes the key foundations that play can give for social relationships, for good physical and emotional health as well as for children's love of learning. Alongside these fundamentals we also seek to understand which aspects of play and playfulness can lead to more effective, long-term learning for children – right from the start of life. PEDAL's role is to conduct research of the highest quality and to interrogate existing research to find its strengths and limitations to yield lessons for teaching practice in primary schools and the early years. This involves work in the UK but also collaborations with colleagues in many countries, including Ghana, Kenya, South Africa, Mexico, Brazil, Denmark and Bangladesh.

In the UK, a large part of our work is based in primary schools and conducted in collaboration with teachers and other key staff. We consider approaches to learning that can incorporate play and the essential ingredients of play – not for the sake of it, but because some elements of the playful approach can enhance learning and lead to more effective teaching (Skene et al., 2022).

For example, in a two-form entry school in the East of England, year 1 teachers had the backing of their headteacher to reorganise their classrooms to align with their continuous provision. They removed most of the tables and chairs to enable children to work in more creative ways, collaborating in pairs on the floor on a number line, or conducting investigations outside, with children recording their findings by taking photos and writing in a notebook they carried around. The teachers also repurposed the shared space between their two year 1 rooms into a dedicated science and creative arts area (it was near the sinks!).

In a school in Stratford in London, we worked with teaching assistants who were focused on their use of questioning to extend pupils' learning. Engaging in reflections on the skills they are learning, whether in PE or a phonics session, allows children even from the earliest phases of primary school to develop metacognition and a sense of themselves as learners.

We have also worked with colleagues in initial teacher training programmes who want to incorporate more on the pedagogy of play into early career teachers' practices. For those colleagues, playful approaches were being woven into thinking about classroom management. Involving children in establishing classroom rules, as well as reviewing them, can be engaging and gives both children and staff ownership and responsibility over the classroom climate.

There are a wide range of projects running at the PEDAL Centre. If you wish to find out more about PEDAL's work, you can find more on the website (www.pedalhub.net).

Playful enquiry: one school's journey

Many years before the foundations were laid in 2014, a large triangle of land to the west of Cambridge was earmarked for a new development. The University of Cambridge decided, as part of the requirement for a large housing development, that it would open a primary school. Its conception and development were captured in *A University's Challenge, Cambridge's Primary School for the Nation* (Gronn and Biddulph, 2016). James Biddulph (author of Chapter 10 in this book), the inaugural headteacher of the country's first university primary school made a bold move to place play at the centre of the curriculum. Working with Penny Coltman and David Whitebread, both with considerable expertise in the academic knowledge and practitioner wisdom of early years practice (having both been early years teachers) outlined this play-based vision in their 2015 chapter, 'within UCPS, a play-based pedagogical approach will be extended into Key stage 1' (p. 119). However, James was unsure why play had to end at the beginning of children's first year in primary school. Could it be possible to extend playful enquiry through to year 6 (11-year-old children)? Could it expand children's imaginations, understanding of self and other, demand deeper thinking from them or help build synapses across the diverse knowledges within the UK curriculum? Through his knowledge of creativities and understanding of children, James promoted an approach of playful enquiry from the youngest in the school to the oldest. Initially this was a relatively easy task because the school opened to only 120 children: two reception classes, one year 1 class and one year 2 class.

As the years passed and the school grew, play took on many different guises – not just the usual free play experienced during the break from classroom learning but also play that was central to the learning experiences within curriculum time. Teachers and teaching assistants grappled with the competing demands placed on them for knowledge-rich acquisition compared with the freer opportunities that playful enquiry afforded them. James informed his team that all aspects of the school day should feature playful learning opportunities. But how did this manifest and what was the impact?

Elsewhere, we have described the curriculum design in detail (Coltman and Rolls, 2020). In Figure 1.1, the central focus of compassionate citizenship is supported by a pedagogy that has oracy and dialogue, habits of mind and playful enquiry as 'golden threads' to frame the learning `experience for all children, including the oldest in the school and also including the adults during their own professional development and learning (Biddulph and Cariss, 2020).

For the children at University of Cambridge Primary School (UCPS), playful enquiry involved the following guiding principles:

- Creation of open-ended spaces (Fox, Clarke, Winstanley and Warwick, 2020; Bellfield, Dyer, McAleavey and Erskine, 2021)
- Child-led and adult-guided tasks and activities (Sutton, Downham and Rhodes, 2020)

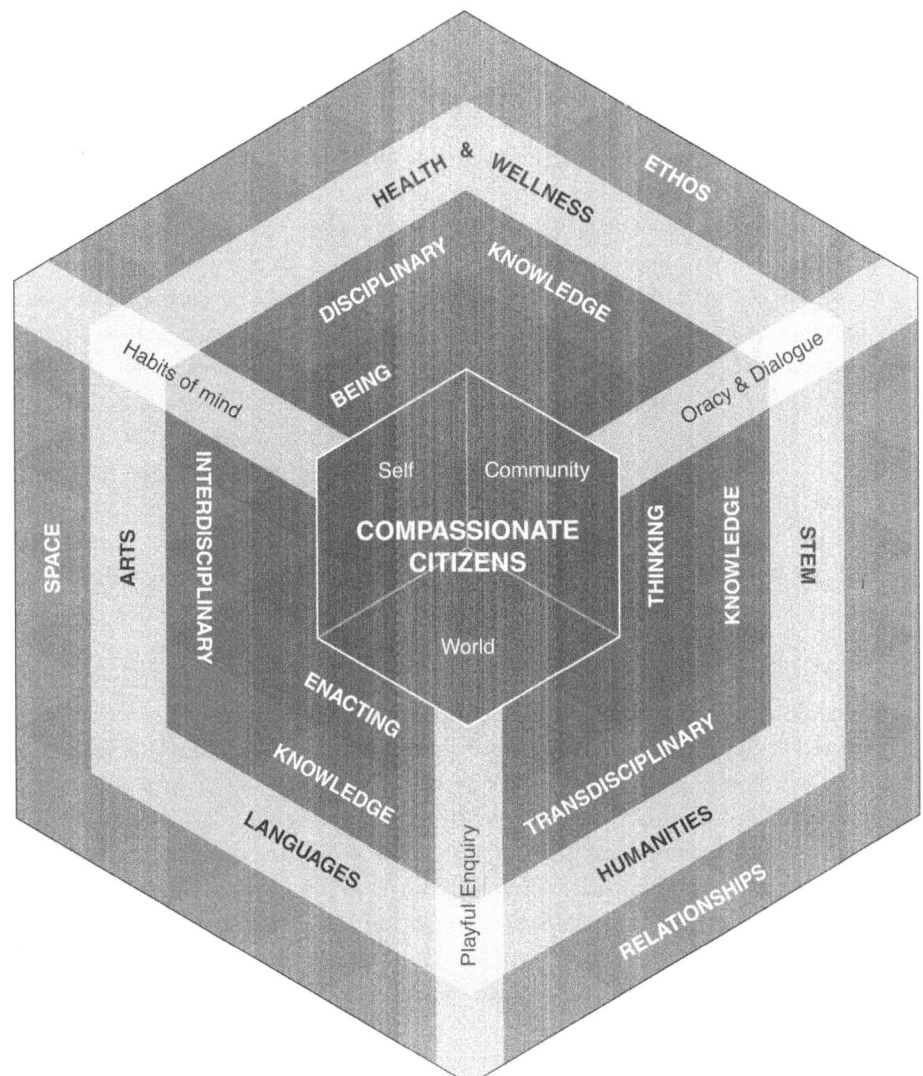

Figure 1.1 UCPS curriculum model

- Linked with the curriculum and not seen as a separate 'activity', e.g. play is part of learning (Whitebread and Basilio, 2012)
- Encourages teachers and teaching assistants to stand back and observe for the following: wonder, joy and delight; social interactions; oracy and dialogue (e.g. what children talk about in and through play); how knowledge is developed through play (e.g. role playing the Great Fire of London would include substantive vocabulary (e.g. that they would not include use of mobile phones during the role play) (Biddulph and Baldacchino, 2022)

Playful enquiry is described on the UCPS's website as follows:

It is recognised that children experiencing some feeling of being in control of their environment and their learning is fundamental to them developing confidence in themselves, and their responsibility to positively manage setbacks and challenges (Goswami, 2015). In play, children set their own tasks, which may or may not be goal oriented. Sometimes the pleasure in a playful activity is gained through engaging with and exploring a process, with no particular end in mind. Children spontaneously set themselves challenges in their play and, given a choice, will often choose a task which is more challenging than one which an adult might have thought appropriate. Providing children with achievable challenges, and supporting them so they can meet them, is a powerful way to encourage positive attitudes to learning, and the children's independent ability to take on challenging tasks (Whitebread and Coltman, 2016).

(UCPS Website 2023: Learning & Curriculum Pedagogical Approach, Playful Enquiry)

As we explored and played with our practice at UCPS, we started asking questions about the quality of learning that was happening through these playful moments: were the children aware that they were *learning* through playful moments? Probably not. What does play look like in a year 6 class? Did play have to be planned? Or was the phenomenon of play present in some lessons and not in others? As the years passed and the curriculum developed, these moments became intwined with project learning (enquiry), STEAM lessons (STEM) (science, technology, engineering and maths) plus the A which refers to the Arts and related to creativities) and, for our youngest children, the concept of playful enquiry.

For the team, many playful moments were witnessed in classrooms, learning streets (corridors) and outside. What became surprising was that through their play, there was a releasing of imagination, or an emancipation from formal learning, which for some children was a time to shine. Aimee's experience of this 'ah-ha moment' was captured in her journal:

One playful occurrence that is etched in my mind was Year 6, taking on the role of evacuees during their World War 2 project. In groups they stood outside with numerous props, waiting at an imaginary railway station. Alone, fearful and immersed in 1939 London. For half an hour the play was reminiscent of how children played half a century ago before the inventions of mobile phones, social media, and games consoles.

Educators at UCPS have been encouraged to trust in the power of play to support development, socialisation and learning beyond the usual remit of early years. Many in key stage one and beyond have witnessed the children grow in confidence, understanding and knowledge in a particular curriculum area because of playful moments. The Teaching and Learning Policy guides educators in their understanding of play and empowers them to offer choice, challenge and memorable learning opportunities to all children. In Figure 1.2, an extract from the Teaching and Learning Policy.

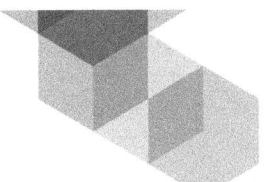

Figure 1.2 UCPS Playful enquiry poster

Bridging research to practice

One of the ways in which the PEDAL Research Centre has engaged with schools is through a project called 'Play, Learning and Narrative Skills (PLaNS)'. Within the research, the concept of guided play rather than free play was explored. Readers can have full access to the teacher handbook which explains the research and how to enable play practice in classroom contexts (https://www.pedalhub.net/?library=plans-handbook).

At UCPS, the research was incorporated into English lessons and involved the following:

- Integration with the planned curriculum and not an 'add on'
- Direct teaching of knowledge and vocabulary (e.g. about Christopher Columbus and the ethics of invasion. The teacher taught the children the relevant curriculum knowledge content so that during their play, there was accuracy about the historical period.)
- Well-considered groupings – children were placed into triads, building from oracy and dialogue research (Mercer and Littleton, 2007)
- Setting expectations – the children were taught the rules of dialogue (Talk Agreements, see PLaNs Handbook)
- Professional development for teachers and teaching assistants to understand how they could support, intervene and stand back from guided play
- Ensuring inclusion for all children through planning

Exploring the impact of play for one adult's practice – Aimee's playful journey

As Paul Ramchandani writes, 'Play gives children opportunity – to develop skills, to learn, to solve problems and grow healthy relationships. If they are physically active during play, it also brings health benefits. Widening access to play, particularly early in life, is one way of reducing the differences in life chances that we see in society' (Ramchandani, 2019, p. 6).

This quote frames my thinking in this section. How fortunate I have been to work in a school which understands the value of play. So much so, that play is considered a golden thread which runs through the curriculum, as a major artery providing each classroom, child, educator with playful opportunities.

Through my continuous development at UCPS, I consider myself an advocate for play in schools because formal learning can be experienced by children as a serious acquisition of knowledge, devoid of playful characteristics for many children, which unfortunately can extinguish any desire to love the experience of learning. My experiences as a teaching assistant and school leader have afforded me to have witnessed the power of play and its numerous health (both physical and mental) benefits. In this section, I share my personal reflections and insights as I grappled with trying to develop playful enquiry in my own practice.

Reflections from a teaching assistant in one school

My own unlocking of play research occurred when I encountered a curriculum design which featured playful enquiry. Figure 1.1 explains the central focus of the curriculum design, the three golden threads of habits of mind: oracy & dialogue and play! My knowledge and understanding about the power of play has developed, as has our curriculum design. I have acquired knowledge about child development and how play provides opportunities to reach developmental milestones.

As a practitioner and the unlocking of research, this has occurred via my own professional development as a student with the Open University, through additional academic reading and by carefully observing the interactions between children at school. I also visited the PEDAL Hub and completed The LEGO Foundation's short professional development online course: *Social Learning and Collaboration in Schools: Learning to Thrive through Play*. This course has created numerous pathways to explore in relation to play and primary education at my school.

During the years at UCPS, I have become interested in those children who do not have the skills to meet a 'good level of development' at the end of their reception year (even after a year of play-based learning) and those who, through no fault of their own, find themselves unable to play with other children or adults because of some degree of missed socialisation in their lives. This could possibly be due to trauma or periods of national lockdown or causes yet to be discovered.

Back in 2015, I had no idea what playful enquiry would look like in the primary classroom. That was my first mistake! Play happens everywhere in school, as the headteacher kept reminding us! What do I mean by play? What type of play? Many educators consider play as children's unstructured time away from the classroom. This is certainly what I thought before I joined the UCPS. Pre-UCPS I believed classroom learning to be a time of serious concentration and listening from the children as the class teacher gifted their knowledge to the class. Slowly, I began to realise that play comes in many forms and that children would experience different feelings and emotions during play. I began to notice the playful learning opportunities afforded to the class that I was working in with Mr Rolls (year 2, class teacher) and how important unstructured playtimes are. Playtime is an essential part of the school day for some children to unwind and engage with their peers away from the interference and demands of adults and the curriculum. Some children, as we know, find school difficult and playtime becomes the time shine, a time to shake off a sense of academic dread, a time to connect and belong.

Throughout the years at UCPS, I was to discover and witness the power of classroom play. I can imagine that there are some educators who consider that play should happen only at playtime. These educators may struggle to understand the value of play and how play can support learning behaviours. For the team at UCPS and the children we educate during their primary school years, play provides a powerful pedagogical device within our teaching, learning and development toolkit.

Playful enquiry: one child's journey

As educators, we assume that children are naturally able to play, and they arrive in school with these skills fully embedded and ready to take part in playful learning opportunities in early years classrooms. Or there are children who are in the development stage of their play skills as they enter nursery or reception. Instead of discussing play skills, we talk about school readiness and whether children can follow instructions, adult-led agendas, and are socialised to an acceptable level in order to withstand the demands of primary education. How often do educators assess play skills beyond EYFS (Early Years Foundation Stage)? Or think about play skills beyond EYFS? Fortunately, I have collaborated with Stephen Kilgour (co-author of Chapter 4) who worked at Cherry Graden School in London. At Cherry Garden School they created a play assessment tool, enabling educators to assess where individual children were in their play development. From this assessment they were able to plan so that children could meet crucial play mini-developmental steps. I now understand and believe that these steps provide the pathway to formal learning. As educators, if we consider where children are in their play development, as well as their learning journey, we are on the way to developing well-rounded human beings. We are attending to the whole child (socially, emotionally and cognitively), not just the pupil or student. For many children, enabling time and space to develop their play skills is the way into friendship groups and happiness with their peers. For some children, play makes school worthwhile.

For children who have some sort of development delay or sadly their development has been damaged due to neglect and other forms of abuse, playing with others does not come naturally. For these children at UCPS, we have prescribed play but, most importantly, play with peers. Not 1:1 time with a teaching assistant away from classroom, teacher and curriculum, as is so often the case for children with an Educational Health Care Plan.

Could play make a huge difference to the life chances of one child in your school? Have our educational establishments the time to consider one vulnerable child and their play needs? Educators should consider play because play consists of wonder, stirs emotions and creates a wonderful sense of belonging. Play releases the imagination and takes the child on unexpected journeys, which in turn create long-lasting memories.

As a team at UCPS we have applied our practitioner wisdom and knowledge of play and entered a phase of understanding and attending to the developmental needs of individual children in our classrooms. Of course, this happens in some schools for children who are diagnosed with complex trauma, through the PACE (Playfulness, Acceptance, Curiosity and Empathy) approach (Hughes, 2019). Every child matters and therefore we should be finding ways to support each and every child during their time in education and especially primary education, to set them up for the rigors of secondary school. I am not suggesting that children are left to their own devices with 6 and a half hours of free unlimited and unstructured play during the school day. I am suggesting that for some children (a very small minority), play becomes the motivator during the school day. This is until they are ready to socially interact and engage with classroom learning and adult-led agendas. Play with a peer/s becomes the pedagogical tool which fosters a sense of belonging and in turn provides an invitation to join the classroom.

Recently, I have witnessed the reimagining of primary education for children who are unable to access formal learning. Yes, state-funded primary education is not alternative provision where some of our most vulnerable children find themselves! Fortunately for one child, who I shall refer to as Billy, this reimagining took place in 2021, where he experienced a year of play. The team at UCPS has been empowered to place play at the heart of their pedagogy for those vulnerable children who require a different approach. This is an approach to pre-national curriculum school participation beyond Early Years Foundation Stage. This approach considered development as well as learning, and with time, we believed that this could transform a child's learning experience in a formal classroom setting. A transformation to accelerated progress nurtured in a compassionate, collaborative socio-cultural environment.

This journey was difficult on occasions as Billy learnt how to interact and play with others. His play skills were limited when he joined us in December of 2021. He was able to sit alongside his peers and push cars around a road mat or build his own Lego creations. On reflection we, as a team, should have taken time to watch him interact with others, rather than placing him straight in the classroom environment. This would have allowed us the opportunity to discover his level or stage of socialisation development. Instead, we felt a pressure from external agencies that he must 'catch up' on missed learning. Within his first days, we realised that a different approach would be needed for Billy to experience success. Fortunately, for the teaching assistant team at UCPS, their own pedagogical development has involved scaffolding instruction. Scaffolding play is similar to scaffolding classroom learning opportunities. We set about modelling

> playful interactions on the playground during playtime. A colleague and I would play alongside the football match that was taking place. We would gently pass the ball to one another. Billy would eventually join us. Then he would attempt to take shots at our small goal. To develop these skills and interest, we created an after-school football club that Billy and his friends attended. This wasn't always a success, and on reflection, maybe we acted too soon – we should have waited until Billy was joining in team games during PE. Our enthusiasm for play got the better of us.
>
> Older children in the school sensed that there was something different with Billy and often paused when passing to enquire how he was. He didn't always respond, so we would model how the interaction could look. On occasions, a couple of year 6 would demonstrate and scaffold Billy when he received a new Lego set. They would carefully follow the instructions with Billy sat in the middle of them. It was to be several months before he would follow the instructions himself and carefully construct a Minecraft Lego set and then play with a friend. The teaching assistants who supported him had plenty of patience, playing the same games over and over again: table football, dodge ball and zombie tag. Eventually, other children would join in his preferred games, the repertoire of zombie Tag or MineCraft Lego. The team also attended to his physical development by taking him to the local park and modelling how to climb and balance. We experienced a breakthrough one lunchtime, when we discovered him playing 'sloth wars'. This was a wow moment for the team. Not only was he playing a new game, but he was also following the rules which had been created by a friend.
>
> This playful journey, which of course had moments of classroom learning along the way, continues to the present day. The power of play has nurtured and prepared Billy for formal learning, and as a result we have witnessed accelerated progress. Most importantly, Billy has friends and enjoys school very much.

Come and play

In the reflective journal entries in this chapter, the reader was guided through the *playing with ideas* which brought new insights and understanding. In a world that is increasingly fraught with insecurities about resources, sense of self and purpose and in which mass migration is challenging communities' sense of identity and purpose, mental health crisis, our education system and those who work within it are asking bigger, bolder and more far-reaching questions. Much like the Cambridge Primary Review (2010), this book, as indeed do all the books in the *Unlocking Research* series, goes some way to inspire new questions, in your own contexts with your own communities and in which you bring your own vital expertise. What is the purpose of childhood? What is the purpose of education? How do educators invite playful opportunities into their own lives and into the lives of children in their care? Play can repair the human spirit (Johnson et al., 2022). Educators have the capacity to develop the toolkits to help this reparation and to help children heal. What the COVID pandemic taught us all is that we need social connection, that we need to keep learning and, importantly, that we need love and laughter in our lives. This book argues that play is a vital tool in our toolkits.

References

Bellfield, T., Dyer, E., McAleavey, K. S., & Erskine, B. (2021). Using school corridors to support learning: spatial creativity driving primary education. In *Sculpting New Creativities in Primary Education* (pp. 26–44). Routledge.

Biddulph, J., & Baldacchino, J. (2022). Wilful strangers in a possible democracy. *Unleashing Children's Voices in New Democratic Primary Education* (pp. 43–62). Routledge.

Biddulph, J., & Burnard, P. (2021). Storying the journey to new spaces of intercultural creative learning. In *Sculpting New Creativities in Primary Education* (pp. 45–61). Routledge.

Biddulph, J., & Cariss, J. (2020). Creative ways of learning: Using therapeutic arts to inspire professional learning. In *Reimagining Professional Development in Schools* (pp. 164–185). Routledge.

Coltman, P., & Rolls, L. (2020). Nurturing compassionate citizens of the future: Weaving together pedagogy and curriculum. In *Inspiring Primary Curriculum Design* (pp. 27–42). Routledge.

Fox, K., Clarke, J., Winstanley, J. M., & Warwick, J. (2020). Rethinking spaces for learning: Designing a curriculum with freedom and flexibility at its heart. In *Inspiring Primary Curriculum Design* (pp. 43–62). Routledge.

Gronn, P., & Biddulph, J. (Eds.). (2016). *A University's Challenge: Cambridge's Primary School for the Nation*. Cambridge University Press.

Hughes (2019) Daniel Hughes PhD. Creating PACE for the special children in our lives. http://www.danielhughes.org/p.a.c.e.html (accessed 16 October 2023).

Johnson, J. E., Roopnarine, J. L., & Patte, M. M. (2022). A playful introduction to 11:1. *International Journal of Play, 11*(1), 1–2.

Mercer, N., & Littleton, K. (2007). *Dialogue and the Development of Children's Thinking: A Sociocultural Approach*. Routledge.

Ramchandani, P. (2019). In White Paper. Play Facilitation: the science behind the art of engaging young children. https://cms.learningthroughplay.com/media/ok2hjrbh/play-facilitation_the-science-behind-the-art-of-engaging-young-children.pdf (accessed 16 October 2023).

Skene, K., O'Farrelly, C. M., Byrne, E. M., Kirby, N., Stevens, E. C., & Ramchandani, P. G. (2022). Can guidance during play enhance children's learning and development in educational contexts? A systematic review and meta-analysis. *Child Development, 93*(4), 1162–1180.

Sutton, R., Downham, L., & Rhodes, H. (2020). "Why do I have to sit down?": Designing an age-appropriate curriculum for children in Year 1. In *Inspiring Primary Curriculum Design* (pp. 63–80). Routledge.

The University of Cambridge Primary School (Website) Learning & Curriculum Pedagogical Approach, Playful Enquiry. https://universityprimaryschool.org.uk/learning-curriculum/pedagogical-approach/ (accessed 16 October 2023).

Whitebread, D., & Basilio, M. (2012). The emergence and early development of self-regulation in young children. *Profesorado, Revista de currículum y formacíon del profesorado, 16*(1), 15–34.

Whitebread, D., & Coltman, P. (2016). Ensuring developmentally appropriate practice in the early years of primary schooling. In *A University's Challenge: Cambridge's Primary School for the Nation* (pp. 119–140). Cambridge University Press.

CHAPTER 2

Play instead of learning, or play as learning? Reconceptualising play for a new generation of children

Sarah Seleznyov

Introduction

Why has play become disassociated from learning? In the early years, play is seen to be crucial to learning. In advanced studies in any field, playing with ideas, experimenting, tinkering and enabling students to follow their own lines of enquiry is seen to be crucial to learning. What happens in the intervening years? Is it really the case that play loses its currency as a learning experience between the ages of 4 and 18? It's definitely not the case that children and parents do not believe in the importance of play for learning and well-being:

- 92% of children say they want more play in their lives;
- 93% of children say that play makes them feel happier;
- 83% of children say they learn better when it feels like play;
- 95% of parents believe play has a positive impact on the development of pro-social skills such as empathy;
- 82% of parents believe that children who play more will be more successful in education and later life (Real Play Coalition, 2019).

One of the main issues is that play is generally seen to be entirely child-directed and therefore a bit of a hit-and-miss approach to learning (Smith, 2015).

This narrow view of play fails to capture the rich and varied possibilities for learning through play and playful learning: physical play, playing with objects, role play, symbolic play, playing with rules (Whitebread et al., 2012); as well as failing to mention how play can be carefully shaped and structured through the selection of resources, the organisation of space and quality adult interactions.

We know that children learn best when they are engaged and experience autonomy and agency (McMahon and Portelli, 2004; Niemiec and Ryan, 2009). And, as Jensen et al. (2019) state:

> Having autonomy in a situation is about feeling ownership and making choices, rather than being free from all constraints.
>
> (2019: 20)

Guided play even offers a teacher-led version of play which merges the best of the 'telling' and 'discovery' approaches to learning: the child has some free choice within a playful activity so that they can make their own discoveries, and the adult provides guidance based on the individual child's interests, needs and understanding to support them towards a predetermined learning goal (Skene, 2022).

And the evidence speaks for itself. Many high-performing Scandinavian and Asian countries, for example, focus on play-based approaches to learning for longer and formalise much later than in England. They see a distinction between free play, which might happen at breaktime in an English school, and structured play-based learning experiences, which might happen in the classroom and beyond, with the careful support of skilled adults (Grindheim and Ødegaard, 2013). Just over the border in Wales, play-based learning until the age of seven was introduced in 2011, and studies found that both attainment and well-being improved (Taylor et al., 2015).

So, what happens when play becomes one of the underpinning principles of a school curriculum in England?

In September 2021, when we first opened School 360, a new state primary in Newham, London, we were just emerging from the COVID-19 lockdown. One of the things we had all learnt during this lockdown was how important play was for children, not only for their well-being but also for their learning (Rogers, 2022). All parents had seen their children struggle to stay positive and happy, when they could no longer go out and play with their friends. All teachers had seen how difficult it was to motivate their pupils, when sitting alone at a computer screen was the only way to introduce learning. We agreed that play should become one of the underpinning pedagogical principles of the school and that the curriculum should be shaped around the importance of play.

We started our first professional development session with the new team by asking them what childhood memories of learning through play they could recall. The team came from four different countries, from urban, suburban and rural contexts, and yet all our memories had the same features in common: we were in multi-age groups, there were adults available but not interfering in our play, we had freedom to choose where we went and what we did, and there were elements of risk-taking, which helped us learn both how to achieve things and to keep ourselves safe. We asked the team to consider how we could replicate this kind of experience in school, so that children experienced memorable learning experiences rooted in play.

We included all staff in our professional development sessions (teachers and teaching assistants) and simplified our professional development offer to focus on one thing only: the effective interaction of adults and children in playful learning experiences. These experiences would encompass 'playtime', guided play opportunities and independent play in the classroom, known at School 360 as COOL (Choosing Our Own Learning) Time. We decided that all our professional development time would involve cycles of learning about the role of the adult in play, videoing ourselves interacting with children in play and reflecting on these videos collectively, and offering each other constructive feedback and agreeing on joint next steps. In this way, the professional development curriculum offered teaching staff a chance to play around with their practice, to take risks and to explore possibilities. It also created a flat hierarchy – teaching assistants were expected to be critical about the headteachers' videos of practice, and the videos were not an opportunity for appraisal or judgement.

We knew that in Wales, extensive staff training had been needed to make sure all children accessed high-quality play and to avoid a slip back into formal learning (Taylor, Rhys and Waldron, 2015). One study warned against assuming that a play-based curriculum would solve the issue of underachievement, noting that in Wales, boys and those living in poverty benefitted, but not as much as others, partly attributing this to the unconscious lack of warmth and positivity of interactions with adults during their play (Power et al., 2019). Reading these papers, and analysing our videos against them, helped us become more conscious of our own bias and self-fulfilling prophecies.

We also knew that when adults intervened in play, they were often too formal and directive, and children therefore did not perceive situations in which adults engaged as playful (McInnes, 2019). The TRAIL (Teachers Reflecting on Agency in Learning) materials developed by the Centre for Play in Education, Development and Learning (PEDAL), University of Cambridge, provided a brilliant support for us in enhancing play in the best way possible and we used them to structure our reflection sessions. The five 'trails' (see Figure 2.1) were each broken down into individual strategies (see Figure 2.2), and each had descriptions and brief vignettes of classroom examples. These were really easy for both teachers and teaching assistants to use both when planning playful activities and when analysing videos of their own practice.

We were naturally anxious about progression between Reception and Year 1 and, like all schools, felt the pressure of Ofsted looking over our shoulders. It was important to us that all children were challenged and we had a very diverse intake of pupils, with a wide range of attainment levels. Inspired by a chance meeting with some inspirational Steiner school leaders (Jenkinson, 2002) and

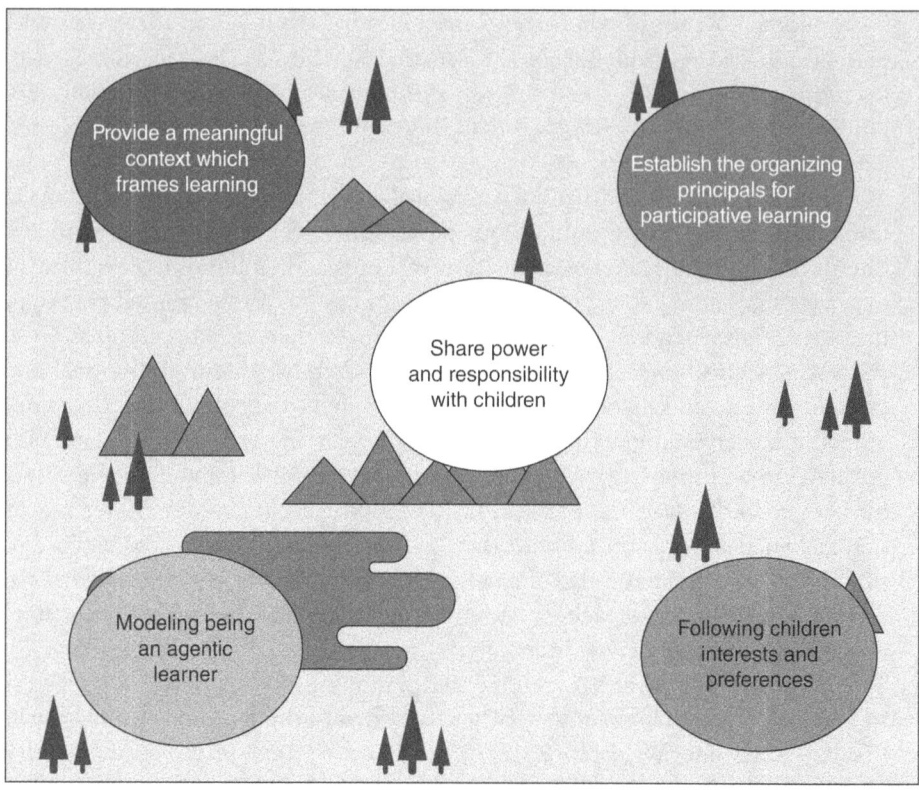

Figure 2.1 Five 'trails'

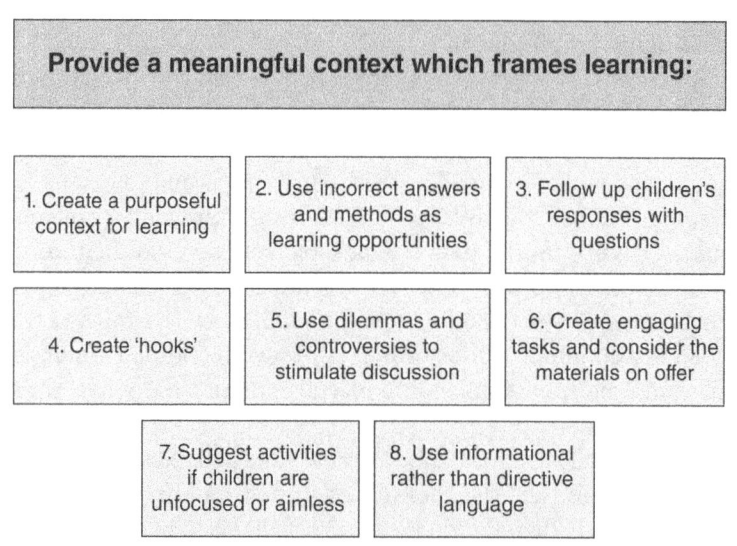

Figure 2.2 Strategies for the first 'trail'

reading about Froebelian approaches to teaching and learning (Tovey, 2020), we carefully developed continuous provision progression grids that mapped progression in teaching and learning across the different play areas of the classroom, from Reception through to the end of Year 1.

We were cautious not to overload teachers with too much guided groupwork, as we knew this would leave them with limited time to interact with children in independent play (Seleznyov et al., 2020), so we focused on one carefully researched programme with evidence to show impact on learning across the curriculum when taught once a fortnight: this was Let's Think (or Cognitive Acceleration), a series of guided play and practical problem-solving activities that draw on the theories of Piaget and Vygotsky (Adey, Robertson and Venville, 2002). This programme gave us a series of high-ceiling, low-threshold guided play activities, which both teachers and teaching assistants could lead. Through learning how to teach Let's Think, teaching staff also learned the importance of creating a meaningful concrete context for learning which motivates children to engage (Adey, 2008); of being an enthusiastic participant in play (Moe et al., 2021) rather than the arbiter of 'correct' work; and of encouraging metacognitive talk and modelling it yourself (Larkin, 2002).

Let's Think also helped us prioritise the development of social construction and oracy, and especially peer-to-peer listening. We drew heavily on the wonderful material developed by the national oracy charity Voice 21 and worked with them to develop a progression map for oracy across Reception, Years 1 and 2 that would support both the teaching of oracy and the assessment of children's development. Using a class set of iPads, we began to teach children how to take pictures, videos and audio clips to record and explain their learning independently. They would upload these to the assessment app we used to track progress and to communicate with parents. They would then watch them back during whole class carpet sessions and give each other feedback on how well they had explained their learning. This produced an ongoing feedback loop that helped children understand how to improve their work and value feedback from their classmates. But crucially, they chose what to record and when, meaning they shaped their own learning trajectory, choice being a crucial element of play (Parker and Thomsen, 2019).

We knew that if we wanted children to engage constructively in an independent play environment, trust needed to be high and the children needed to understand behaviour expectations and self-manage. We started with our values (see Figure 2.3), as we wanted these to shape the way everyone in the school interacted with each other. However, we soon realised that our youngest children needed more concrete teaching about the behaviours we needed in a play-based learning environment. Thanks to the Montessori experience of one member of staff, we learnt about the 'grace and courtesy' approach (Soholt, 2015) where there is explicit teaching, discussion and modelling of the behaviours that children and adults are expected to show each other when they are in the classroom. We had sessions on tidying up; saying please and thank you; greeting visitors to the classroom; waiting for your turn to speak in a conversation; and solving problems and conflicts through talking.

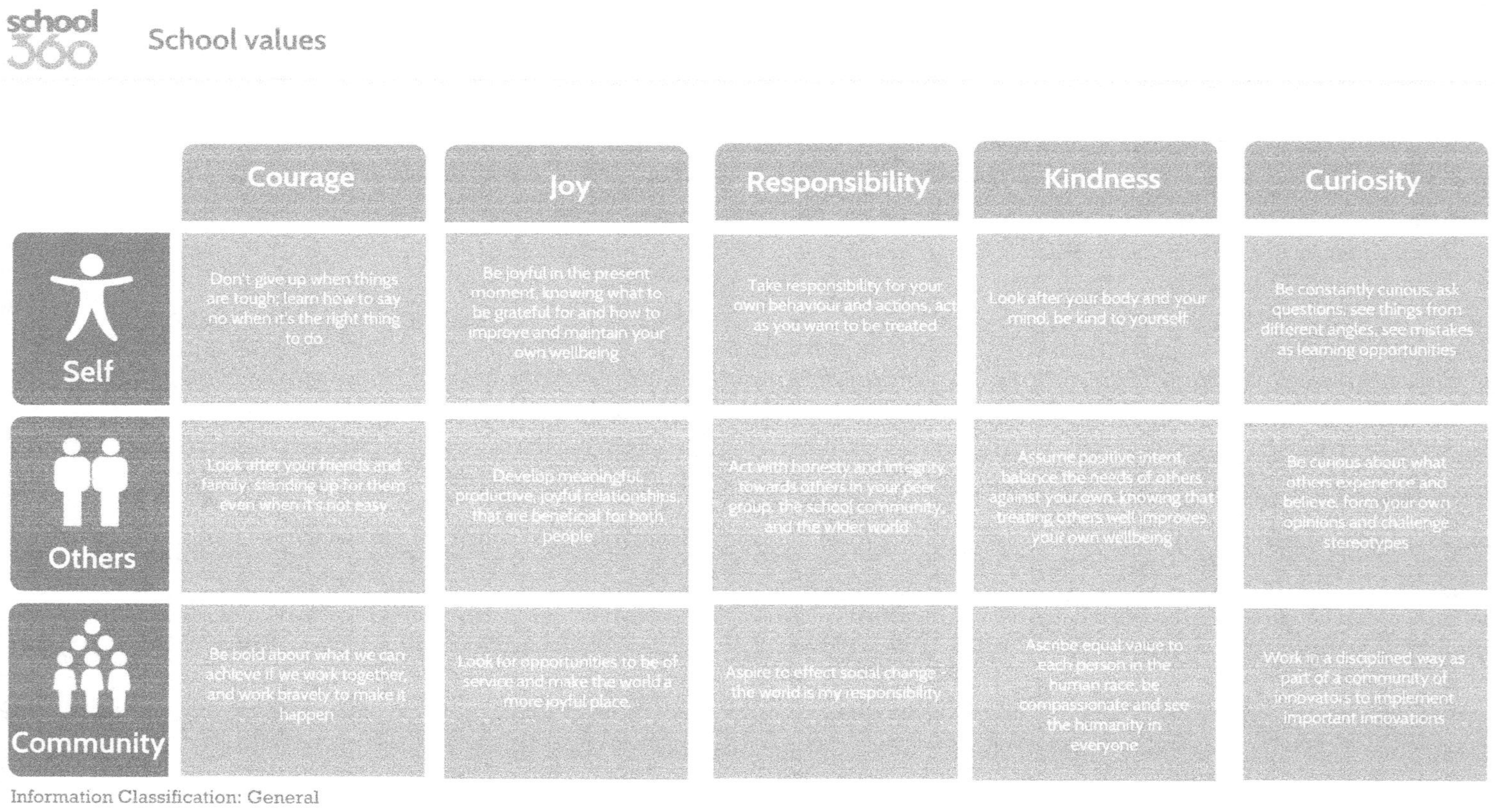
school 360
School values
Courage
Joy
Responsibility
Kindness
Curiosity
Self
Don't give up when things are tough; learn how to say no when it's the right thing to do
Be joyful in the present moment, knowing what to be grateful for and how to improve and maintain your own wellbeing
Take responsibility for your own behaviour and actions, act as you want to be treated
Look after your body and your mind, be kind to yourself
Be constantly curious, ask questions, see things from different angles, see mistakes as learning opportunities
Others
Look after your friends and family, standing up for them even when it's not easy
Develop meaningful, productive, joyful relationships that are beneficial for both people
Act with honesty and integrity towards others in your peer group, the school community and the wider world
Assume positive intent, balance the needs of others against your own, knowing that treating others well improves your own wellbeing
Be curious about what others experience and believe, form your own opinions and challenge stereotypes
Community
Be bold about what we can achieve if we work together, and work bravely to make it happen
Look for opportunities to be of service and make the world a more joyful place
Aspire to effect social change - the world is my responsibility
Ascribe equal value to each person in the human race, be compassionate and see the humanity in everyone
Work in a disciplined way as part of a community of innovators to implement important innovations
Information Classification: General

Figure 2.3 School 360 values

We knew we wanted to implement a project-based learning approach (Berger, 2003) for the older years, as an 'older sibling' of continuous provision in Reception and Year 1 (Parker and Thomsen, 2019). However, we wanted to ensure that having a project would not impinge on children's freedom to choose what to play and when. Reggio Emilia inspired our approach to this (Fraser and Gestwick, 2002) with their explanations of projects arising from children's lines of enquiry. The most successful approach to teaching a project was borrowed from a wonderful primary school in Bedfordshire called Great Denham. They created challenge and progression within an environment of choice and independence, using 'must do' tasks. Linked to the twice daily short whole-class teaching sessions, these were tasks for children to complete independently at a time of their own choosing during the week. Each one was linked to a QR code that children could access via the class iPads, so that they could hear the teacher explain the task as many times as they liked. The teacher would be able to track the completion of the tasks via the iPad and remind children daily of the tasks they had yet to complete that week. Some chose to do them all on Monday or Tuesday, some spread them out across the week and some needed adult support to get them done on Thursday or Friday, but everyone made the choice that was right for them.

Great Denham also inspired us to reconsider the classroom environment. If children were going to make choices about what they learnt and when, the standard classroom setup of 30 chairs and some clusters of tables would not suffice. We needed to set up areas in the classroom that reflected the choices we would offer children in their play: a creative area in which the children could make their own choices about art and design and learn the importance of process (Tate Modern, 2022); a construction area with various different construction kits; a science area in which children could carry out investigations; a role play area which would reflect the children's current interests and become a doctor's surgery, a fire station, a shop. This meant there was not a chair for every child, nor a table, and that did not detract from learning.

Free access to the outdoors was also crucial (Dillon, Rickinson and Teamey, 2016). If children were going to be able to go outside and play in all weathers, we needed to have sets of waterproof clothing and wellies for them to wear. We needed more green spaces, so we dug up concrete from the playground and planted trees. We fundraised and installed a rooftop garden for the children to grow their own food. We wanted to include opportunities for the sorts of risky outdoor play offered in a Scandinavian learning environment (Grindheim and Ødegaard, 2013), so bought in climbing frames, monkey bars, climbing walls and woodwork benches with tools. We installed bird boxes, bird baths, bug houses and a wormery. We learned about the value of loose parts play (Casey et al., 2016), participated in a den-building workshop and collected old tyres, pushchairs, tarpaulins, cable reels and suitcases for imaginative and construction play.

We wanted to teach literacy in a playful way, so decided to use a storytelling approach. We read about Mantle of the Expert (Taylor, 2016), Helicopter Stories (Faulkner, 2016) and Storytelling Schools (Smith and Guillain, 2014) and used these readings to design and test our own teaching methodology, starting with a high-quality text, moving into storytelling and oracy work, and then into writing. Props and costumes were crucial to this approach: we collected these from the parent community and borrowed specialist items from the education library service.

This is still a work in progress and we definitely do not have a perfect model of learning through play, but what has been the impact so far? Walk into our Year 1 classroom, and you will see a general atmosphere of happy purposefulness. All the children are engaged in playful learning tasks, adults are interacting with small groups and those not with an adult are engrossed in learning in the various different areas of the classroom. We have some children with special needs and disabilities, but you would not notice these children, as they are also generally calm, settled and working hard. In fact, the time we notice them most is during the short whole class carpet sessions, when they struggle to focus and sit still. They can learn as productively as everyone else when they are able to learn through play. And the tracking of progress shows that this learning through play is also having an impact on results. Our children are confident speakers, good listeners, able to collaborate and support each other and happy to have a go, even when learning is tricky. They are creative learners, producing the most wonderful art, woodwork, scientific investigations and design projects. They are learning to read, write and do mathematics, as well, if not better than their peers in more formal learning environments.

Parents could not be happier. Firstly, their children love coming to school, have happy productive friendships and are clearly making progress in their learning. Secondly, this learning is open access to all parents via a simple app on their phone, and they can also use this to upload evidence of learning at home.

And what about staff? We do not want to give the impression that this has been an easy journey for us: teaching this way is more difficult. We have needed to work hard on our practice, ask for lots of help and give each other more feedback. But the well-being and learning of the children are visible, and that is what really motivates us to continue.

We now begin to think about what happens in Year 2 and beyond. How will we progress play as the children mature and the learning becomes more challenging? One thing we do know is that we now have some key pedagogical principles that will help us embed play into the curriculum as we grow and expand:

- Any concept, skill or knowledge can be taught playfully;
- Giving children choices enables them to take charge of their own learning and become more engaged;
- There is a range of play that spans free play through to more structured guided play, and all are valid and important for learning;
- Skilful adult interactions in play are crucial for high-quality learning through play;
- Playful learning requires staff to rethink the classroom environment, including the spaces and the equipment.

As long as we remain true to these principles and continue to value well-being and creativity as highly as literacy and mathematics, we hope to offer children at School 360 an experience in which play is integral to learning at all ages, learning is hard but fun and it is something you self-manage rather than something which is done to you.

Questions to consider:

How might you reimagine the role of play in your own setting?

What does playful learning look like and how might it benefit pupils?

What would be the barriers to implementing playful pedagogies in your context?

What kinds of play would pupils in your setting gain the most learning from?

What might a progression in play look like from Nursery through to Year 6?

References

Adey, P. (2008). *Let's Think Handbook*. London: GL Assessment.

Adey, P., Robertson, A., & Venville, G. (2002). Effects of a cognitive acceleration programme on Year I pupils. *British Journal of Educational Psychology*, 72(1), 1–25.

Berger, R. (2003). *An Ethic of Excellence: Building a Culture of Craftsmanship with Students*. 361 Hanover Street, Portsmouth: Heinemann, a division of Reed Elsevier Inc, NH 03801-3912.

Casey, T., Robertson, J., Abel, J., Cairns, M., Caldwell, L., & Campbell, K. (2016). *Loose Parts Play*. Scotland: *Inspiring Scotland*.

Dillon, J., Rickinson, M., & Teamey, K. (2016). The value of outdoor learning: Evidence from research in the UK and elsewhere. In *Towards a Convergence Between Science and Environmental Education* (pp. 193–200). London: Routledge.

Faulkner, D. (2016). Young children as storytellers: Collective meaning making and socio-cultural transmission. In *Storytelling in Early Childhood* (pp. 99–114). London: Routledge.

Fraser, S., & Gestwicki, C. (2002). *Authentic Childhood: Exploring Reggio Emilia in Theclassroom. Canada*: Delmar.

Grindheim, L., & Ødegaard, E. (2013). What is the state of play? *International Journal of Play*, 2(1), 4–6.

Jenkinson, S. (2002). *Genius of Play*. Stroud, UK: Hawthorn Press.

Jensen, H., Pyle, A., Zosh, J., Ebrahim, H., Scherman, A., Reunamo, J., & Hamre, B. (2019). *Play Facilitation: The Science Behind the Art of Engaging Young Children: White Paper*. Billund: The LEGO Foundation.

Larkin, S., (2002). Creating metacognitive experiences for 5- and 6-year old children. In Shayer, M, & Adey, P (Eds.). *Learning Intelligence: Cognitive Acceleration Across the Curriculum from 5 to 15 Years*. Milton Keynes: Open University Press.

McInnes, K. (2019). Playful learning in the early years – Through the eyes of children. *Education 3-13*, 47(7), 796–805.

McMahon, B., & Portelli, J. (2004). Engagement for what? Beyond popular discourses of student engagement. *Leadership and Policy in Schools*, 3(1), 59–76.

Moe, A., Frenzel, A.C., Au, L., & Taxer, J.L. (2021). Displayed enthusiasm attracts attention and improves recall. *British Journal of Educational Psychology*, *91*(3), 911–927.

Niemiec, C.P., & Ryan, R.M. (2009). Autonomy, competence, and relatedness in the classroom: Applying self-determination theory to educational practice. *Theory and Research in Education*, 7(2), 133–144.

Parker, R., & Thomsen, B. (2019). Learning through play at school. *A Study of Playful Integrated Pedagogies That Foster children's Holistic Skills Development in the Primary School Classroom. White Paper*. Billund, Denmark: The LEGO Foundation.

Power, S., Rhys, M., Taylor, C., & Waldron, S. (2019). How child-centred education favours some learners more than others, *Review of Education*, 7(3), 570–592.

Real Play Coalition. (2019). *Value of play report*. National Geographic, LEGO, UNILEVER & IKEA. Available at: https://www.ikea.com/ca/en/files/pdf/bb/2f/bb2f0627/the-real-play-coalition_value-of-play-report_a.pdf Accessed on: 28 December 2022.

Rogers, S. (2022). Play in the time of pandemic: Children's agency and lost learning, *Education 3-13*, 50:4, 494–505, DOI: 10.1080/03004279.2022.2052235

Seleznyov, S., Sprakes, A., Shields, P., Nakkas, N., Crank, A., & Finbow, K. (2020). Play based learning in Year 1: A practical guide for schools.

Skene, K. (2022). *Juggling play and learning: The role of guided play*. Available at: https://www.pedalhub.net/play-pieces/post/j-juggling-play-and-learning-the-role-of-guided-play Accessed on: 28 December 2022.

Smith, S. (2015). *Playing to engage: Fostering engagement for children and teachers in low socio-economic regions through science and mathematics play-based learning*. (Doctoral Dissertation). Retrieved from https://researchonlinend.edu.au/theses/116/

Smith, C., & Guillain, A. (2014). *Storytelling School: The Handbook for Teachers (Storytelling Schools)*. Stroud, UK: Hawthorn Press.

Soholt, P. (2015). Living grace and courtesy in the primary. *NAMTA Journal*, *40*(1), 51–61.

Tate Modern. (2022) *Process art*. Available at: https://www.tate.org.uk/art/art-terms/p/process-art Accessed on: 28 December 2022.

Taylor, T. (2016). *A Beginner's Guide to Mantle of the Expert: A Transformative Approach to Education*. Norwich, UK: Singular Publishing.

Taylor, C., Davies, R., Rhys, M., & Waldron, S. (2015). Evaluating the Foundation Phase: The of Foundation Phase Pupils up to 2011/12 (Report 2), Social Research No. 01/2015, Cardiff: Welsh Government.

Taylor, C., Rhys, M., & Waldron, S. (2019). Implementing curriculum reform in Wales: The case of the foundation phase. In *Education in a Federal UK* (pp. 51–67). London: Routledge.

Tovey, H. (2020). Froebel's principles and practices today. Froebel Trust. Available at: https://www.froebel.org.uk/uploads/documents/FT-Froebels-principles-and-practice-today.pdf Accessed on: 28 December 2022.

Whitebread, D., Basilio, M., Kuvalja, M., & Verma, M. (2012). *The Importance of Play*. Brussels: Toy Industries of Europe.

CHAPTER

Practices of play in education: play at home, school readiness, and a positive transition to school

Beth Barker and Christine O'Farrelly

Starting school marks a significant milestone in the lives of children and their families. Children's experiences, adjustment, and feelings towards school during this important transition are shaped by myriad factors. A child's family, their experiences of early childhood education and care, their community, public services, their new school and teacher can all play a supportive role in a positive transition to school. Of key importance both before and during the adjustment to school are the relationships, resources, and opportunities that children bring from their lives at home. Play with caregivers lies at the heart of these experiences as it nurtures children's development, builds their confidence, and seeds curiosity and a love of learning. In this chapter we introduce different perspectives on school readiness, explore children's own priorities for their early school adjustment, discuss the powerful role of parent–child play in children's development, and consider how programmes that support play at home in children's first years can contribute to a positive start in school.

Perspectives on school readiness

School readiness is a widely used term and a concept that increasingly lies at the centre of contested discourses within early childhood (see Georgeson et al., 2022). 'School readiness' is often used to convey a goal or outcome of early childhood. This is seen in both international and UK policy where school readiness is frequently situated as a means of reducing inequalities in children's life chances. For example, the purpose of the Early Years Foundation Stage is to promote teaching and learning to ensure children's school readiness (Department for Education, 2023) while target 4.2 of the Sustainable Development Goals is to ensure children have access to quality early childhood development, care and pre-primary education so that they are ready for primary education. From this perspective, school readiness assessments provide a useful means of identifying the need for early intervention and redressing inequalities in children's life chances as early as possible. However, many have criticised that these policies have led to an outcome-based culture and a deficit focus, which has encroached on the provision of developmentally appropriate and enriching early years experiences for children in the here and now of their early childhoods (Brown, 2017; Mashburn, 2014).

Although the term 'school readiness' clearly has 'conceptual baggage', many agree with the idea that readiness is not just for children (Georgeson et al., 2022). Viewed as a multidimensional construct, readiness extends to incorporate not only the child's readiness for school, but the school's readiness for the child, and the capacity of families and communities to provide opportunities and support that promote children's development and learning (Dockett, Perry, & Kearney, 2010). This perspective is helpful in situating school readiness more in an ecological systems approach that recognises multiple spheres of influence in children's lives as well as the active role that children play in their own development. Nonetheless, we lack clear consensus around what expectations should be placed on children themselves, as well as schools, early years settings, families, and communities, to ensure that every child is able to experience success and contentment in the classroom.

Traditionally, ideas surrounding the child's school readiness have focused on their individual level of development in terms of their cognitive, behavioural, socio-emotional, and physical capabilities. Although these skills are important, a more helpful perspective is put forward by Ladd (2009) and Ramey and Ramey (2004), who suggest that readiness is characterised when children, like school, are able to establish supportive connections with teachers and peers, feel comfortable and happy, and are interested in learning and motivated to participate. Ladd's research suggests that a positive start in school and a smooth adjustment to the classroom can pave the way for positive and enjoyable educational experiences, achievement, and attainment. Moreover this work indicates that it is children's early feelings towards school and the quality of their relationships, rather than academic skills, that foster ongoing participation and school achievement (Ladd, Buhs, & Seid, 2000). Indeed, recent research from Morris, Dorling, Davies, and Davey Smith (2021) demonstrated that children's feelings about school at age six were associated with higher educational achievement at age 16. This is striking and suggests that in overlooking children's feelings about school, we are missing an important opportunity to provide positive transition experiences that set children on strong paths for their learning.

There can also be tensions between teachers and parents' views of school readiness. Research suggests that teachers tend to identify readiness as children's ability to communicate wants, needs, and thoughts, having curiosity and enthusiasm for learning, and strong self-regulation and social skills, whereas parents typically prioritise literacy and numeracy skills (Rimm-Kaufman & Sandilos, 2017). In the UK a survey conducted by the Professional Association for Childcare and Early Years (Professional Association for Childcare and Early Years [PACEY], 2013) reported that, compared to a quarter of parents and a third of childcare professionals, only 4% of teachers thought a definition of school readiness should include a stipulation that children need an understanding of reading, writing, and arithmetic before school. These differences are important as work by Abry, Latham, Bassok, and LoCasale-Crouch (2015) found that greater misalignment between kindergarten and preschool teachers' priorities for children's competencies was associated with poorer outcomes, especially for children from lower socioeconomic backgrounds. We also know that children tend to do better in school where preschool and kindergarten teachers have time to meet to share information about the curricula and individual children (LoCasale-Crouch, Mashburn, Downer, & Pianta, 2008) and where families are supported to become involved in children's learning and school life (Schulting, Malone, & Dodge, 2005). Moreover these practices are especially beneficial for children experiencing socioeconomic risk. Taken together this suggests that children benefit when contexts have shared expectations and offer consistent experiences, and teachers and schools have the opportunity to learn about children as individuals from the people who know them best.

Children's own priorities for their early school adjustment

Despite this increasing attention on how children feel about school, we know remarkably little about what matters to children themselves. What helps children to feel positively about and have a sense of belonging in school? What challenges are most salient to children and where do they want support? Where do children's priorities diverge from what typically gets prioritised by adults?

A number of important studies stand out as exceptions, as they have sought to elicit the perspectives of young children directly. This includes, but is not limited to, work by Dockett and Perry (2004), Murray and Harrison (2005), and Margetts (2006) in Australia, Einarsdottir (2010) in Iceland, Peters (2003) in New Zealand, and Keating, Fabian, Jordan, Mavers, and Roberts (2000) and Brooker (2008) in the UK. However, many of these studies have been conducted in mixed or high socioeconomic communities meaning that we know less about the priorities of children who are most at risk of a poorer transition to school. To help tackle this gap we conducted the Children's Thoughts about School Study, which involved participatory interviews with 57 four- and five-year-olds living in a socioeconomically deprived suburb of Dublin, Ireland. The Children's Thoughts about School Study was embedded within the Preparing for Life study, a randomised controlled trial (RCT; see Doyle, 2020, 2022) that was testing a home-visiting programme delivered from pregnancy until the start of school to enhance children's school readiness (Preparing for Life & The Northside Partnership, 2008). The Children's Thoughts about School Study set out to interview children in the Preparing for Life communities, including those whose families had participated in the RCT, about their priorities for their early school adjustment.

Using more traditional question-and-answer interview methods with very young children often only leaves room for the loudest, brightest, and clearest voices. To counter this, we tried to cast the methodological net wide, inviting children to respond to line drawings of everyday school experiences, offer advice for a character 'Riley Rabbit' starting school for the first time, draw a 'special picture just about them in school', and answer semi-structured and structured questions about their feelings towards school. The use of multiple participatory methods can stimulate and maintain children's interest, helping to maximise the opportunity for as many children as possible to contribute insights and to minimise bias from relying on one approach.

We analysed the data using inductive thematic analysis. Through this process, we drew out 25 priorities that children themselves identified as important in their transition to school. These priorities converged on four big ideas for children's early school adjustment: feeling able and enthusiastic for school; being able to navigate friendships; having supportive environments with opportunities to play; and strong bridges between school and family life. More information on these four areas is included below and the full findings are reported in O'Farrelly, Booth, Tatlow-Golden, & Barker (2020).

Feeling able and enthusiastic for school: For children it was important to like school and look forward to going to school, to have a sense of confidence in their skills (including academic skills) and be able to persist in the face of challenges. Children also wanted to have independence in toileting, and be able to regulate their emotions, behaviour, and attention; and to have encouragement from their teacher and peers in all of these efforts.

Ability to navigate friendships: Being able to initiate and maintain relationships with peers was strongly linked to children's descriptions of well-being, with many sharing a sense of risk and uncertainty that often characterised these early relationships.

Having supportive environments with opportunities to play: The emphasis on play was striking in children's accounts. Rather than lamenting the loss of play as is typical for children starting school, children strongly endorsed the playful learning curriculum that was being employed in the community's schools. Play was the best thing about school, allowed children to feel happy, and it was important for other children starting school to get to know that they would get to play. Children valued rich and varied play opportunities both in the classroom and outdoor spaces, with outdoor spaces providing a wider space for movement, freedom, and imagination. As well as play, children also emphasised the value of supportive and encouraging relationships with teachers and clear expectations and routines.

Strong bridges between school and family life: Children's family lives were also closely entwined with how they discussed school, with family members featuring in about half of children's drawings. Children highlighted the challenge of dealing with the separation from their parents, the social safety net provided by siblings and cousins while in school, and (for a smaller number of children) the ways family members could help with learning. A small number of children also spoke about how their participation and attendance in school was linked to their family's well-being.

We looked at how well these priorities were captured across a gold standard battery of school readiness measures used in the Preparing for Life trial. We identified which of children's priorities were measured, which were partially captured, and which were overlooked by available school readiness measures (see Figure 3.1). We found that there are multiple areas of children's early school experiences that tend to be missed by the outcome measures often used in school readiness assessments.

Captured	Partially captured	Not captured
Writing	Enthusiasm for learning	School liking
Reading	Academic self-efficacy	Access to friends for enjoyment and support
Counting	Drawing	Absence of social distress and victimisation
Behavioural regulation	Independence in toileting	Regular access to play and supportive outdoor space
Following direction	Balance	Clear rules and routines
	Social skills to establish and maintain friendships	Supportive and encouraging teacher relationships
	Avoiding rejection	Strong family-school involvement
	Conflict resolution	Supportive social networks
	An ability to think and play creatively	

Figure 3.1 Degree to which children's priorities were captured by school readiness outcomes

As an example, intrinsic motivation for school and learning, and a strong sense of self-efficacy, seemed to be so salient for these young children, but little is captured about children's beliefs in their ability and their zest for learning in existing measures.

We also used children's priorities to generate a multi-faceted model of early school adjustment based on children's own priorities. Figure 3.2 shows the model including individual, relational, and environmental factors that contribute to school adjustment and the reciprocal relationship between these. Children's intrinsic motivation lies at the centre of the model and includes children's enthusiasm for school and learning, their sense of self-efficacy, and their capacity to persevere. These factors underpin children's capacity and skill in five priority areas: reading, writing, counting, and drawing; thinking and playing creatively; navigating peer interactions; physical

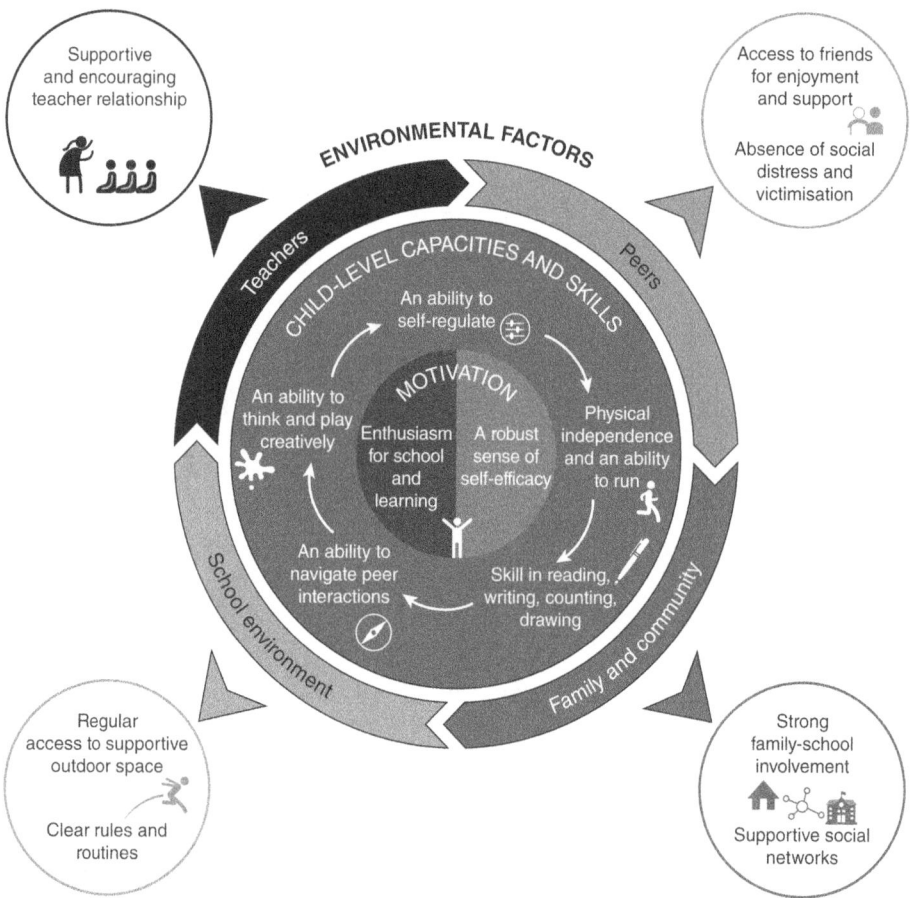

Figure 3.2 A model of school readiness through the lens of the child

Source: A version of this figure was first published in Early Childhood Research Quarterly, Vol 50, O'Farrelly et al., Reconstructing readiness: Young children's priorities for their early school adjustment, p. 3–16, Copyright Elsevier (2020).

independence; and self-regulation. These skills both underpin and are shaped by the teacher-child relationship, the peer group, school environment, and relations between family, school, and wider community contexts.

Overall, these children, and their peers who have provided insights in previous studies (see Educational Transitions and Change (ETC) Research Group, 2011), challenge us to consider them as rich and competent beings who come to school as unique individuals with ample experience, knowledge, and creativity; to invest in their families and communities right from the start of life; to support strong relationships across settings and services; and to embrace curricula that are playful and responsive to their interests.

The powerful role families can play in promoting school readiness

Parents[1] can play a rich and varied role in facilitating and supporting their children's transition to school. For many children, their parents are not only their very first teacher but also their most frequent playmate during their earliest years. A home environment that is safe and nurturing and encourages curiosity, exploration, and learning can support multiple aspects of a child's social-emotional, cognitive, and language development. In this section, we consider the features of parent-child interactions that seem to be particularly beneficial for children's development, and the unique role that specific types of family play can have in sparking positive interactions and a natural context for learning.

Parent-child interactions are important

Understanding the varied ways in which parenting and the parent-child relationship shape child development has been a consistent focus for researchers, practitioners, policymakers, and families themselves for decades. An ever-growing evidence base demonstrates that strong foundations for children's development and learning can be laid through strong parent-child relationships. Responsive, nurturing, and consistent parent-child interactions can be an especially powerful influence across multiple developmental domains and a promising target for intervention. Here, we focus closely on just one aspect of parent-child interaction that has been consistently linked to positive aspects of children's development: parental sensitivity.

Parental sensitivity describes the caregiver's ability to be aware of the signals and communications of a child and their capacity to respond to these signals in a prompt and appropriate way (Ainsworth, Bell, & Stayton, 1974). According to Ainsworth, the sensitive parent reads the baby or child's communication and gives the child what they want and need in that moment; for example, she responds playfully to their invitations to play, soothes the baby when they are distressed, picks them up when they want to be cuddled, and puts them down when they are ready to explore. Under attachment theory, a caregiver's capacity to provide sensitive and consistent care feeds into the child's internal perception of that caregiver and contributes to a secure attachment (Fearon & Belsky, 2016). Experiences with multiple attachment figures are believed to be internalised and generalised into a set of continually updated assumptions and expectations about how attachment and wider social relationships work (Society for Emotion and Attachment Studies, 2021). Attachment to a protective and reliable caregiver helps children to manage their emotions when faced with stress, to engage positively with their peers, and to explore the environment with confidence (Van IJzendoorn & Bakermans-Kranenburg, 2019).

Research exploring the links between children's early experiences of caregiving and their wider development suggests that sensitive and responsive parental behaviours are important (but not the only) mechanisms for children's social, emotional, and behavioural functioning (DePasquale & Gunnar, 2020). Robus links have been found between parental sensitivity and children's behavioural and cognitive development (see systematic reviews from Cooke et al. [2022] and Prime et al. [2023]). These findings situate children's experiences of parental sensitivity as a significant factor not only in family functioning but also in children's longer term educational experiences. Sensitive and responsive caregiving can also act as a protective factor for children growing up in adversity (The World Health Organisation, 2004). Research shows that the everyday, informal, but highly meaningful experiences and interactions taking place in children's homes and communities form the basis of their learning, exclusively in the first few years, and then as a complement to school learning through childhood (Whitebread, 2015).

Play sparks positive parent-child interaction and a natural context for learning

Play is one of the main contexts in which parent-child interactions take place, and a natural context for parents and children to share responsive and enriching interactions. In play, bonding and learning can thrive. When parents join their children in play, they are given a unique opportunity to pay close attention to their child, to view the world from their child's perspective, and to connect and communicate in a child-centred way. Even in infancy much of the infant's interactions with the parent occur in playful moments through gaze, facial expressions, and physical touch.

Examining play as a rich and important context for parent-child interaction offers us a valuable opportunity to better understand the pathways through which parenting may impact upon child development. Play is said to be particularly beneficial for children's learning and development because children enjoy it and so it tends to be motivating in and of itself. Child-led play fosters children's autonomy and reduces pressure by providing a low-stakes environment for learning and increases the likelihood of children adopting creative problem-solving behaviours (Gray, 2013).

Play facilitated by interactions with sensitive and responsive adults is an especially powerful context for playful learning (Skene et al., 2022; Weisberg, Kittredge, Hirsh-Pasek, Michnick Golinkoff, & Klashr, 2015). Children can benefit from a whole range of play experiences and research suggests that more parent-initiated play opportunities at home can enhance early learning and socialisation (e.g., Kenney, 2012). By adopting a playful approach to children's learning, caregivers can support children to develop the skills, attitudes, and understanding needed for success in the classroom (O'Sullivan & Ring, 2018). Here, we refer to four different kinds of play that parents can take part in with their children and introduce some of the evidence that discusses their potential benefits.

Play with objects and spatial reasoning. Materials like stacking blocks, building bricks, shape sorters, and puzzles can provide children with an accessible and playful introduction to spatial concepts and skills (Byrne, Jensen, Thomsen, & Ramchandani, 2023). Early spatial reasoning skills, including spatial visualisation, mental rotation, and shape transformation, have been linked to skills that can support learning in science, technology, engineering, and maths. For instance, Levine, Ratliff, Huttenlocher, and Cannon (2012) observed parent-child play at home for 90 minutes every four months between two and four years of age. When children were four-and-a-half, they were asked to complete a task involving mental transformations of 2D shapes. Children who had played with puzzles during the earlier observations performed better on the spatial transformation task, particularly if their parents had been more engaged and used more spatial language in the early observations. Foster and Hund (2012) considered the ways in which parents can 'scaffold' children's learning in more directive ways when introducing complex spatial terms (e.g., 'between' and 'middle') and pointed to the important role of parental sensitivity in this process, as caregivers were required to notice and respond to their child's individual cues and needs. This work highlights that it is not just the presence of the play but also the presence of a supportive adult who knows that child that can make a real difference to learning complex concepts.

Sharing books and language development. Sharing books and stories together can be a playful and intimate way for parents to support their children's early language and literacy-related skills, as well as other parenting and child development outcomes. The benefits of book sharing have been shown starting right from the earliest months of children's lives (Leech, McNally, Daly, & Corriveau, 2022; O'Farrelly, Doyle, Victory, & Palamaro-Munsell, 2018). Logan, Justice, Yumus, & Chaparro-Moreno (2019) estimated that a child experiencing just one-book-a-day of shared reading would enable them to hear 78,000 words per year. The formative role of the home learning environment and children's early literacy experiences on children's later language and cognitive development have been found to be especially apparent in children living in families with a low income (Rodriguez et al., 2009). In their meta-analysis of 19 studies of book-sharing programmes for one- to six-year-olds, Dowdall et al. (2020)

found positive overall effects for children's expressive and receptive language as well as caregiver's book-sharing skills. This is in keeping with findings from a recent study by Murray et al. (2023) who tested a seven-week, picture-book, dialogic book-sharing intervention with 218 families of two- to four-year-olds. The authors reported positive effects of the book-sharing training on children's expressive and receptive language and attention, as well as parental sensitivity and cognitive scaffolding.

Physical play, rough-and-tumble, and self-regulation. Physical play involves any activity that raises children's metabolic rate. This kind of play peaks during children's preschool years and often involves energetic, competitive, and body-contact kinds of play like rough-and-tumble, bouncing and lifting, chasing games, and playful swinging, spinning, and tickling. In the early years especially, parents are one of the main play partners for children's physical play, especially rough-and-tumble, where parents can encourage children to exert their bodies and strength. Rough and tumble play can include play fighting, chasing, wrestling, and lifting. It gives young children the opportunity to experience more intense, sometimes difficult emotions (e.g., feeling scared when being chased) in a safe context (Murray, 2014). This provides the caregiver with the opportunity to support the child in exploring their emotional limits as well as reading the child's cues to dial down the play before emotions spillover; helping to scaffold the child's emotion regulation (Murray, 2014). Of course, any caregiver can enjoy rough-and-tumble with their child; interestingly though, literature has consistently reported that fathers engage in more physical play when compared to mothers (Craig, 2006; Paquette, Carbonneau, Dubeau, Bigras, & Tremblay, 2003). Rough-and-tumble play has been linked to a range of behavioural, emotional, and physical benefits for young children including self-regulation (Amodia-Bidakowska, Laverty, & Ramchandani, 2020). It should be noted though that the findings in this area are mixed, with some studies reporting associations between a greater frequency of rough-and-tumble play and higher aggression in early childhood (e.g., Veiga, O'Connor, Neto, & Rieffe, 2022; O'Connor, Neto, & Rieffe, 2020). This suggests that it is not simply the presence or absence of rough-and-tumble that is important but also the quality of the play and the ways in which the parent can support children's regulation throughout.

Pretend play and children's socio-emotional development. Pretend play, also known as imaginative play or make-believe play, is considered to be a central component of early childhood development, peaking when children are three to five years old (Piaget, 1962). In their earliest years, young children spend a significant portion of their play in the roles of others (e.g., teachers, doctors, nurses, mechanics, chefs), pretending one object is another (e.g., boxes are rocket ships, saucepans are cauldrons, and washing baskets are cars), and imagining that non-existent things are entirely visible to them (e.g., volcanoes exploding around action figures, fairies flying through the garden). Again, parents play a key role in helping children to develop their imaginative play skills. Children's pretend play is initially more advanced with caregivers than with peers, although by age four pretend play with peers takes centre stage and is relatively more sustained (see Lillard, 2012). Parent-child pretend play is thought to boost varied aspects of their socio-emotional development. During imaginative play with parents, children can experience different emotions and work with their caregiver to reflect upon and understand these feelings. Pretend play also encourages children to take on the perspective of other people, to try to understand others' feelings and beliefs, and offers an opportunity for children to try out different 'solutions' to problems that come up in the play (Jankowska & Omelańczuk, 2018). One proposed mechanism for these benefits is that parental involvement in pretend play can increase a child's sensitivity to social signals and help them to learn that pretence is different from reality, which in turn is thought to promote their social understanding of others (Lillard, 2017). Studies of pretend play in toddlers and preschoolers have reported that children who engage in more frequent pretend play, particularly with their caregivers, have higher ratings on aspects of their socio-emotional development (Weisberg, 2015). However, a review from Lillard et al. (2013) found mixed evidence of the importance of pretend play for development and emphasised the need for more research in this area.

Drawn together, this research exploring different kinds of parent-child play tells us that simple, everyday play shared between caregivers and their young children can help to set children up for a good start in school, especially for those children who may be more at risk of experiencing difficulties during the transition. However, research into parents' perspectives on school readiness suggests that parents often underestimate the role of play in nurturing skills related to school readiness (O'Sullivan & Ring, 2018).

Poverty and inequalities in children's school readiness

Growing up in poverty can mean that children start school behind their peers in terms of their school readiness skills, gaps which tend to widen over time and can affect children's life chances (e.g., Claessens, Duncan, & Engel, 2009; Condron, 2009; Shonkoff, 2015). Poverty carries a range of risk factors that can undermine families' ability to provide care as optimally as they would like, including the home learning environment and the responsive and stimulating interactions that nurture development (see Oppenheim & Milton, 2022). Importantly, findings from the Effective Provision of Pre-School Education (EPPE) project show that when families provide stimulating learning opportunities in the home this can buffer against the effects of poverty on children's development (see Sylva et al., 2012). Thus, equitable access to support for the home learning environment is important so that all families have the same opportunity to experience enjoyable and enriching learning experiences.

In response to the far-reaching consequences of these early skills gaps, interest is growing in early interventions that target school readiness and early school adjustment, particularly for children facing more disadvantage. Interventions designed to raise parents' awareness of the important role they hold in their children's lives and the value of play in children's development, as well as supporting responsive interactions, can be a powerful way to promote children' outcomes across multiple domains (for example, see the systematic review from Jeong, Franchett, Ramos de Oliveira, Rehmani, & Yousafzai, 2021).

Parenting programmes to promote child development

In this section, we discuss three different early interventions that have play-based components and have been shown to have positive effects on factors frequently associated with children's school readiness.

The preparing for life programme

The Preparing for Life Programme is an intensive parenting programme that aims to improve children's school readiness skills which began as a community-led initiative in a deprived area of North Dublin, Ireland (see Doyle, 2020). This manualised early intervention provided a range of support for families from pregnancy until their child started school, including regular home visiting, a baby massage course, and the Triple P parenting programme (Triple P; Sanders, 1999). Home visits supported parents to identify developmental milestones, adopt parenting practices, and provide enhanced stimulation.

A key feature of the *Preparing for Life* Programme is the use of engaging, easy read 'Tip Sheets' which cover a range of topics, including pregnancy, parenting, health, and development, and are delivered through the home visits. The Tip Sheets offer practical suggestions about a range of strategies, activities, and approaches that parents can try out in everyday moments with their children. Play features regularly throughout the 210 Tip Sheets including 14 dedicated Tip Sheets on topics such as learning through play, messy play, playing outdoors, sand play, water play, play dough, role play and playing with toys (see Doyle, 2020). For example, one Tip Sheet encouraged parents to create play opportunities for them and their children using both traditional toys and everyday objects from around the house that would be engaging and safe for play with babies and toddlers. Another sheet provided ideas for play like 'treasure baskets' and emphasised the role parents can play in expanding their child's vocabulary and building up their self-esteem by taking notice of the child's actions and commenting on the things they are doing and achieving.

The randomised controlled trial evaluation found large positive impacts on multiple aspects of children's skills including their cognitive ability that were sustained at age nine, although earlier effects on children's behaviour problems were not sustained (see Doyle, 2020, 2022). Doyle (2022) also found that about 46% of the effects in children's skills at age nine were explained by earlier improvements in parenting and the home environment. While it is not possible to isolate the effect of individual components of the extensive and diverse supports made available to families, it is notable that the programme placed such an emphasis on the important and powerful role that parents play in shared everyday moments with their children.

Video-feedback intervention to promote positive parenting and sensitive discipline

Video-feedback intervention to promote Positive Parenting and Sensitive Discipline (VIPP-SD; Juffer, Bakermans-Kranenburg, & van IJzendoorn, 2008) is a manualised, home-based parenting programme delivered across six sessions taking place every two weeks. A key aim of the programme is to enhance parental sensitivity by promoting parents' capacity to observe and interpret their child's behaviour and emotions and respond in a prompt and responsive way. VIPP-SD uses a video-feedback approach. Short video clips of the parent and child interacting are used by the programme facilitator to reflect on the child's communication and behaviour, to bring to life the bond the parent and child share, and to offer tips on parental responsiveness and sensitive discipline strategies.

The majority of the interactions included in the programme are play-based. In some of the interactions, the parent is asked to play freely with their child using simple toys like blocks, puppets, and books. In other interactions, they are asked to support their child with a tricky task like a puzzle. Moments of play where the child is exploring a toy a little beyond their developmental capabilities can be useful to highlight both the benefits of the caregiver sitting back and letting the child have a go themselves, as well as moments where the caregiver increasing their level of support can scaffold the child's experience. In some interactions, the parent is asked to help the child through a task that the child is likely to resist or find challenging, like tidying up the toys. Clips of these more challenging interactions can be used to highlight to the caregiver the important role their support provides for their child's emotion regulation using strategies such as empathising, distraction, and praise.

The VIPP model has been tested across numerous populations. A meta-analysis of 25 randomised controlled trials testing VIPP identified positive effects for parenting behaviour and for children's attachment, but not children's behaviour problems (van IJzendoorn et al., 2022). In the Healthy Start, Happy Start study (O'Farrelly et al., 2021; Ramchandani et al., 2017), we tested whether the use of VIPP-SD delivered in health visiting services in the UK could prevent enduring behaviour problems for children showing elevated signs of difficulties at one to three years old. In this randomised controlled trial of 300 families, we found that children in the VIPP-SD group showed lower levels of behaviour problems following the programme than children whose parents did not receive the programme. When we visited families again two years later, the children in the VIPP-SD group continued to show lower levels of behaviour problems. This study indicates that the VIPP-SD programme is effective in promoting aspects of parenting and child behaviour for children who are at risk of behaviour problems, benefits which are likely to offer children a stronger start in school.

The reach up programme

The Reach Up early childhood programme was designed to support mothers in teaching their children, to interact with them in consistent and responsive ways, and to provide stimulating home environments for their children's play and learning (Walker, Chang, Smith, & Baker-Henningham, 2018). This home-visiting intervention was developed in Kingston Jamaica in the 1970s in response to the identification of a decline in young children's development, relatively low levels of resource in children's homes (toys, books), relatively low levels of parental responsiveness and nurturing care seen in parent-child observations, and high levels of malnutrition in toddlers (Grantham-McGregor, Desai, & Back, 1972). In Jamaica, an estimated one in three children under the age of four live in poverty. Given the high costs and lack of access to centre-based care for children under three years (only ~14% of under 3s attend childcare, compared to 85% of four- to five-year-olds), home-based early childhood programmes are considered to be a powerful tool in breaking the cycle of poverty in these communities (Scott-McDonald, 2002).

The goal of the manualised home-visiting programme is to improve child development by enhancing the responsiveness and stimulation provided by mothers and increase their capacity to draw enjoyment from helping their child to play and learn (Smith, Baker-Henningham, Brentani, Mugweni, & Walker, 2018). The programme has been delivered to families with children aged 6–48 months old. Families typically receive visits for 18 months, and the programme has been designed to be low cost, using paraprofessionals (i.e., community mothers) as the programme facilitators. During the weekly visits, the home visitor uses books and homemade toys to demonstrate play activities to mothers and model behaviours that promote responsive parent-child interactions. Toys and materials are then left in the family home between weekly visits and replaced with new play materials each time the home visitor returns. The curriculum includes sorting and matching activities, puzzles, and word games. The visitor also places a general emphasis on the power of the parent spending time playing, chatting, looking at books, and singing with their child.

Since its development and implementation in Jamaica, the intervention has been adapted for different cultures and tested in over a dozen studies across a number of low- and middle-income countries, including Bangladesh, Colombia, and Peru. In a review of 13 studies testing the Reach Up programme, Grantham-McGregor and Smith (2016) reported that all included studies indicated benefits to children's cognitive, language, and/or behavioural development, with some evidence of long-term benefits into adolescence and early adulthood.

We have the evidence to tell us that well-run parenting interventions, delivered by dedicated teams, can have immediate and sustained effects for child development. The challenge now is to better understand how we can take these programmes effectively to scale so that they can reach more families.

Steps forward: a whole systems approach to school readiness

This chapter has drawn together evidence that highlights the positive and powerful role parents can play in supporting and facilitating children's early school adjustment. However, parenting and family life do not take place in a vacuum. It can be shaped, sustained, and enhanced by supportive and playful opportunities in early childcare settings, in schools and classrooms, and in the community and wider society. This must be coupled with efforts to tackle the rising tide of poverty, so that families can enjoy and enrich the early years of their children's lives and all children are offered a fair start.

Discussion starters around school readiness

School, early years settings, and families are already using lots of techniques to help promote children's school readiness. The following discussion starters could be helpful for staff to consider ways to build upon the work they're already doing to continue to support children and families during this important milestone.

- What practices seem to already be working well in supporting children through their transition to school? Are there ways these activities can be built upon?
- How can we ensure that these practices are supportive of children from a range of backgrounds and experiences?
- What opportunities are there to integrate play into these transition practices?
- What can we do to maintain and nurture the links between home and school for children?

Further information

The following resources tell us more about supporting children's transition to school.

- **Encyclopaedia on Early Childhood Development** – This provides resources that highlight key skills and abilities that contribute to school readiness and discusses the role of parents and early years settings in supporting a successful start in school.

- **Position statement from the Educational Transitions and Change Research Group** – This has been developed as an aspirational document for all those involved in the education and care of young children and focuses on the transition to school in the context of social justice, children's rights, educational reform, and ethics.
- **Mo Scéal (My Story) from the Irish National Council for Curriculum and Assessment** – This provides materials designed to support the transition from preschool to primary, including information about the skills and dispositions commonly associated with school readiness, information about Children's Thoughts on moving to primary school, and ideas for activities focusing on transitions, building relationships, and working with parents.
- **PEDAL Research Centre: Play and the transition to school** – This is a short blog written by PEDAL researchers summarising what we know about the ways play can help build relationships, spark joy in learning, and boost learning during children's early years of school.
- **Nursery World: Children's perspectives on starting school** – This book summarises our research about children's views on their school readiness from the Children's Thoughts about School Study.

Key terms

- **A randomised controlled trial** is widely considered to be the 'gold standard' in producing empirical evidence looking into the effects of an intervention. In randomised controlled trials, participants are randomly assigned to one of two groups. One group receives the intervention that is being tested. The other group acts as a comparison or control group by receiving an alternative treatment or services as usual. Randomisation balances participant characteristics between groups. This means that differences in outcome between the two groups can be attributed to the intervention with a high degree of confidence.
- **A systematic review** is a type of literature review that collates empirical evidence that fits pre-specified eligibility criteria to answer a specific research question. The structured, transparent, and reproducible techniques are used while drawing together literature in a systematic way that helps to minimise bias and increase reliability in the findings.
- **A meta-analysis** builds on the techniques of a systematic review by synthesising the findings of single studies using statistical techniques to calculate an overall effect. Findings from meta-analyses can help us to understand the strength and quality of the evidence for a specific intervention or condition.

Note

1 Please note, we intend for the term 'parent' to represent all parental figures that take responsibility for children's day-to-day care and upbringing.

References

Abry, T., Latham, S., Bassok, D., & LoCasale-Crouch, J. (2015). Preschool and kindergarten teachers' beliefs about early school competencies: Misalignment matters for kindergarten adjustment. *Early Childhood Research Quarterly, 31*, 78–88.

Ainsworth, M. D. S., Bell, S. M., & Stayton, D. F. (1974). Infant-mother attachment and social development: Socialization as a product of reciprocal responsiveness to signals. In M. P. M. Richards (Ed.), *The integration of a child into a social world* (pp. 99–135). London: Cambridge University Press.

Amodia-Bidakowska, A., Laverty, C., & Ramchandani, P. G. (2020). Father-child play: A systematic review of its frequency, characteristics and potential impact on children's development. *Developmental Review, 57*, 100924.

Brooker, L. (2008). *Supporting transitions in the early years*. Maidenhead: Open University Press McGraw Hill.

Brown, C. (2017). School readiness. In L. Miller, C. Cameron, C. Dalli & N Barbour (Eds.), *The Sage handbook of early childhood policy* (pp. 287–302). SAGE Publications.

Byrne, E. M., Jensen, H., Thomsen, B. S., & Ramchandani, P. G. (2023). Educational interventions involving physical manipulatives for improving children's learning and development: A scoping review. *Review of Education, 11*(2), e3400.

Claessens, A., Duncan, G., & Engel, M. (2009). Kindergarten skills and fifth-grade achievement: Evidence from the ECLS-K. *Economics of Education Review, 28*(4), 415–427.

Condron, D. J. (2009). Social class, school and non-school environments, and black/white inequalities in children's learning. *American Sociological Review, 74*(5), 685–708.

Cooke, J. E., Deneault, A. A., Devereux, C., Eirich, R., Fearon, R. P., & Madigan, S. (2022). Parental sensitivity and child behavioral problems: A meta-analytic review. *Child Development, 93*(5), 1231–1248.

Craig, L. (2006). Does father care mean fathers share? A comparison of how mothers and fathers in intact families spend time with children. *Gender & Society, 20*(2), 259–281.

Department for Education (2023). *Early years foundation stage statutory framework for group and school-based providers: Setting the standards for learning, development and care for children from birth to five*. Department for Education. https://assets.publishing.service.gov.uk/media/65aa5e42ed27ca001327b2c7/EYFS_statutory_framework_for_group_and_school_based_providers.pdf

DePasquale, C. E., & Gunnar, M. R. (2020). Parental Sensitivity and Nurturance. In J. Brooks-Gunn & A. Aizer (Eds.), *Future of children: Supporting development from three trimesters to three years* (pp. 53–70). Princeton, NJ: Princeton-Brookings.

Dockett, S., & Perry, B. (2004). Starting school: Perspectives of Australian children, parents and educators. *Journal of Early Childhood Research, 2*(2), 171–189. https://doi.org/10.1177/1476718X04042976

Dockett, S., Perry, B., & Kearney, E. (2010). *School readiness: What does it mean for indigenous children, families, schools and communities? Issues paper no. 2*. GPO Box 570, Canberra, ACT 2601, Australia: Australian Institute of Health and Welfare.

Dowdall, N., Melendez-Torres, G. J., Murray, L., Gardner, F., Hartford, L., & Cooper, P. J. (2020). Shared picture book reading interventions for child language development: A systematic review and meta-analysis. *Child Development, 91*(2), e383–e399.

Doyle, O. (2020). The first 2,000 days and child skills. *Journal of Political Economy, 128*(6), 2067–2122.

Doyle, O. (2022). Can early intervention have a sustained effect on human capital? *Journal of Human Resources, 58*(3), 1–51. https://doi.org/10.3368/jhr.0321-11557R1

Educational Transitions and Change (ETC) Research Group (2011). *Transition to school: Position statement.* Albury-Wodonga: Research Institute for Professional Practice, Learning and Education, Charles Sturt University.

Einarsdottir, J. (2010). Children's experiences of the first year of primary school. *European Early Childhood Education Research Journal, 18*(2), 163–180. https://doi.org/10.1080/13502931003784370

Fearon, R. M. P., & Belsky, J. (2016). Precursors of attachment security. In J. Cassidy & P. R. Shaver (Eds.) *Handbook of attachment theory and research* (3rd ed.) (pp. 291–313). New York: Guilford Press.

Foster, E. K., & Hund, A. M. (2012). The impact of scaffolding and overhearing on young children's use of the spatial terms between and middle. *Journal of Child Language, 39*(2), 338–364.

Georgeson, J., Roberts-Holmes, G., Campbell-Barr, V., Archer, N., Lee, S. F., Gulliver, K., Street, M., Walsh, G., & Waters-Davies, J. (2022). *Competing discourses in early childhood education and care.* British Educational Research Association. Available at: https://www.bera.ac.uk/publication/competing-discourses-in-early-childhood-education-and-care

Grantham-McGregor, S. M., Desai, P., & Back, E. H. (1972). A longitudinal study of infant growth in Kingston, Jamaica. *Human Biology, 44*(3), 549–561.

Grantham-McGregor, S., & Smith, J. A. (2016). Extending the Jamaican early childhood development intervention. *Journal of Applied Research on Children: Informing Policy for Children at Risk, 7*(2), 4–38.

Gray, P. (2013). *Free to learn: Why unleashing the instinct to play will make our children happier, more self-reliant, and better students for life.* Basic Books.

Jankowska, D. M., & Omelańczuk, I. (2018). Potential mechanisms underlying the impact of imaginative play on socio-emotional development in childhood. *Creativity. Theories–Research-Applications, 5*(1), 84–103.

Jeong, J., Franchett, E. E., Ramos de Oliveira, C. V., Rehmani, K., & Yousafzai, A. K. (2021). Parenting interventions to promote early child development in the first three years of life: A global systematic review and meta-analysis. *PLoS Medicine, 18*(5), e1003602.

Juffer, F., Bakermans-Kranenburg, M., & van IJzendoorn, M. (2008). *Promoting positive parenting: An attachment-based intervention.* New York: Routledge.

Keating, I., Fabian, H., Jordan, P., Mavers, D., & Roberts, J. (2000). 'Well, I've not done any work today. i don't know why i came to school'. Perceptions of play in the reception class. *Educational Studies, 26*(4), 437–454. https://doi.org/10.1080/03055690020003638

Kenney, M. K. (2012). Child, family, and neighborhood associations with parent and peer interactive play during early childhood. *Maternal and Child Health Journal, 16*, 88–101.

Ladd, G. W. (2009). School transitions/school readiness: An outcome of early childhood development ~ Perspective: Children's social and scholastic development – Findings from the pathways project. In R. E., Tremblay, M. Boivin, & R. Peters (Eds.), *Encyclopaedia on early childhood development.* (pp. 1–11) Retrieved from: http://www.child-encyclopedia.com

Ladd, G. W., Buhs, E. S., & Seid, M. (2000). Children's initial sentiments about kindergarten: Is school liking an antecedent of early classroom participation and achievement? *Merrill-Palmer Quarterly, 46(2)*, 255–279.

Leech, K. A., McNally, S., Daly, M., & Corriveau, K. H. (2022). Unique effects of book-reading at 9-months on vocabulary development at 36-months: Insights from a nationally representative sample of Irish families. *Early Childhood Research Quarterly, 58*, 242–253.

Levine, S. C., Ratliff, K. R., Huttenlocher, J., & Cannon, J. (2012). Early puzzle play: A predictor of preschoolers' spatial transformation skill. *Developmental Psychology*, *48*(2), 530–542. https://doi.org/10.1037/a0025913

Lillard, A. S. (2012). Mother-child fantasy play. In P. Nathan & A. D. Pellegrini (Eds.), *The Oxford handbook of the development of play* (pp. 285–295). Oxford Academic.

Lillard, A. S. (2017). Why do the children (pretend) play? *Trends in Cognitive Sciences*, *21*(11), 826–834.

Lillard, A. S., Lerner, M. D., Hopkins, E. J., Dore, R. A., Smith, E. D., & Palmquist, C. M. (2013). The impact of pretend play on children's development: A review of the evidence. *Psychological Bulletin*, *139*(1), 1–34.

LoCasale-Crouch, J., Mashburn, A., Downer, J., & Pianta, R. (2008). Pre-kindergarten teachers' use of transition practices and children's adjustment to kindergarten. *Early Childhood Research Quarterly*, *23*(1), 124–139. https://doi.org/10.1016/j.ecresq.2007.06.001

Logan, J. A., Justice, L. M., Yumus, M., & Chaparro-Moreno, L. J. (2019). When children are not read to at home: The million word gap. *Journal of Developmental & Behavioral Pediatrics*, *40*(5), 383–386.

Margetts, K. (2006, September). Teachers should explain what they mean": What new children need to know about starting school. *Paper presented at the EECERA 16th Annual Conference*, Reykjavik, Iceland.

Mashburn, A. J. (2014). The importance of quality prekindergarten programs for promoting school readiness skills. In C.L. Cooper & S.H. Landry (Eds.) *Wellbeing in children and families.* (pp. 271–296). Wiley Blackwell. https://doi.org/10.1002/9781118539415.wbwell012

Morris, T. T., Dorling, D., Davies, N. M., & Davey Smith, G. (2021). Associations between school enjoyment at age 6 and later educational achievement: Evidence from a UK cohort study. *Science of Learning*, *6*(1), 1–18. https://doi.org/10.1038/s41539-021-00092-w

Murray, L. (2014). *The psychology of babies: How relationships support development from birth to two*. Hachette UK.

Murray, E., & Harrison, L. (2005). Children's perspectives on their first year of school: Introducing a new pictorial measure of school stress, *European Early Childhood Education Research Journal*, *13*, 111–127. https://doi.org/10.1080/13502930585209591

Murray, L., Jennings, S., Perry, H., Andrews, M., De Wilde, K., Newell, A., ... & Cooper, P. J. (2023). Effects of training parents in dialogic book-sharing: The early-years provision in Children's Centers (EPICC) study. *Early Childhood Research Quarterly*, *62*, 1–16.

O'Farrelly, C., Booth, A., Tatlow-Golden, M., & Barker, B. (2020). Reconstructing readiness: Young children's priorities for their early school adjustment. *Early Childhood Research Quarterly*, *50*(2), 3–16.

O'Farrelly, C., Doyle, O., Victory, G., & Palamaro-Munsell, E. (2018). Shared reading in infancy and later development: Evidence from an early intervention. *Journal of Applied Developmental Psychology*, *54*, 69–83.

O'Farrelly, C., Watt, H., Babalis, D., Bakermans-Kranenburg, M. J., Barker, B., Byford, S., ... & Ramchandani, P. G. (2021). A brief home-based parenting intervention to reduce behavior problems in young children: A pragmatic randomized clinical trial. *JAMA Pediatrics*, *175*(6), 567–576.

O'Sullivan, L., & Ring, E. (2018). Play as learning: Implications for educators and parents from findings of a national evaluation of school readiness in Ireland. *International Journal of Play*, *7*(3), 266–289.

Oppenheim, C., & Milton, C. (2022) *Changing patterns of poverty in early childhood: The changing face of early childhood in the UK*. Nuffield Foundation. Available at: https://www.nuffieldfoundation.org/wp-content/uploads/2021/09/Changing-patterns-of-poverty-in-early-childhood-Nuffield-Foundation.pdf

Paquette, D., Carbonneau, R., Dubeau, D., Bigras, M., & Tremblay, R. E. (2003). Prevalence of father-child rough-and-tumble play and physical aggression in preschool children. *European Journal of Psychology of Education, 18*, 171–189.

Peters, S. (2003). "I Didn't Expect That I Would Get Tons of Friends More Each Day": Children's experiences of friendship during the transition to school. *Early Years, 23*(1), 45–53. https://doi.org/10.1080/0957514032000045564

Piaget, J. (1962). *Play, dreams, and imitation in childhood*. New York: Norton.

Preparing for Life & The Northside Partnership (2008). Preparing for Life programme manual. Dublin: Preparing for Life and the Northside Partnership.

Prime, H., Andrews, K., Markwell, A., Gonzalez, A., Janus, M., Tricco, A. C., Bennett, T., & Atkinson, L. (2023). Positive parenting and early childhood cognition: A systematic review and meta-analysis of randomized controlled trials. *Clinical Child and Family Psychology Review, 26*, 362–400.

Professional Association for Childcare and Early Years (PACEY) (2013) *What does "school ready" really mean? A research report from Professional Association for Childcare and Early Years*. Available at: https://www.pacey.org.uk/Pacey/media/Website-files/school%20ready/School-Ready-Report.pdf

Ramchandani, P. G., O'Farrelly, C., Babalis, D., Bakermans-Kranenburg, M., Byford, S., Grimas, E., … & Scott, S. (2017). Preventing enduring behavioural problems in young children through early psychological intervention (healthy start, happy start): Study protocol for a randomized controlled trial. *Trials, 18*(1), 1–11.

Ramey, C. T., & Ramey, S. L. (2004). early learning and school readiness: Can early intervention make a difference? *Merrill-Palmer Quarterly, 50*(4), 471–491. https://doi.org/10.1353/mpq.2004.0034

Rimm-Kaufman, S., & Sandilos, L. (2017). School transition and school readiness: An outcome of early childhood development. *Encyclopaedia on Early Childhood Development*, 1–7.

Rodriguez, E. T., Tamis-LeMonda, C. S., Spellmann, M. E., Pan, B. A., Raikes, H., Lugo-Gil, J., & Luze, G. (2009). The formative role of home literacy experiences across the first three years of life in children from low-income families. *Journal of Applied Developmental Psychology, 30*(6), 677–694.

Sanders, M. R. (1999). Triple P-positive parenting program: Towards an empirically validated multilevel parenting and family support strategy for the prevention of behavior and emotional problems in children. *Clinical Child and Family Psychology Review, 2*(2), 71–90. https://doi.org/10.1023/A:1021843613840

Schulting, A. B., Malone, P. S., & Dodge, K. A. (2005). The effect of school-based kindergarten transition policies and practices on child academic outcomes. *Developmental Psychology, 41*(6), 860–871. https://doi.org/10.1037%2F0012-1649.41.6.860

Scott-McDonald, K. (2002). Elements of quality in home visiting programs: Three Jamaican models. In M. E. Young (Ed) From early child development to human development: Investing in our children's future (pp. 233–256). Washington, DC: The World Bank.

Shonkoff, J. P. (2015). The neurobiology of early childhood development and the foundation of a sustainable society. In P. T. M. Marope & Y. Kaga (Eds.), *Investing against evidence: The global state of early childhood care and education* (pp. 55–71). UNESCO Publishing.

Skene, K., O'Farrelly, C. M., Byrne, E. M., Kirby, N., Stevens, E. C., & Ramchandani, P. G. (2022). Can guidance during play enhance children's learning and development in educational contexts? A systematic review and meta-analysis. *Child Development, 93*(4), 1162–1180.

Smith, J. A., Baker-Henningham, H., Brentani, A., Mugweni, R., & Walker, S. P. (2018). Implementation of reach up early childhood parenting program: Acceptability, appropriateness, and feasibility in Brazil and Zimbabwe. *Annals of the New York Academy of Sciences, 1419*(1), 120–140.

Society for Emotion and Attachment Studies. (2021). Explanations of attachment theoretical concepts. Version April 2021. Retrieved from https://seasinternational.org/explanations-of-attachment-theoretical-concepts/

Sylva, K., Melhuish, E., Sammons, P., Siraj-Blatchford, I., Taggart, B., Toth, K., ... & Welcomme, W. (2012) *Effective pre-school, primary and secondary education 3–14 project (EPPSE 3–14) final report from the key stage 3 phase: Influences on students' development from age 11–14*. London: Department for Children, Schools and Families. Available at: https://assets.publishing.service.gov.uk/government/uploads/system/uploads/attachment_data/file/184087/DFE-RR202.pdf

Van IJzendoorn, M. H., & Bakermans-Kranenburg, M. J. (2019). Bridges across the intergenerational transmission of attachment gap. *Current Opinion in Psychology, 25*, 31–36.

Van IJzendoorn, M. H., Schuengel, C., Wang, Q., & Bakermans-Kranenburg, M. J. (2023). Improving parenting, child attachment, and externalizing behaviors: Meta-analysis of the first 25 randomized controlled trials on the effects of video-feedback intervention to promote positive parenting and sensitive discipline. *Development and Psychopathology, 35*(1), 241–256.

Veiga, G., O'Connor, R. A., Neto, C., & Rieffe, C. J. (2020). Rough-and-tumble play and the regulation of aggression in preschoolers. *Early Child Development and Care*, 1–13. doi:10.1080/03004430.2020.1828396.

Veiga, G., O'Connor, R., Neto, C., & Rieffe, C. (2022). Rough-and-tumble play and the regulation of aggression in preschoolers. *Early Child Development and Care, 192*(6), 980–992.

Walker, S. P., Chang, S. M., Smith, J. A., & Baker-Henningham, H. (2018). The reach up early childhood parenting program: Origins, content, and implementation. *Zero to Three, 38*(4), 37–43.

Weisberg, D. S. (2015). Pretend play. *Wiley Interdisciplinary Reviews: Cognitive Science, 6*(3), 249–261.

Weisberg, D. S., Kittredge, A. K., Hirsh-Pasek, K., Golinkoff, R. M., & Klahr, D. (2015). Making play work for education. *Phi Delta Kappan, 96*(8), 8–13.

Whitebread, D. (2015). Introduction: Young children learning and early years teaching. In *Teaching and learning in the early years* (pp. 1–22). London: Routledge.

World Health Organisation (2004). *The importance of caregiver-child interactions for the survival and healthy development of young children: A review*. Department of Child and Adolescent Health and Development.

CHAPTER

Inclusive practice and play in primary education

Lenka Janik-Blaskova and Stephen Kilgour

Introduction

In this chapter, we explore how play is key in developing inclusive practice in schools. The concept of inclusive education implies that all children are learning together in mainstream classrooms; or does it? We argue that play makes classrooms more inclusive. It comes naturally to children, fuels their interest in discovery and enables interactions with other children. Social play has its own universal rules that apply to all, equally. How can we harness the benefits of play when educating children in schools? What can teachers do to incorporate the inclusiveness of play into their classrooms? What do children need to feel included and to what extent can play facilitate these needs? And what if some children are simply not ready to be included? Can playful approaches assist the unique inclusion needs of all children?

This chapter aims to encourage practitioners to reflect on the extent to which their practice is truly inclusive. It will consider play-based approaches as facilitators of inclusive practice. The chapter highlights some of the opportunities available to educators and how they may implement them in their learning spaces. We will start by looking closely at the terminology around inclusion, as it can have a powerful influence on an educator's approach.

It is worth clarifying our view on 'education', which we perceive broadly. We believe that schools are places for attaining knowledge and developing important life skills, such as communication, resilience and the ability to navigate through interpersonal relationships. Our examples will demonstrate our holistic view, which, in the context of inclusion, seems the most natural one to adopt.

We have developed our views through our personal and professional experiences. Stephen is an Education Advisor with 15 years' experience working with 2–11-year-olds, including 7 years as a senior leader in an outstanding specialist school in London. He is passionate about child-centred teaching and assessment. Lenka is a psychologist and a trained guidance counsellor. When supporting children and young people in schools, she learned that children's well-being mainly depends on their interactions and relationships with peers. Using play-based approaches, she has conducted studies on the friendships and well-being of children with language difficulties. As a lecturer in the Psychology of Education, Lenka continues exploring school interventions supporting peer inclusion.

Inclusive language

It is our aim throughout this contribution to be considerate of the language that we include in relation to special educational needs and disabilities (SEND). Over time, the terminology we use linked to disability has changed significantly, and language that was acceptable 50 years ago seems alarming when reflected on today. Our language is likely to continue to evolve, and it is up to us to be mindful of this in our practice.

The most obvious starting point for unpacking current commonplace language is the term 'special needs' itself. The word 'special' may have been deemed positive and gentle when it first came into use to describe people with differences and disabilities, but in essence it is an unhelpful term. A child with learning differences or a physical disability doesn't have extra special 'needs' in life. Just like any of their peers, they need love, warmth, nutrition, security and opportunities for learning through play (not an exhaustive list). To label this child's needs as 'special' or even 'additional' is doing them a disservice. They are entitled to the same opportunities as anyone else, but they may require some additional support in order to have their needs fully met. For this reason, we will occasionally refer to 'support needs'. Lees (2022, p. 6) states that 'language shapes our beliefs and attitudes'. If we continue to use language that reinforces a view that people with a disability have needs that are above and beyond those of any other human, then we will perpetuate this harmful narrative – this is a form of ableism. Ableism is a type of discrimination which favours people without disabilities and, as a consequence, harms people with learning differences or disabilities. It can present in many different forms such as policies, society values, people's beliefs, attitudes and actions.

Unfortunately, the language used across the sector and from the Department for Education often fails to be progressive. In March 2022, the UK government released their long-anticipated SEND review green paper entitled: 'Right Support, Right Place, Right Time'. There were 296 mentions of the word 'needs' across the document, including 46 references to 'high needs' and 22 references to 'complex needs'. There were also numerous mentions of 'identifying needs'. It is time for a change in mindset. 'Needs' should not require deeper scrutiny or identification for our children with learning differences or disabilities, because those basic needs are the same for all children and they should therefore be obvious before a child even arrives at a setting or school. It is the provision that adapts accordingly, to make sure that those needs are met for all children. It was also striking that there was no mention of the importance and power of play in the paper – all children should be entitled to motivating and engaging education.

In order to combat ableism in education, it is important that we embrace neurodiversity, affirming practice in the language we use and in the provision we offer. The word 'neurodiverse' describes all types of brains, whether they are 'neurotypical' or 'neurodivergent'. 'Neurodivergent' describes a person whose brain functions in a way that diverges from the dominant society standards of 'normal' or 'neurotypical'.

The medical model of disability is currently dominant in terms of practices in health, education and social care. It focuses on reducing symptoms or treating. In contrast, rather than focusing on what is 'wrong' with the person, the social model and the neurodiversity paradigm consider the context and surrounding environment, and how they may be impacting that person negatively.

A change in the language that we use linked to learning differences and disability in our settings and schools can help to change the attitude of the educators who work in them. If we look for strengths in the children who we work with as opposed to seeking out the deficits, it can lead to a more celebratory approach to assessment which in turn can contribute to a more positive, child-centred environment.

LANGUAGE COMPARISONS

Ableist/Medical model terminology	Neurodiversity affirming terminology
Deficits	Strengths
Disorder	Difficulties
Symptoms	Characteristics
Challenging behaviour	Distress
Person with autism	Autistic person

Source: A Beginner's Guide to Ableism (Lees, 2022)

Figure 4.1 Language Comparisons: Medical model terminology verses neurodiversity affirming terminology

History of inclusion

Traditionally, the concept of inclusion targeted children and young people with special education needs and disabilities (SEND). This understanding was based on the origins of inclusive education principles, which were formulated at the United Nations' World Conference on Special Education Needs in Salamanca in 1994, and later restated at the UN's World Education Forum in Dakar in 2000. Although *Education for All* has been the key idea from the beginning, the understanding of inclusion has shifted. We have moved from identifying and lifting barriers for children with SEND to creating an accommodating educational environment for all children, without any discrimination with regard to culture, ethnicity, faith, language, sexual orientation and so on. This broader understanding of inclusion is reflected in the current discourse in the UK. Governmental bodies (for example, the Department for Education, Ofsted), educational organisations and schools have been referring more often to equality and diversity alongside inclusion.

Ableism linked to play and assessment

It is vital that we are truly inclusive when it comes to our provision and assessment. If we are to value the power of play, then we also need to ensure that we avoid ableist mindsets when it comes to planning our environment and resources. Murphy (2022, p. 152) highlights: 'The issues that can sometimes emerge with SEND play is that the child is just assumed to be displaying SEND behaviours and fewer efforts are made to understand how this might link to learning'. It is this judgement of play for children with learning differences that can lead to attempts to 'normalise' play behaviours or 'train' a child to play in a typical way. Susan Isaacs, an early years educationalist and psychologist, explained that children's play should be respected and left free to evolve on their own terms because '….play has the greatest value for the young child when it is really free and his own' (Isaacs, 1971, p. 133). A child's unique play characteristics should be celebrated and valued if we are to achieve what should be a key aim – learning through genuine engagement.

As with any child in a group, when we first meet them, we need to observe their play and interactions and respond appropriately. Where does their interest lie? What makes them feel safe, happy and comfortable? Conversely, we also need to attempt to have an acute awareness of what makes them feel unsafe, unhappy or scared. We should ensure that the learning environment is inclusive – especially if a child has sensory sensitivities. This could mean building in flexibility to a child's routine or adapting areas of the space. It would be ableist, for example, to expect a child with noise sensitivity to cope in a busy classroom without appropriate support or adjustments in place.

Knowledge of the way children typically develop is important for an educator. If we know the order in which learning generally takes place, we can support and respond appropriately in our teaching, particularly when we are considering a child-led scenario. As an educator we are constantly evaluating the learning that is taking place and adjusting what we do next – skilled practitioners can use their experience and knowledge to respond and adjust in the most purposeful manner at the very moment it is required. The need for an understanding of typical development comes with a caveat though – not all children will follow the same pathways, particularly those with learning differences or disabilities. We should not make assumptions about the route a child's learning journey will take. There is a significant chance that a child who is neurodivergent will progress with their learning in a manner that is not comparable to their neurotypical peers – or, importantly, their peers who also have learning differences.

Assessment of children's play and learning can be a contentious issue. For many years, those working in the early years or in specialist settings were required to assess children's learning in a formulaic way, based on banks of statements which described milestones you would typically expect to find in young children. These processes created a wealth of 'data' and 'evidence' that could be provided when Ofsted called, to clearly demonstrate the quality of education being provided. The fact that these procedures are no longer required (Inspectors will not use schools' internal assessment data as evidence, Ofsted School Inspection Handbook, 2022) shows that they weren't a particularly accurate reflection of quality (and also incredibly time-consuming). UK nurseries and schools now find themselves in a position where they can develop assessment approaches that are bespoke to their particular situation. This is a very positive development – but it is important that we devise approaches which do not exclude certain children or require them to fundamentally change in order to achieve. Our assessment systems should be like our learning environments – inclusive, responsive and adaptable.

Representation and inclusive practice

When reflecting on inclusivity in our settings and schools, it is essential that we take into account the diversity and representation on offer in our provision.

Have you ever considered the whiteness of educators working in education? A report from University College London's Institute of Education in 2020 found that 46% of schools and nurseries in England have an entirely white teaching staff (Tereshchenko et al., 2020). What impact could this have on a Black or Brown student in these settings or schools? Representation is a powerful concept. If a child sees someone who looks like them carrying out a role, then they are more likely to feel that they have an opportunity to follow in those footsteps. In addition, to spend time at school/early years setting with someone who can genuinely relate to them is very significant – particularly for a child with learning differences who may need comforting during moments of distress on a more regular basis. Representation obviously is not exclusive to race. We need to be considerate of the identities of every child and their families when we make decisions in schools.

Representation is addressed not only in the makeup of our staff teams but also in the resources that we provide. Do we consider the characters in the books on our shelves, or the images on our displays? How would it feel as a Black or Brown child to only ever read books where the hero is white? Do we genuinely embrace the cultural differences amongst our pupils through high-quality engagement with families? How does that manifest itself in the role play area of our learning space or in the dressing up box? Does Black History Month constitute a plastic storage box of resources that gets wheeled out each October? Or are we considering Black history and its place in our curriculum all year round? If you are working in a school that has an entirely white cohort of children, this is not an excuse to deny the children rich and diverse provision. Once we have made considerations and adjustments to our environment to ensure that it is actually inclusive, it is imperative that we then embrace the newfound resources we have brought in by having necessary conversations about race. Pemberton (2022, p. 4) states:

> By ignoring race whilst openly discussing with children other protected characteristics such as disability or sex, it transmits a message that race is a bad thing. For example, if a child asks a question about why their skin colour is different to that of another child's, it is important to be equipped to be able to communicate this in a positive and meaningful way that is age, stage and ability appropriate which is not rooted in shame, guilt or embarrassment.

The term 'intersectionality' is very prevalent when reflecting on the needs of Black and Brown children in our setting or school who have learning differences or disabilities. Kimberlé Crenshaw coined the term 'intersectionality' in 1989 to describe how systems of oppression overlap to create distinct experiences for people with multiple identity categories (Crenshaw, 1989). Reflecting on intersectionality should help us to better understand the multiple barriers that these young children are facing in our education system and wider society.

To counter systemic racism in education, educators can take steps to become actively anti-racist in their practice. This may be through the additional considerations given to resources and provision as mentioned previously, or by having more conversations about race in our classrooms. It may also be refusing to attend or take part in education conferences where entire panels are made up of white 'experts'. If we are attending events specific to SEND, then are there a diverse range of voices being given a platform, including experts who are neurodivergent or have a disability?

Inclusive play and well-being

In schools, educators can capitalise on play and create a unique, nurturing environment for inclusion and well-being. Play has the power to remove barriers, and this is especially important for children with learning differences and disabilities. Children do not notice or pay attention to their differences as play seems to have unifying language and rules. In playful interactions, children connect with peers by sharing, helping, collaborating and problem-solving. They test out different strategies of working with other children and these experiences help them navigate through relationships later in life. Playful learning activities with peers often lead to making new friends or strengthening existing relationships. Peer interactions motivate children to engage in learning activities, which leads to positive well-being experiences in schools. Additionally, social bonding at peer level helps children overcome potential setbacks. They build their social capital and networks, which can provide emotional and practical support such as getting help from adults, acting as facilitators to more friends or even overcoming physical and communication barriers. Play-based learning enhances chances to relate to peers and creates a sense of belonging, which drives improvements in well-being.

Indeed, we have noted many examples of inclusive play in our work and research. Observing and talking to children playing with their peer with speech, language and communication needs (SLCN), we have learned about their ways of staying connected. For example, they respond to even an inarticulate question of their peer with SLCN. When explicitly asked about this situation, which was recorded on a video, the child mentioned that although they did not understand what their peer with SLCN was saying, they felt they need to respond, even if with an 'uhm'. This example of social connection was complemented by more active strategies of including peers with SLCN in play. If a peer with SLCN has difficulties with speaking and expressing themselves, children give their friends with SLCN options of a game to play, or they act as gatekeepers and invite peers with SLCN to join in games they play with other children. Perhaps the most eye-opening moment was to learn that children do not always see the differences. When asking a child '*How do you speak to your friend with SLCN because sometimes I find it difficult?*', they responded '*Just like anybody else*'. This could show that children either do not make the distinction or do not pay attention to the differences and simply play together as if with any other peer. More examples of an 'inclusive mindset' in children playing with peers with SLCN can be found in Janik Blaskova and Gibson (2023) paper.

Inclusion and peer relationships

Efforts to create an inclusive learning environment may tend to omit peers and the active role they can play in creating truly inclusive settings and schools. However, many educators support social inclusion in learning spaces and encourage peer interactions. For example, they arrange their classroom seating so that children with learning differences are mixed with typically developing peers and encourage them to play together during break times. This is their day-to-day reality, which does not stem from a specific policy. In fact, the Department for Education's (2015) guidance on inclusive education, titled 'Special educational needs and disability code of practice: 0 to 25 years', focuses on removing the barriers to learning, not peer interaction and play. In this document, the DfE presents a somewhat narrow perspective and pays little attention to the socialising aspect of inclusion. The Department for Education (2015) makes a reference to peers as follows:

1. A comparative baseline to the skills, abilities and attainment of children with SEND;
2. Additional time that college students with SEND may need for homework and socialising with peers;
3. A potential communication channel supporting children with SEND;
4. An alternative provision, which should support some face-to-face contact with peers in case of online learning (Department for Education, 2015).

While there are some hints to promoting contact with peers, these do not seem to capture the richness of the social aspect of inclusion and feeling connected with peers. Instead, peers seem to be considered a comparative benchmark and potential source of academic support to children and young people with learning differences and disabilities.

Six years after the SEND code of practice was published, the DfE introduced the relationship curriculum, suggesting that the DfE understands the need for developing relevant skills. Since 2021, schools should have been delivering Relationship Education, Relationships and Sex Education, and Health Education (RSHE), which touches on peer relationships. For primary schools, the RSHE specifies 'caring friendships' and 'respectful relationships' as themes supporting children in developing their understanding of healthy relationships and friendship development (Department for Education, 2019). While these are essential and inclusion-relevant skills, the RSHE does not specify means to support play, inclusion, equality or diversity.

Even in the absence of governmental guidance, teachers show their awareness of the need for social inclusion. They implement day-to-day strategies and consider what systemic changes could support social inclusion at peer level. Teachers from language units[1] illustrate that this is the case, when they create space for children with speech, communication and language needs (SCLN) to meet with their mainstream peers during break times and join mainstream classrooms in the afternoons. In Cambridgeshire, teachers observed the tendency of the children from the language base unit (LBU) to play together and asked researchers to find out how children with SCLN could develop more friendships with their mainstream classroom peers.

The study, which was conducted as doctoral research, involved children from the LBU and their peers from afternoon classes. Classroom and playground observations, video recordings of free play and interviews with children revealed what kind of barriers children perceive in their peer interactions and relationships. Interestingly, these were not language and communication based.

Mainstream classroom peers did not know what the children from the LBU do in the morning, or where they are in the school building. To uncover this 'mystery', children with SCLN conducted a guided tour around their morning classrooms and showed peers what part of the school they attend and activities that they do through drawings and photographs.

The study deliberately prompted mainstream peers about their communication with children with SCLN. Many of them did not talk about having difficulties in understanding, but then there were a few moments on the video recording of peer play where peers asked for clarification when a child with SCLN spoke. One of the peers even responded with 'mhm' to an inaudible utterance and when asked about this specific situation, they said they did not understand but felt they should respond anyway. Other peers revealed specific strategies that they used if they could not understand their friends, many of whom were non-speaking. Mainstream peers gave children with SCLN options about games that they could play so that their friends could choose. They pointed at toys or school aids, utilising non-speaking communication channels. None of the mainstream friends mentioned learning about these strategies from someone else.

Although this was a small-scale qualitative study, it demonstrates that there are children in mainstream settings who tend to have an inclusive mindset. Perhaps these are the peers whom teachers could work with as potential communication channels, as suggested by the Department for Education's (2015) Code of Practice.

Framework for inclusive learning through play

Let us consider the design of an inclusive play-based learning environment. Danniels and Pyle (2021) surveyed teachers and learned that they are very much aware of how play supports academic learning and inclusion, but interestingly not many of them could share strategies promoting inclusion within play. The tendency is to consider inclusion outside of the play context: this could be linked to the perceived separate objectives of play, including academic learning, social and emotional development.

Conceptualising the understanding of learning through play is a good starting point for noting the relationships between learning, play and inclusion. Drawing on recent studies on children's play and learning outcomes, Parker and colleagues (2022) define play-based approaches to learning as myriads of child-led and teacher-facilitated activities, aiming at the holistic development of children who are actively engaged and internally motivated to interact socially. Children's internal motivation stems from their experiences of positive emotions and their perceptions of the meaningfulness of activities (Parker et al., 2022). Designing play-based learning involves an effective use of available resources that help with achieving the intended learning outcomes (Parker et al., 2022). The use of resources and how they are adjusted to support children with learning differences and disabilities makes this aspect very relevant for inclusive play-based activities.

As the definition of play-based learning suggests, there are many elements to this approach. Adding the inclusion lens enhances the complexity of delivering learning through play. What can teachers do to implement a play-based learning environment that would also be inclusive? To start with, Parker and colleagues (2022) provide a framework to support teachers in reflecting on quality learning through play. In Figure 4.2 the framework specifies facilitation, experience, design and outcomes as interconnected elements of play-based learning, which resonates with the earlier definitions.

Facilitation represents a flexible means of content delivery that can be led either by a child or teacher, or skilfully guided through scaffolding. Although teachers have a variety of facilitation approaches at hand, they need to remain open and observant to adjust their choices reflecting on the learning objectives and children's responsiveness to the selected approach. For example, if a teacher plans to follow child-led learning when delivering a lesson on gravity, and children are not discovering the relevant forces, teachers may need to adjust to either scaffolding or teacher-directed learning of the content. With inclusion in mind, it is likely that teachers' facilitation will vary from child to child, and that teachers might build in peer-led activities.

Experience relates to children's perceptions and emotional responses to learning. In a play-based approach, children's experience is given equal weight to the other elements because it taps into children's engagement and motivation to pursue the learning activity. Experience shifts the view of children as active learners. Teachers,

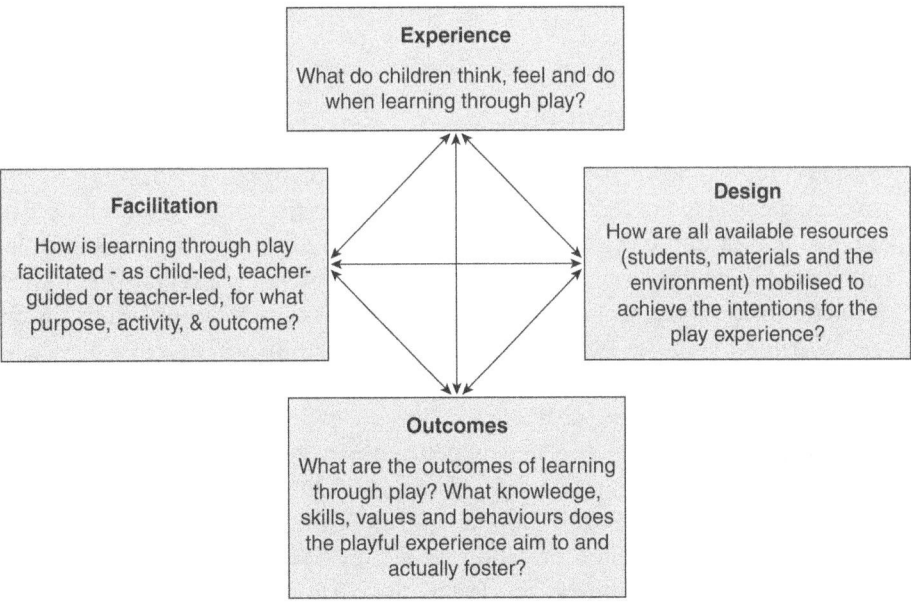

Figure 4.2 Quality learning through play at school (Parker et al., 2022, p. 8)

as well as schools, need to consider children's perspectives and experiences in order to deliver quality learning through play. Considering the specific experiences of children with learning differences and disabilities, teachers can also get important insights from parents/carers, SENDCOs, therapists and other experts in the field.

Design specifies that resources need to be effectively managed to support the delivery of play-based learning and achieve the desired learning objectives. Materials, physical environment and children are the key resources, which need adjustment to support ALL children. Teachers can get specific recommendations and requirements about materials and the environment from parents and those supporting individual children. When it comes to peers and peer interactions, teachers can build on the strategies that they find useful in their own interactions with children with learning differences. We offer some ideas relevant to communication in the Planning and Implementation section.

Outcomes, or learning objectives, are perhaps the first element of learning that teachers have in mind when reflecting on their practice. In play-based learning, the outcomes include learning gains as well as holistic development of inter- and intra-personal skills and understandings. Inclusion could be considered one of the intended learning outcomes that can be measured either through acquired knowledge of differences and disabilities or through newly developed communication skills. Enhanced well-being and relationships are inclusion-related outcomes that can be achieved for all children through play-based approaches to learning.

The framework for quality learning through play by Parker and colleagues (2022, above) outlines areas that teachers can use to reflect on their own methods or to be inspired when designing new strategies introducing more play to learning activities.

Planning and implementation

Establishing a high-quality play-based learning environment can lead to much increased engagement levels amongst children. The freedom to make choices from a range of motivating opportunities should lead to happier students who relish the newfound autonomy over their learning: 'Choice plays a critical role in promoting students' intrinsic motivation and deep engagement in learning. Across a range of academic outcomes and student populations, positive impacts have been seen when student autonomy is promoted through meaningful and personally relevant choice' (Evans & Boucher, 2015).

One primary specialist setting which embraced this child-led approach was Cherry Garden School in London. The leadership team were keen to take their existing successful Early Years model and replicate it across their full age range (2–11 years old). Although the children in Key Stage 1 and Key Stage 2 previously accessed opportunities for play in their day, this was usually outweighed by structured sessions or group work. It was felt that there should be more opportunities for explorative learning and choice making to enhance engagement and learning.

As this was a significant shift for some of the classrooms and educators at the school, it was decided that a 'Classroom Handbook' would be created to share the expectations of what resources should be on offer and how the environment and timetable should be organised. The first port of call was to make use of established environmental rating scales to create a 'bottom line' of expectations. The school chose to use the 'Infant/Toddler Environment Rating Scale®, Revised (ITERS-R™)' (2017) – 'The 39 items are organised into seven subscales: Space and Furnishings, Personal Care Routines, Listening and Talking, Activities, Interaction, Program Structure, and Parents and Staff. The ITERS-R™ contains items to assess provision in the environment for the protection of children's health and safety, appropriate stimulation through language and activities, and warm, supportive interaction'. The straightforward organisation of the scale meant it was easily understood by the staff team, and, as many of the children at the school were at a stage where they liked to explore items and objects orally, the health and safety messages from the Infant/Toddler scales were a good fit. As the school became more confident in creating motivating and engaging learning spaces, less rigidity was required in terms of resourcing, and class teams could tweak their environments to suit their particular cohort of children.

Simon Wright led a KS2 class of seven children aged 9–11, all with complex support needs at the time the new systems were established. Simon reflects:

> Introducing a play-based approach to my classroom had many instant and obvious benefits. I felt that the children were able to make more choices and lead their own learning, which in turn increased the level of opportunity for staff to engage the children in motivating and meaningful learning opportunities. It was clear that the children developed their confidence and were then, as a result, able to apply their skills in a wider range of settings, including the community. We had a big push on using real items such as tools, rather than 'play' ones, which increased the children's ability to use tools for purpose in a functional way. Some of the class would previously struggle to cope at school on a fairly regular basis, but by being able to plan more in the moment and link this to children's interests, I noticed a big improvement in their well-being.
>
> (Simon Wright, personal communication, 21st June 2022)

Designing an inclusive play-based learning environment

In designing an inclusive play-based learning environment, we should consider the environment and methods, as well as peer interactions. Making play-based learning accessible to all children requires adjustments that can be universal or very individual, depending on the support needs of a child or children in the class. Some of the most common practices draw on as follows:

- Physical safety, ensuring enough physical space is available for any role play activities, particularly for children experiencing challenges with coordination and spatial awareness.
- Reducing the level of noise, for example, by moving a speaker further away from an autistic child or children experiencing noise anxiety, or by installing panels with acoustic noise absorption in classrooms.
- Visualisation strategies – for example, using a picture of the activity or a comic book outlining the steps via illustrations will assist children with language support needs. Alternatively, there are commercial tools such as © Widgit Software that can assist with generating visual representations of instructions.

Each child with learning differences is unique and it is best to consult their families or those working closest with the child in school learn how best to support them.

Equally, recent trends in educational research promote a more active voice of children in matters that affect their lives. The project 'Look Who's Talking: Eliciting the Voices of Children from Birth to Seven' led by Professor Kate Wall explored meaningful ways for engaging even very young children coming from a variety of backgrounds. Six seminars connected practitioners and researchers in discussions that are captured as visual minutes posters designed by Albi Taylor. These 'Talking Point Posters' are available at the project website and can serve as user-friendly starting points for an open dialogue between schools and families. Kate Wall and colleagues (2019) offer tools to help practitioners in eliciting children's voices.

Getting help from peers

In the light of our earlier discussion about the importance of peers, practical considerations around designing inclusive play-based learning should actively take peers into account.

It may be useful to consider to what extent peers need to be aware of some of the specific support that their classmates may need. This can be done in a generic way, when children learn about differences more broadly. For example, Favazza and colleagues (2016) structured an activity that is part of their evidence-based Making Friends programme:

1. A story reading on the theme of diversity followed by a short discussion:
    Depending on the age group, a story reading could be replaced with a short movie or video testimonies.
2. Creating small learning groups of children with mixed abilities:
    Small groups give a more immediate space for children to work together, learn about each other and create bonds. Children can take turns in leadership roles and divide tasks based on their strengths, which will help them appreciate and value their differences.

3. Expanding the discussion to home by sharing the story books with the families: Story books can be replaced with leaflets and resources available at the charity/organisation websites supporting families and individuals with learning differences or disabilities.

In addition to raising awareness of differences in a generic way, peers could be informed about the specific differences of their fellow classmates. Retrospective studies with adults with a history of language support needs reveal that many appreciated others being aware of their support needs and adjusting their communication accordingly (Dockrell et al., 2014). However, sharing diagnosis could be perceived as controversial by some children and carers.

In fact, we lack evidence that would evaluate whether disclosing a diagnosis is beneficial. Our limited knowledge draws on a review of previous studies that looked at experiences and perceptions of disclosing an autism diagnosis to others (Thompson-Hodgetts et al., 2020). The results were mixed across the reviewed studies. They varied from an increased acceptance and support to unfulfilled expectations of greater social inclusion (Thompson-Hodgetts et al., 2020). These findings imply that people can react in an unpredictable way. Therefore, any disclosing efforts have to be managed with great sensitivity and the decision needs to depend on the child and their family. Not all children and carers prefer disclosing information with the child's peers. However, if they decide to do so, the approach should be agreed in collaboration with the family, therapists, teachers and other school staff involved. This will help with identifying the best strategy and having follow-up support in place.

The field of autism offers some examples of how the diagnosis can be disclosed to friends and family. Disclosure as an inclusion strategy involves highlighting the unique abilities and strengths of a child to their peers and is best applied in collaboration with clinicians and therapists (e.g., Donaldson, 2016; Law, 2020). Having external support reflects the needs identified by teachers, who are tasked with facilitating inclusive education. Mainstream teachers in England are mainly concerned about the lack of resources (e.g., support staff, infrastructure, finances) that needs to assist them and schools in promoting inclusive education (Warnes et al., 2021).

Disclosing is only one and rather specific strategy to raise awareness of differences among children. Teachers could address inclusion-supporting strategies more broadly. For example, the children's communication charity I CAN (2021) proposes that peers are encouraged to speak slower than usual and make pauses more often (I CAN, 2021). As this could be an unusual way of talking to children, it may be presented to them as a part of their play. Inspired by preschool teachers, Danniels and Pyle (2021) further recommend reading stories that portray diversity; labelling children's strengths to peers; and giving direct support in play. Teachers can provide children with strategies, facilitating peer interactions, perhaps even sharing their own methods for interacting with a child with SEND.

Next steps/summary

Our understanding of inclusion needs to broaden and shift beyond the rather narrow lens of 'SEND'. The term neurodiversity captures the unique skills and abilities of each child, acknowledging that they do not necessarily need a 'special' support but an approach that facilitates their unique development and learning. This child-centred approach to teaching needs to become an essential part of training if we are to support inclusion in settings and schools. Teachers remain the key facilitators of inclusion, and through their relationships with children, they can uncover the unique characteristics that each child brings into their classroom. Moreover, teachers are the role models for inclusive behaviours, which they can facilitate with peers and through play.

Children reveal their best selves in play – it provides a sense of belonging by removing barriers, which ultimately leads to enhanced learning and well-being of ALL children. There is a need for more progressive thinking from policy makers when it comes to children with learning differences and disabilities. They are not an add-on or an extra – they have the same needs as any child and deserve the same level of respect.

Suggested further resources and readings

Casey, T. (2010). *Inclusive Play: Practical Strategies for Children from Birth to Eight*. SAGE Publications Ltd. https://dx.doi.org/10.4135/9781446288252

- Book outlining inclusive play strategies to use in classrooms.
- The author specifies methods of how teachers could assess the inclusion activities.

Information and Communication Technology for Inclusion. (2023). *European Agency for Special Needs and Inclusive Education*. https://www.european-agency.org/activities/ict4i/international-resources

- Outputs (e.g., education toolkits, reports, policy templates) from a project that ran in 2012–2013
- Includes links to Country Reports, Country Resources, and International Resources
- Countries involved: Belgium (Flemish-speaking community), Cyprus, Czech Republic, Denmark, Estonia, Finland, France, Germany, Greece, Hungary, Iceland, Italy, Latvia, Lithuania, Luxembourg, Malta, the Netherlands, Norway, Poland, Portugal, Slovakia, Slovenia, Sweden, Switzerland, the UK (England), the UK (Northern Ireland) and the UK (Scotland).

Favazza, P. C., Ostrosky, M. M., & Mouzourou, C. (2016). *The Making Friends Program: Supporting Acceptance in Your K-2 Classroom*. Baltimore, MD: Brookes.

- A comprehensive guide to changing attitudes in children.
- Educators will find specific activities supporting the understanding of diversity in children.

Jenkins, R. (2021). *Resources Catalogue: Teaching and Learning Resources for Professionals and Parents Working with Children with Disabilities*. UNICEF Education Section. https://www.unicef.org/media/101006/file/RESOURCES%20CATALOGUE.pdf

- List of teaching and learning resources.
- Resources are mostly in English but represent a variety of cultures and geographical locations.

Wall, K., Cassidy, C., Robinson, C., Hall, E., Beaton, M., Kanyal, M., & Mitra, D. (2019). Look who's talking: Factors for considering the facilitation of very young children's voices. *Journal of Early Childhood Research*, 17(4), 263–278. https://doi.org/10.1177/1476718X19875767

- Talking Point Posters: https://www.voicebirthtoseven.co.uk/talking-point-posters/

World Family Education. (2023). *Special Needs Resources by Location*. https://worldfamilyeducation.com/special-needs-resources-by-location/

- A compiled list of local organisations supporting SEND.
- Countries include Australia, Bahamas, Bahrain, Belgium, Bermuda, Brunei, China, France, Guatemala, Hong Kong, India, Ireland, Jordan, Kenya, Malaysia, Mexico, the Netherlands, New Zealand, Peru, the Philippines, Singapore, South Africa, Spain, Thailand, Scotland.

Note

1 Language Units, or specialist resources bases, provide specialised educational provision to children with profound speech, language and communication needs. These specialist units hold small number of children and are attached to some mainstream schools in England.

References

Blaskova, L. J., & Gibson, J. L. (2023). Children with language disorder as friends: Interviews with classroom peers to gather their perspectives. *Child Language Teaching and Therapy*, *39*(1), 39–57. https://doi.org/10.1177/02656590221139231

Crenshaw, K. (1989). Demarginalizing the intersection of race and sex: A Black feminist critique of antidiscrimination doctrine, feminist theory and antiracist politics. *University of Chicago Legal Forum*, Iss. 1, Article 8. https://chicagounbound.uchicago.edu/cgi/viewcontent.cgi?article=1052&context=uclf

Danniels, E., & Pyle, A. (2021). Promoting inclusion in play for students with developmental disabilities: kindergarten teachers' perspectives. *International Journal of Inclusive Education*. DOI: 10.1080/13603116.2021.1941316

Department for Education. (2015). Special educational needs and disability code of practice: 0 to 25 years. DFE-00205-02013. https://assets.publishing.service.gov.uk/government/uploads/system/uploads/attachment_data/file/398815/SEND_Code_of_Practice_January_2015.pdf

Department for Education. (2019). Relationships education, relationships and sex education (RSE) and health education: Statutory guidance for governing bodies, proprietors, head teachers, principals, senior leadership teams, teachers. https://assets.publishing.service.gov.uk/government/uploads/system/uploads/attachment_data/file/1019542/Relationships_Education__Relationships_and_Sex_Education__RSE__and_Health_Education.pdf

Dockrell, J., Lindsay, G., Roulstone, S. & Law, J. (2014). Supporting children with speech, language and communication needs: An overview of the results of the Better Communication Research Programme. *International Journal of Language & Communication Disorders, 49*. https://doi.org/10.1111/1460-6984.12089

Donaldson, A. (2016). Fostering friendship: An expert explains how SLPs can encourage social interaction among preschool-age peers. *The ASHA Leader*. https://doi.org/10.1044/leader.OV.21052016.np

Evans, M., & Boucher, A. R. (2015). Optimizing the power of choice: Supporting student autonomy to foster motivation and engagement in learning. *Mind, Brain, and Education, 9*(2), 87–91. https://www.researchnet/publication/276074224_Optimizing_the_Power_of_Choice_Supporting_Student_Autonomy_to_Foster_Motivation_and_Engagement_in_Learning

I CAN. (2021). Developmental Language Disorder: A guide for every teacher on supporting children and young people with Developmental Language Disorder (DLD) in mainstream schools. United Kingdom.

Isaacs, S. (1971). *The Nursery Years: The Mind of the Child from Birth to Six Years*. London: Routledge.

Law, B. M. (2020). Strengthening families by involving siblings in autism treatment: Including siblings in autism intervention may reduce stress and fortify not just siblings, but the fabric of the whole family. *The ASHA Leader, 25*, 48–58. https://doi.org/10.1044/leader.FTR1.25042020.48

Lees, E. (2022). A beginner's Guide to ableism. *Tapestry: Online Learning Journal*. https://tapestry.info/wp-content/uploads/sites/2/2022/01/A-Beginners-Guide-to-Ableism-1.pdf

Murphy, K. (2022). *Supporting the Well-Being of Children with SEND: Essential Ideas for Early Years Educators*. London: Routledge.

Ofsted. (2022). *School Inspection Handbook*. England. https://www.gov.uk/government/publications/school-inspection-handbook-eif/school-inspection-handbook#fn:54

Parker, R., Thomsen, B. S., & Berry, A. (2022). Learning through play at school–A framework for policy and practice. *Frontiers in Education, 7*(February), 1–12. https://doi.org/10.3389/feduc.2022.751801

Pemberton, E (2022). A beginner's guide to anti-racism. *Tapestry: Online Learning Journal.* https://tapestry.info/wp-content/uploads/sites/2/2022/06/A-Beginners-Guide-to-Anti-Racism.pdf

Tereshchenko, A., Mills, M., & Bradbury, A. (2020). *Making progress? Employment and retention of BAME teachers in England.* London: UCL Institute of Education.

Thompson-Hodgetts, S., Labonte, C., Mazumder, R., & Phelan, S. (2020). Helpful or harmful? A scoping review of perceptions and outcomes of autism diagnostic disclosure to others. *Research in Autism Spectrum Disorders, 77,* 101598. https://doi.org/10.1016/j.rasd.2020.101598

Warnes, E., Done, E.J., & Knowler, H. (2021). Mainstream teachers' concerns about inclusive education for children with special educational needs and disability in England under pre-pandemic conditions. *Journal of Research in Special Educational Needs, 22,* 31–43. https://doi.org/10.1111/1471-3802.12525

CHAPTER

Designing opportunities for play in primary education: A no-trade off approach to play and learning

Luke Rolls, Rachel Lownsbrough and Liam Connolly

To bring our lives under control and exert agency has been argued to go to the very heart of what it means to be human (Storoni, 2022). From the earliest stage, children are born with an in-built sense of curiosity and meaning-making and their understanding of the world is based on both 'reality' and 'magical thinking'. As children grow older, they face a potential trade-off between their growing wisdom and understanding of the world with their inherent sense of wonder. But does it have to be this way? Are curiosity and a sense of awe necessary casualties in the mission of 'educating' children?

Since we established our school in 2015, the first University Training School in the UK, we have always held dear the challenge of growing both children's sense of agency alongside their wisdom in a way that compromises neither. Such an effort brings into focus a pedagogical question around what qualities a playful approach to learning fosters and whether such an approach can be successfully integrated within the teaching of substantive and disciplinary forms of knowledge. Can play be harnessed as a super-tool to power up more traditional forms of learning?

Having a sense of agency over yourself as a learner and the wider world is hard to contest as desirable outcomes of education. More controversial though is how such autonomy is best generated and whether certain pedagogical approaches are misguided in their attempt to do so. Would a solely play-based or direct instruction approach imbue children with the types of powerful knowledge that by the time they leave school represent true learner autonomy and the types of knowing that can change the world? What constitutes a balanced diet of learning that includes a diverse range of 'knowing'? Rather than polarising different pedagogies, we part from traditional dichotomies to consider the affordances and limitations of pedagogical approaches and situate these within the context of teachers developing repertoires (Alexander, 2010), ones that can be used for different aims and purposes.

An unnamed academic collaborator to this chapter whom we would like to write in dedication to is the late Dr David Whitebread. David was the inaugural director of the Centre for Research on Play in Education, Development and Learning (PEDAL) at the University of Cambridge and, with colleague Penny Coltman, had a significant influence on the pedagogical approach of our school. David was always hopeful for our school to demonstrate how play could work across the age groups and across the curriculum. We learned from David and Penny that research into play showed significant potential for physical, social-emotional and cognitive benefits for children's development and its real potency to develop metacognitive thinking and self-regulation, collaborative learning and dialogic skills. In the UK context, play had been historically poorly researched in education, misrepresented in extreme forms such as 'discovery-only learning' and generally bound to the early years of primary school. In support of such viewpoints were poor examples of 'progressive' schooling that lacked sufficient rigour and therefore seemingly affirmed suspicions that play does not happily co-exist with academic achievement. David and Penny gave us the opportunities to think about how we could integrate theory and research into play with the practical wisdom of designing learning in the classroom. We enquired into using Lego for developing young children's story writing and started to quickly see some interesting pay-offs. The children appeared motivated to write in a way that joining our school they didn't seem to be, and with this will to write came opportunities to develop their skill to write.

Alongside the benefits of a playful approach, we also found plenty of pitfalls awaiting. These are important to address in order to not underplay the complexity of developing meaningful agency in children. Here are some of the bumps in our opinion, to avoid the following:

Play as activity. Where play is only activity, exactly what the learning can be is insufficiently clear. David used to refer to the phrase used in education, 'the children don't even realise they're learning' with frustration. Children do not need to be tricked into learning; learning can be interesting in itself(!), but in order to reflect on something, we need to know what we are learning. If the learning was exploratory, were the children really exploring what was intended? Inconveniently, experienced curriculum does not necessarily neatly link to that which was intended and where children are not aware of what their learning focus is, it is questionable what they are learning; metacognitive processes about such learning then seem very unlikely.

Play as additional time. In the UK context, play is not easily scheduled as additional time in what tends to be an already packed curriculum timetable. If our aim is to give children exploratory learning time and opportunities for play, additional sessions *can* be carved out in classes' timetable but with what trade-off?

Any primary teacher will tell you that they struggle to fit in the competing demands of the many important curriculum areas they are required to teach. Rather than there being 'playful' times in the school week, a different perspective would be to embed playfulness into different subjects, lessons or projects.

Play as only something unstructured. The interactions between learners and what they are learning, other learners and the teacher could be thought of as a delicately balanced eco-system. One skill of teachers is to create this high functioning learning environment – one that keeps personal, social-emotional and academic goals in equilibrium. While playful learning tends to be motivating for children, there needs to be enough structure that sets the boundaries within which children can explore and be creative, what American psychologist Hirsh-Pasek refers to as 'guided play' (Weisberg et al., 2016). Where guidance is not there, playful learning can easily become unhinged and may well not lead to desired learning for all children. It seems likely that within a balanced diet of learning, some unstructured play opportunities might ask children to 'raise their game' and, without the added support, find new possibilities of ways to solve problems and resolve issues with peers. During curriculum lesson time, our experience is that children in practice benefit from inspiration, provocation, extension and guidance to move their learning on.

Play as discovery only. Unstructured play is unlikely to support children's understanding of difficult or counterintuitive concepts. Learning often involves 'desirable difficulty'; concept such as 'subtraction as difference' is not something young mathematicians are likely to discover through play, nor is how to write using a semi-colon for effect. Over-relying on play to fulfil all functions and outcomes of the intended curriculum can serve to undermine what an inclusive education aims to be. This is distinct from exploratory and practical opportunities for learning concepts which is of course vital. In mathematics, for example, children might be helped to understand concepts like conservation in the context of measurement. How meaningful are these without children having had the opportunity to pour liquids into different-sized beakers in trying to solve a problem like what half of a measurement looks like in different containers? Curriculum goals in different subjects show that many skills and knowledges which curriculums demand benefit from foundational work and concrete preparation. In the early years, children become used to seeing groups of things like pairs of scissors or children set them up to have an understanding of cardinality, which leads to multiplicative reasoning later on. In geography, having a sense of where they are in their environment, travelling to somewhere else develops their understanding of location which then gives meaning to abstract representations of space such as maps.

It is important to note that the definition of play, and the relationship of teaching and learning to it, is not resolute (Hirsh-Pasek, Golinkoff, Berk and Singer, 2009). Smith and Vollstedt write that 'it may well be that it is a combination of features, rather than the presence or absence of one defining characteristic, that leads observers to characterise behaviour as play' (1985). Various features are often used to rate the playfulness of an activity, focussing on pleasure, intrinsic motivation, process, a measure of free choice, the active engagement of the participant and the presence of make-believe (Krasnor and Pepler, 1980; Rubin, Fein and Vandenberg, 1983). Guided play is a term used to describe adult-facilitated learning situations that revolve around or involve play (Fisher et al., 2011). White writes that 'intrinsically motivated free play provides the child with true autonomy, while guided play is an avenue through which parents and educators can provide more targeted learning experiences' (2012). We build on this provenance of research to suggest that a conception of play that is considered in broader terms of choice and challenge enables its potential to extend beyond being tied to certain limited conditions.

In this chapter, we try to give some examples of play that take account of the pitfalls above to spotlight cases where play can

- Be learning-focussed
- Be integrated into a coherent learning sequence
- Harness children's curiosity and agency
- Promote high quality dialogic and recorded outcomes
- Be exploratory and set the foundations and source material for more formal learning
- Be motivating and seen as purposeful by children
- Lead to children independently extending their learning outside of the classroom

To illustrate this approach, we draw on the metaphor of movements in a piece of music. Movements are defined as:

A self-contained part of a musical composition or musical form. While individual or selected movements from a composition are sometimes performed separately, a performance of the complete work requires all the movements to be performed in succession.

We note that similarly, a teaching sequence is made up of different 'movements' that express different types of learning and bring with them a unique contribution to the composition. They are of different tempos, moods and elicit different forms of motivation and affect in those that experience them. Movements in teaching are things that teachers do instinctively and tacitly; they know that having children sat down for 6 hours a day is not only counter-productive but with younger children at least, near impossible! There is an ebb and flow to school and class life within a lesson, within a day and within a sequence of learning and these are 'performed in succession', orchestrated by the art and skill of a teacher – some parts by design and some by responsiveness, adapting to the needs of the children as they present in real time.

Rachel (below) describes an episode of her teaching a year 5 class a unit on Shakespeare and how embedding these principles of playful opportunities sat alongside and enhanced other movements which included explicitly taught content.

Teacher Reflection

I have always been fascinated by play. It seems to me that as children start school, play is continuously harnessed in early years as a tool for learning. However, as they get older, play is no longer a priority. Instead, teachers favour the more formal approach of direct instruction. I wanted to find out how to strike a balance between children's experimental play and explicit teaching and consider how this would have an impact on their learning and outcomes.

Let me invite you along as I experimented with guided play in a unit of English on Shakespeare. The two-week unit was designed to immerse the children in the world of *A Midsummer Night's Dream* through role-play, drama games, physical 'sculpting' and improvisation. I wanted to harness playfulness, improvisation and experimentation, guiding the children and setting parameters for their play, whilst leaving much decision-making as was productive in their hands. Shakespeare's plays offer an excellent vehicle for this, providing the structure of a script while allowing for many interpretations.

Elements of play I attempted to include in my teaching were **social interactivity, deep immersion and joy** (Unicef, 2018).

Figure 5.1 Image of a theatre auditorium.

Designing opportunities for play in primary education

Elements of play included in my teaching were: **social interactivity, deep immersion and joy** (Unicef, 2018).

This two-week unit would include

- role-play
- drama games
- physical 'sculpting'
- improvisation
- performance

At the beginning of this unit, I explicitly taught who Shakespeare was and where he came from as well as the history of midsummer celebrations in the Tudor period. Children would need to have this information to hand if they were to build on it and understand the context meaningfully.

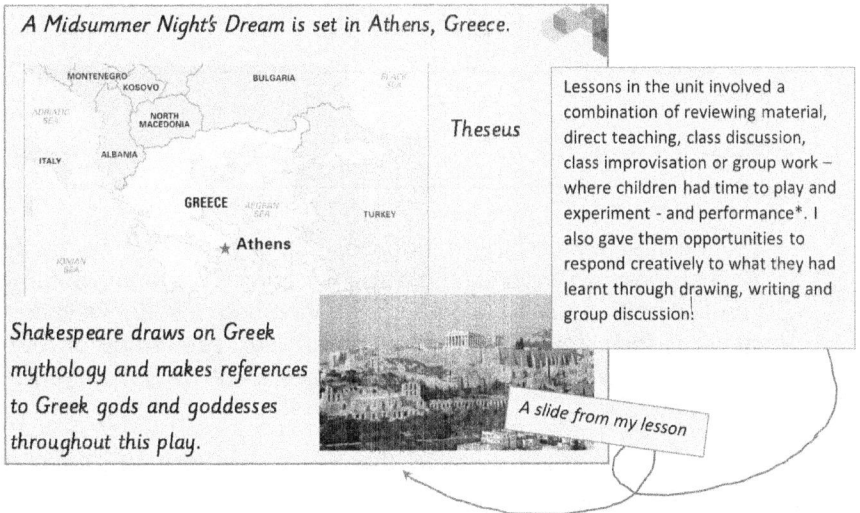

Figure 5.2 Image of a teacher's lesson PowerPoint slide and a description of the overall unit of study.

LOVERS' QUARREL:

One section of the play that we looked at in detail was the 'lover's quarrel' in the Athenian woods, with the objective to understand how the created atmosphere and mood of the woods would impact on the audience. I began the teaching with vocabulary building, prompted by a range of images of woods.

Step 1. Playing: After this, children had their turn build an atmosphere through words and images alongside the use of musical instruments, experimenting with sound and rhythm. Through art and collage, children then explored creating mood boards for setting that would portray a particular atmosphere. This variation was used to immerse and draw children's attention to the setting of the Athenian woods, and to understand that as writers, they could create the mood of their choice. Children were challenged to justify their choices and the reasons for their scenes.

> Later, children appeared to have drawn on these in their poems with rich vocabulary and atmospheric devices evident:
>
> *devoured by demonic air...*
>
> *...an eerie stillness roams the land*
>
> *The forest had crooked, damp trees...*

> In the first part of the sequence, pupils examined contrasting visual images of woods (some spooky, some cold, some autumnal and some tranquil), responding by generating descriptive vocabulary for their image: what would you hear, see, smell or feel in these woods? Some of the responses were 'bright', 'magical', 'screaming'.
>
> *The sounds of crickets in the trees, rustling, proving the sad feeling of loneliness...*
>
> *The atmosphere might be a mystery. Branches breaking and falling...*

Step 2 Playing – Musicking: After examining a range of images, pupils chose small groups and percussion instruments to create a sound scape of the woods that helped to further explore their desired mood. They could choose what sort of mood they wanted to create, which instruments to use and how to use them. They then had to justify their choices to their group and come to agreement on the mood of their composition. I gave them plenty of time to experiment, whilst asking lots of questions about their decisions.

> During these playful episodes, I emphasised our focus 'talk agreement' around justification and children being sure to give reasons for their choices.

During this time of guided play, pupils made decisions in a group and used critical thinking skills to make changes to their composition. They also had a lot of fun with the instruments, exploring the sounds that they made and deciding whether the sound was a good fit for the atmosphere of their Athenian wood (we did this outside so as not to disturb other classes in the learning street). Each child could give a reason for why they had chosen their instrument, and what it was representing. Finally, they performed their soundscapes to the rest of the class using a staged area to present their compositions. Pupils found this performance opportunity made their playful enquiry purposeful and motivating.

> In creating mood boards for their Athenian woods using a range of collage materials, children reflected on the intended impact of their design on an audience:
>
> *I want to make the audience feel creeped and be feeling things like 'Turn around!' and 'Look out!' and be very intimidated.*
>
> *[The woods will be] a dark place full of fear. The only bird in the sky was bats. The only light was the moon.*
>
> *I hope my design makes the audience feel faint and sleepy by essence smells and quiet music.*

The following transcript was taken from a class discussion at the end of the unit:

Teacher Reflection

This sequence of learning provided a scaffold for the children to come to their own creative decisions about the Athenian woods. They realised, through the musical performances, that there were many interpretations of the setting and atmosphere. Through these carefully guided playful activities,

> they understood the mystery and magic of the Athenian woods and how they, as directors, could make creative decisions to have an impact on the audience.
>
> With this deeper understanding of the world of the play, I led the whole class through a rapid improvisation of the plot, called 'active storytelling'. Every child was involved in acting out while the teacher read the story: some were characters with name badges, while others created the setting by becoming the forest. The teacher told the sequence of the lover's quarrel as the children acted it out and brought it to life. Children's attention was captured by this activity, which was fast-paced and fun. All pupils were involved, cast in consecutive order, meaning that several of the roles were played by the opposing gender: boys played Hermia or Helena or girls played Lysander or Demetrius. They loved the freedom to become different people in their imaginations and all entered into the suspended disbelief that they could become someone else. This continued during small group work, where they staged the scene using an edited script and wholeheartedly entered into the character's feelings, motivations and emotions, enjoyment and understanding of the play.

> Many children commented that it was the **role-play** that had the greatest impact on their learning.

Children came to understand the characters in the play and their motivations both through discussing it as a class and through *becoming* that character in their own role-play. One child commented on the following:

> *Well, it's kind of helped our writing with the poems and stuff like that because it went through the story and we were actually in the story kind of and we felt we saw everything going on. And then afterwards you already know the story because we pretended that we were in the story.*

Figure 5.3 One child's reflection.

It was this immersive play – becoming the characters and pretending to be in the story – that really seemed to help the class to know the characters in the play deeply. It particularly supported those who often struggle to come up with their own ideas for writing. The high-quality oracy and dialogue that resulted would be reason enough for me to include this sort of guided play more often in my teaching. However, the children also went on to explore and experiment with language and rhythm to write their own narrative poems based on *A Midsummer Night's Dream*. Children, who had previously been less confident to speak in front of others, performed their poems to the rest of the class – some of them from memory.

> **Teacher:** When you played and acted and did some of the role-play, what did you like about that? If you didn't like doing the role-play you can say why you didn't like it.
>
> **Child 1:** I liked doing Shakespeare because it just didn't feel like we were doing lessons; it feels more like we are playing than doing lessons. You don't feel like it's more of a drag, you feel like you enjoy it.
>
> **Teacher:** Can I ask you if there is anything that makes it feel like playing?
>
> **Child 1:** The role-play and all of the circle time and everything because we don't really do much book work so....
>
> **Child 2:** I like doing role-play because we can be creative with our acting and we are given a set to act and we don't have to stick to it, we can just expand it with everyone.
>
> **Child 3:** I liked the role-play because number one; it was a lot of fun acting with your friends and classmates and number two; it helps me kind of learn more like getting inside the characters' shoes.
>
> **Child 4:** I agree with [Child 3] because it helps you imagine how the character would be in that certain situation and also it's not like you have to rehearse it, you can just do it at random moments.

The narrative poem outcomes at the end of the unit were celebratory and children appeared to take real pride in performing these to their class, particularly for children in the class with additional needs. One such example is given below:

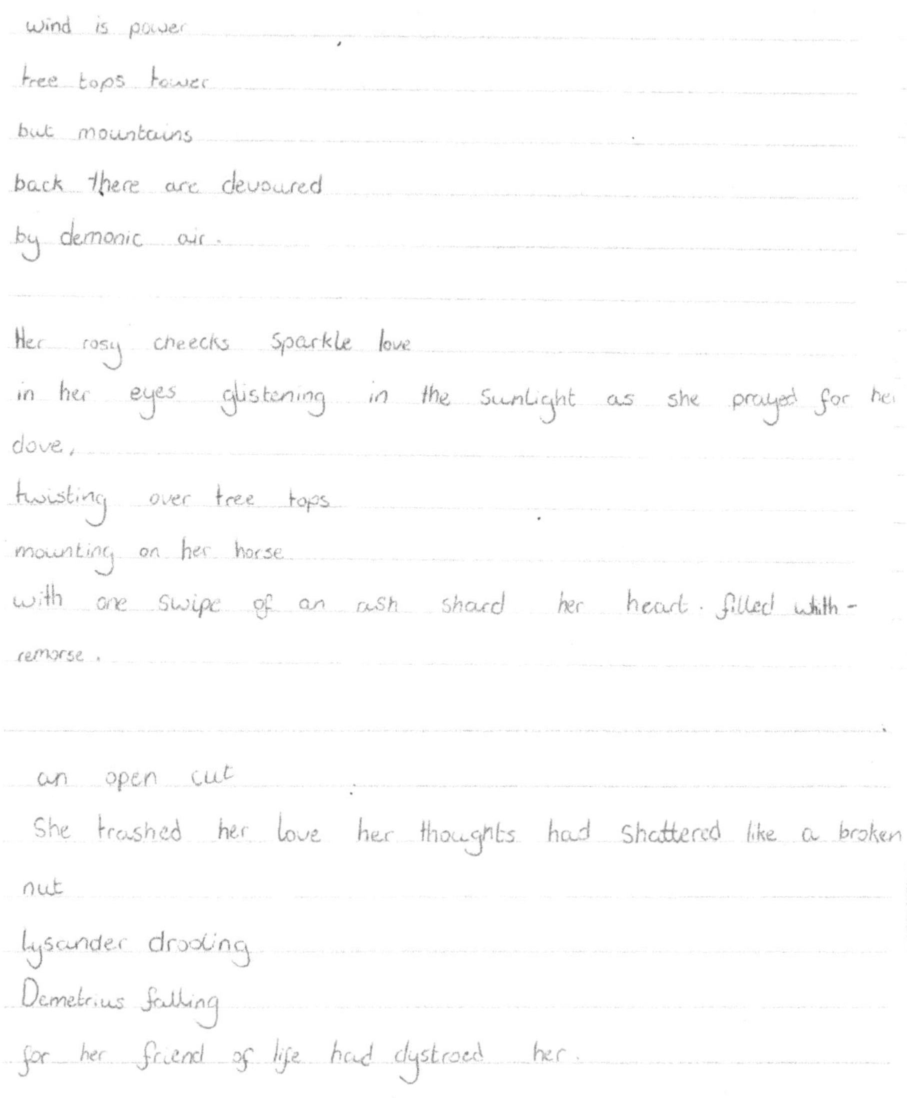

> wind is power
> tree tops tower
> but mountains
> back there are devoured
> by demonic air.
>
> Her rosy cheecks sparkle love
> in her eyes glistening in the sunlight as she prayed for her
> dove,
> twisting over tree tops
> mounting on her horse
> with one swipe of an ash shard her heart. filled whith —
> remorse.
>
> an open cut
> She trashed her love her thoughts had shattered like a broken
> nut
> Lysander drooling
> Demetrius falling
> for her friend of life had dystroed her.

Figure 5.4 Child's Poem.

Some of the most confident writers also appeared challenged by the form and content of narrative poetry. The choice of language, rhythm and rhyme allowed children to stretch themselves and experiment with language in a way they had not previously demonstrated:

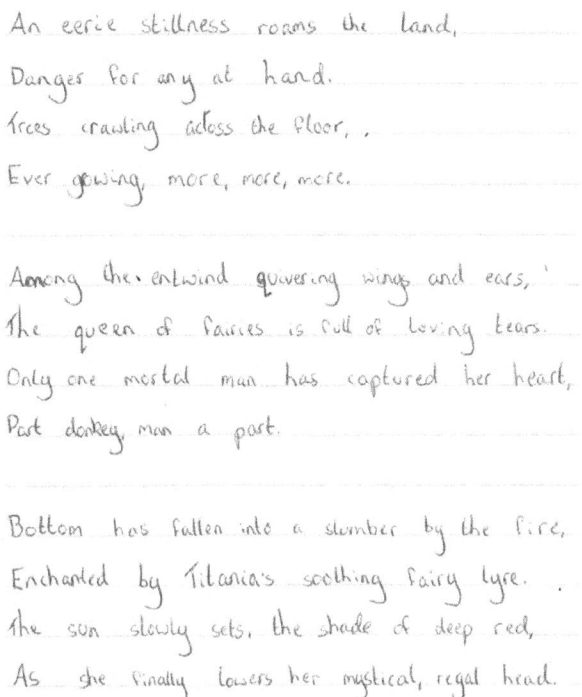

Figure 5.5 Child's poem.

Teacher Reflection

What I have found most incredible in reflecting on this learning sequence is how children take on and bring their learning independently into their play. For a group of children in my class, *A Midsummer Night's Dream* took on a life of its own, spilling out into their playtimes and becoming autonomous and child-led. Pupils decided to write their own script, memorise it, rehearse it and stage it in full costume for the rest of the key stage, even after we had moved on as a class to a different unit. On asking children's reflections of the unit, they most commonly identified role-play as one of the key things that helped them in writing their own poetry. The children said they knew what to write and had ideas because they had been immersed themselves into the play. They mentioned laughter, being with friends, understanding the plot and characters of the play better after having pretended to be those characters, involving everyone and the freedom to not be perfect. If this isn't play, then what is?

Rachel's vignette shows an example of play that is fully integrated into a learning sequence, allowing children opportunities for self-expression, creativity and social-emotional development. The sequences of playful movements enhanced rather than replaced or detracted from accompanying explicit teaching which included a focus on Shakespeare and the historical context, new vocabulary and language, understanding of the plot and characters and knowledge about spoken and written forms of poetry. Children were highly motivated and this even led them to taking their learning outside of the classroom, putting on a performance, relishing the opportunity to act and build on their previous knowledge. Children reflected that while they were aware of what they were learning, it didn't feel like 'book work'; they seemed to sense the authentic purpose to the writing.

Below, Liam describes a second sequence of learning he led with a year 3 class, where he reflects on how playful opportunities interplayed and supported clearly defined learning intentions:

> With my lower key stage 2 team, I had planned an interdisciplinary learning sequence based around the creation and use of shadow puppet theatres. Guided play using the children's own creations was my way to give children some agency in the direction of their learning while still keeping in mind focussed learning outcomes in a range of subject areas, detailed in the table below:

Subject Area	Learning Intentions
Spoken Language	■ Listening and responding appropriately to peers. ■ Articulating and justifying answers, arguments and opinions and participating actively in collaborative conversations. ■ Staying on topic and initiating and responding to comments.
Comprehension	■ Listening to and discussing plays. ■ Preparing play scripts to read aloud and to perform, showing understanding through intonation, tone, volume and action. ■ Checking that the text makes sense, discussing understanding and explaining the meaning of words in context.
Writing	■ Writing a play script that conveys a cohesive narrative, with a grammar focus relating to writing direct speech; this linked to the concurrent grammar learning in our English lessons, where using inverted commas to represent direct speech was introduced. Some difficulty was found in placing the correct words within the speech marks and I wished to use play scripts as a way to address this misconception, with the oral performance of the play working to illuminate what is spoken aloud.
Design and Technology	■ Planning, evaluating and improving a design.
Collaborative Skills	■ Working purposefully in a group: assigning roles, delegating tasks and communicating effectively to achieve a desired result.

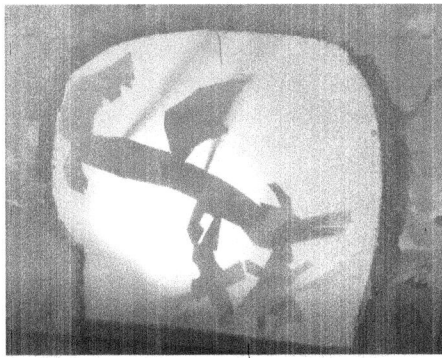

Figure 5.6 Children constructing their shadow puppet theatres.

Having learned about light, dark and shadows in science, the children worked in small groups of two or three to design their shadow puppet theatres. After some initial explicit instruction about creating shadow theatres, I gave no prescription of the forms their theatres had to take and tried to allow for them to be creative and innovative in their designs.

Several of the original or altered stories contained subverted endings where the story's villain was victorious and these children seemed to relish in the freedom to end a story in this unusual fashion. At this point, I did not express or show any opinion on these themes, though I would choose to do so in some instances later in the development of the children's plays only when they were becoming diverted from the learning at hand, for example not developing a narrative sufficiently because they had chosen to have the protagonist be randomly eaten by a monster. I approached this by asking them, 'what do you think the audience will think of that?' or 'that ending is quite sudden, what could you do to make it more satisfying?'. It was clear that in the complete absence of a guiding hand, the playful learning in these particular groups risked becoming desultory. I interjected when necessary but found that I was able to redirect them without becoming overbearing. Other groups needed less prompting and remained more focussed on the end goal independently; notably, these tended to be those with more girls in them.

Teacher Reflection

All groups adopted the basic method, but many embellished or did away with the proscenium arch and one group added scenery that stood in front of the screen itself. In choosing a play to perform, the children could make an original story or choose one they already knew, for example Perseus and Medusa, a story we had recently covered in an English unit. This meant there was the opportunity for agency and meaningful choice alongside and within the established content. They gave reasons to justify their choices of

> story and characters, ranging from 'we've known this story for a long time and it's popular' to 'it's violent'. I used my teacher responsive journal to make notes on these exchanges, which often included the children referencing their cultural backgrounds or previous learning.

Though the children were not instructed to write scripts at this stage, many of them did. One group had difficulty remembering their story and I asked them, 'what could help you remember?' to which they replied, 'writing it down', though most had come to this conclusion by themselves. One group wrote the script in a format of their own creation, using different coloured pencils to denote different character's lines. This idea was observed and adopted by many others in the class, and seeing this, we decided to carry it over to our mainline English lessons, in which one of the tasks that week was to write the script for the play.

Following the completion of the scripts and characters, the children were given more time to playfully rehearse with a focus on oracy, comprehension and performance skills. This was the build-up to a performance afternoon shared with another class, where they would take turns to be the audience and the performers. To help them prepare, I filmed plays and showed them to the children, allowing time for peer and self-assessment. Sentence stems helped scaffold this activity.

The unit culminated with the performance afternoon. The children delighted in seeing each other's performances and remarked on what ideas they would like to emulate next time, and some even developed their plays within the afternoon as they altered details between performances and applied repairs to props that became damaged. Sufficient anticipation was built prior to the event by allowing adequate opportunity for rehearsal and combining classes across year groups to provide the children an audience. Having this opportunity to showcase their learning had motivated the children while practising and writing and was then a basis for further dialogue between children.

> *To empower the children and give their dialogue space to develop, I learned to **bite my lip, step back** and **choose my moments to intervene** carefully.*

Teacher Reflection

This unit made clear to me the power of choice and collaborative learning. The playful learning that took place around creating and rehearsing the plays gave opportunity for meaningful discussion and learning that was child-directed and autonomous. Running parallel to this unit was a practitioner enquiry I carried out surrounding developing meaningful classroom dialogue by knowing when to step back as the teacher. With the shadow puppet theatres, guiding the play was essential to anchoring the learning with scaffolds such as whole-class sentence stems, vocabulary mats and talk agreements. A learning environment with high expectations of behaviour was also crucial to the purposefulness of the oracy and dialogue. In one group, two children took the majority of the tasks in a group while the third member disengaged. I asked prompting questions in a neutral manner to encourage them to re-organise and keep everyone on task. These instances were small, but numerous, and it seemed like these guided elements of the play gave a sense of children's ownership over their learning and learning points.

Figure 5.7 A shadow puppet play being enacted.

Teacher Reflection

It was the children themselves that created a sense of wonder through the having of creative choice of stories, designs and ideas. I scaffolded their learning as lightly as I thought necessary and as subtly as possible to keep the feeling of 'play' and agency alive in the classroom. I was confident to do so because they could talk about their learning and it was evident to see.

Children generating ideas and dialogue through role-play

The freedom and creativity afforded the children was paramount to their consistent engagement with the learning activities and resulted in observable progress in the focus learning areas, detailed below.

Intent	Impact
Spoken language: listening and responding appropriately to peers, articulating and justifying answers, arguments and opinions and participating actively in collaborative conversations, staying on topic and initiating and responding to comments.	All children were observed having constructive discussions within their groups and with other groups on a range of topics, such as which play to perform and why, which characters and props were needed and why. When a group drifted in focus, I was able to help them course-correct by asking questions. Children discussed and planned ahead their group oracy and dialogue 'talk agreement' goals in a session.
Comprehension: listening to and discussing plays and preparing play scripts to read aloud and to perform, showing understanding through intonation, tone, volume and action and checking that the text makes sense to them, discussing their understanding and explaining the meaning of words in context.	Reading each other's scripts as well as their own enabled the children to develop their reading comprehension and here I was able to ask questions to check understanding or help the children to rethink intonation and action. Peer and self-assessment of scripts supported the development of vocabulary in context.
Writing: writing a play script that conveys a cohesive narrative, with a grammar focus relating writing direct speech.	Children working below the age-related expectations for year 3 in writing had previously found the placement of words within speech marks challenging when writing a narrative. There has been development in this area, observed in their daily 'Writing Journal' task, since the completion of the scriptwriting activities in this unit.
	Peer, self and teacher assessment helped the children to develop a cohesive and entertaining narrative in their groups, e.g. I asked clarification questions like 'what do you mean here?' to point out mistakes that the children could then correct, like misuse of words or missing lines of dialogue or stage directions.

(Continued)

Intent	Impact
Design and technology: Planning, evaluating and improving a design.	Creative freedom was afforded the children throughout the design stage and I used my teacher responsive journal and video recordings to formatively assess the children's progress throughout the unit. Peer and self-assessment following the creation of the theatres allowed the children to address flaws and make improvement in their designs, for example, on seeing the video of their play, some groups made alterations to the puppets to make them appear more clearly.
Collaborative learning skills from working in a group.	Children were placed in groups strategically to keep the learning as meaningful as possible: that is to say, most children were placed with those that I had observed them learning well with previously. Adult scaffolding was given sparingly, as I made notes in my teacher 'responsive journal' to formatively assess the group dynamics and progress. I intervened only when I observed a group becoming unproductive.

Liam's vignette above uses the artefact of a puppet theatre as the centre-piece for children to explore and develop many areas of their curriculum learning. The puppet theatre acted as a source material for children's writing. It acted to inspire and motivate, to generate ideas and in turn translated into the dialogue of their stories. Liam's mindful approach of 'stepping back' and giving only as much as is needed is a powerful teacher move in communicating to children that they had agency and responsibility of their learning.

Playfulness as an embedded teaching approach

Coe (2013) points out, rightly, that engagement is a poor proxy for learning. While this is true, it is our experience that engagement, motivation and curiosity can provide important fuel to children's attention and conation (Dehaene, 2018). Engagement alone is insufficient and somewhat rudderless, but when children are given meaningful opportunities that synchronise their curiosity with wider intended learning, examples of practice documented in this chapter suggest to us that targeted learning can be empowered by play. It is important to acknowledge that the relationship and interplay between explicit teaching and more playful enquiry is undoubtedly a tricky one to balance at times. How 'novice' learners are in a particular area and the background knowledge they need to draw will likely mediate their interaction with any designed learning sequences (Clark, Kirschner and Sweller, 2012). We have to reflect on where giving too much autonomy undermines rather than complements learning outcomes, where choice becomes overwhelming and where children need more direction to truly be creative. But the opposite is also true: children generally start school with infinite amounts of curiosity and wonder, and many leave their education with this sense of joy lacking, sometimes even celebratory that they won't need to engage in formal learning again. What goes wrong in between?

Our chapter here attempts to argue that with a commonsense approach about what needs to be taught, wonder and playfulness is still possible within the context of a rigorous curriculum. It is an approach that honours children's curiosity and the benefits of play necessarily alongside and without downplaying the value of external knowledge and the expertise of a teacher. In orchestrating this delicate balance between this science and art of teaching, we seek to avoid simple polarised thinking about singular instruction types meeting all aims of education.

Let's cast our mind back to what it was like for ourselves being a child in a classroom, trying to make sense within a lesson to reflect on some of the nuances and complexities of classroom learning.

- What assumptions do we bring to designing learning sequences about how children learn best? Do these represent a barrier to our understanding of children's real experiences of learning?
- In making our curriculum and teaching decisions as educators, have we listened to the voices of children we seek to represent? What might we learn from them about how they think they will flourish?
- How is learning experienced for a child without a voice or a child coming to school from extremely difficult circumstances?
- To what extent are we honouring children's natural sense of curiosity and wonder alongside teaching them important subject knowledge?
- When are more playful approaches used inefficiently in a way that neither develops curiosity nor knowledge?
- How do we learn from children, observation and reflection to close the gap between the intended and the attained curriculum?

References

Alexander, R. (Ed.) (2010). *Children, their world, their education: Final report and recommendations of the Cambridge Primary Review*. London: Routledge.

Clark, R., Kirschner, P. A., & Sweller, J. (2012). Putting students on the path to learning: The case for fully guided instruction. *American Educator*, 36(1), 5–11.

Coe, R. (2013). *Improving education: A triumph of hope over experience*. Durham: Durham University: Centre for Evaluation and Monitoring.

Fisher, K., Hirsh-Pasek, K., Golinkoff, R. M., Singer, D. G. Berk, L. (2011). Playing around in school: Implications for learning and educational policy. In A. Pellegrini (Ed.), *The Oxford handbook of the development of play* (pp. 341–362). New York: Oxford University Press.

Hirsh-Pasek, K., Golinkoff, R. M., Berk, L. E., & Singer, D. G. (2009). *A mandate for playful learning in preschool: Applying the scientific evidence*. New York: Oxford University Press.

Krasnor, L. R. & Pepler, D. J. (1980). The study of children's play: Some suggested future directions. In K. H. Rubin (Ed.), *Children's play* (pp. 1545–1558). San Francisco: Jossey-Bass.

Rubin, K. H., Fein, G. C., Vandenberg, B. (1983). Play. In P. H. Mussen (Ed.), *Handbook of child psychology* (4th ed., pp. 693–774). New York: Wiley.

Smith, P. K. & Vollstedt, R. (1985) On defining play: An empirical study of the relationship between play and various play criteria. *Child Development*, 56(4), 1042–50.

Storoni, M. (2022). I Am… Dr Mithu Storoni [Podcast]. 28 April 2022. Available at: https://podcasts.apple.com/si/podcast/i-am-dr-mithu-storoni/id1610549437?i=1000558923448 [Accessed 6 March 2024].

Unicef (2018) Learning Through Play (Available Online) UNICEF-Lego-Foundation-Learning-through-Play.pdf (Accessed 6 March 2024)

Weisberg, D. S., Hirsh-Pasek, K., Golinkoff, R. M., Kittredge, A. K., & Klahr, D. (2016). Guided play: Principles and practices. *Current Directions in Psychological Science*, 25(3), 177–182.

White, R. (2012). *The power of play: A research summary on play and learning*. Minnesota: Minnesota Children's Museum.

CHAPTER

Risky play in primary schools

Helen Dodd, Rachel Nesbit, and Matt Robinson

Think back to your childhood and a time when you felt happy and free? What do you think of? Maybe it was going out on your bike all day with friends and only coming home when you got hungry or playing in the waves with siblings on family holidays. Play is a cornerstone of childhood and, for many, their favourite childhood memories involve some form of play, often with an element of risk or out of sight of adults. Children's independence and space to enjoy this type of play, where they have adventures and explore risk, have substantially diminished over recent decades and there is concern about what the consequences of this might be for children's development. Playtimes at primary school offer vital play experiences for children and, with some thought and planning, can even provide children with an opportunity for risk and adventure. In this chapter we describe the latest research about the importance of risky play for children and outline practical steps schools can take to support it based on our experience working with schools.

What is risky play?

> ### Box 6.1 What does risky play mean to you?
>
> Before reading the rest of the chapter, have a think about the following questions. It is likely that you already have some views and experiences of risky play, even if you haven't thought about them consciously for a while. These questions are designed to make you more aware of your existing views before you read more.
>
> - What does risky play mean to you? How would you define it?
> - Do you currently support children's access to risky play inside or outside of education (professionally or as a parent or caregiver)?

- If you do support risky play, what is it that motivates you to support it?
- If you don't actively support children's risky play, would you like to?
- Do you think schools can provide risky play experiences for children? What are the barriers to supporting it? How might you be able to be proactive about supporting it?

When children decide what they would like to play, when they want to start, when they want to stop and who they play with, we call it 'free play'. For children to play in this way they need not only physical space but also psychological space, with adults taking a step back and letting children lead the play. When children are given this space for free play, they naturally explore different roles, styles and emotions in their play, including risk-taking. Risky play specifically is defined as 'thrilling and exciting forms of play that involve a risk of physical injury' (Sandseter, 2007, p. 248). The term adventurous play also captures this type of play, with Dodd and Lester (2021) defining adventurous play as 'child-led play where children experience subjective feelings of excitement, thrill and fear; often this occurs in the context of age-appropriate risk-taking' (p. 164).

To increase understanding of children's risky play, Sandseter (2007) conducted observations and interviews at Norwegian preschools and identified six categories of risky play: Great Heights, High Speed, Dangerous Tools, Dangerous Elements, Rough-and-Tumble, Disappear/Get Lost. An additional two categories have subsequently been added: Vicarious Risk and Play with Impact. These are outlined below.

Category	Description	Examples
Great Heights	Play involving heights	Climbing trees, climbing towers
High Speed	Play involving high speed	Running at high speed, swinging at high speeds
Dangerous Tools	Play involving tools that are sharp or otherwise dangerous	Play with ropes, pound hammers and nails, whittle with knives or use saws and axes
Dangerous Elements	Play near dangerous elements	Playing near water, steep cliffs, fire pits
Rough-and-Tumble	Rough and tumble play	Play fighting, play wrestling, play fencing, chase-and-catch play

(Continued)

Category	Description	Examples
Disappear/Get Lost	Play where children are at risk of getting lost, without adult supervision	Play where children out of the sight of adults, often in their neighbourhood or a forest
Vicarious Risk	Observation of risky play that feels exciting in itself	Children's observations of risk-taking in others play, where the observed child shows clear signs of being exhilarated
Play with Impact	Play involving impact between the child and objects	Crashing tricycles, trolley or other wheeled toy into a fence or wall or other objects

Risky play is generally considered in the context of physical injury risks and, in fact, some definitions of risky play specifically refer to risk of physical injury (e.g., Sandseter, 2007). Nevertheless, thrill, fear and excitement can also be felt when children face risk in other types of play such as creative play or social play. In risky physical play, the fear and risk are around getting physically injured, perhaps from falling. In contrast, in social and creative play, the fear and risk might be linked to looking silly or being rejected. The risks are easier to quantify when we talk about physical risks but risks exist within other domains and exposure to these risks and associated feelings may be equally as important for children's development.

Why is risky play important?

Although children clearly differ from one another in their propensity to take risks, most children seem to enjoy some level of risk-taking in their play. For example, Little and Eager (2010) found that up to 90% of young children expressed a desire to play on equipment that was designed to be risky. Data from the British Children's Play Survey, conducted in 2020, showed that across all play settings other than at home, children played, on average, with at least a mild level of adventure (Dodd et al., 2021). A recent review exploring children's feelings about risky play in school concluded that children want to engage in active, risky play when they are at school but that they are regularly prevented from doing so (Jerebine et al., 2022). If children do not have adequate opportunities to play in a risky way, then they may be more likely to seek out undesirable high-risk activities or play in hazardous places. For example, an estimated 40% of children aged 11–14 years have played in unsafe places such as wastelands, building sites, underpasses, rivers, abandoned buildings and quarries (see Brussoni et al., 2015). Play in these places is associated with a higher risk of injury.

To understand why children might be motivated to play in a risky way and why risky play might be important for children's development, we can begin to get some clues from research with animals. Primates swing in trees, chase one another and leap from one tree to the next. They appear to intentionally switch between being in and out of control during their play, exposing themselves to moderate levels of fear and arousal (Spinka, Newberry, & Bekoff, 2001). It is proposed that this type of play, along with the exposure to moderate fear that it facilitates, helps juvenile animals to learn to cope emotionally with the unexpected (e.g., Spinka et al., 2001). For example, Spinka et al. (2001) argue that this 'risky play' allows animals to learn not only 'increased versatility of movements' but also how to 'avoid emotional overreaction during unexpected stressful situations' (p. 143). Following this same reasoning, Dodd and Lester (2021) propose that adventurous play provides children with 'exposure to fear-provoking situations and…opportunities for children to learn about physiological arousal, uncertainty and coping' which, in turn 'may help to decrease their risk for elevated or clinical anxiety'. These ideas are in keeping with Sandseter and Kennair's (2011) earlier argument that risky play may prevent phobias in children. For example, playing at heights may provide exposure to heights that decreases the risk of a child developing a phobia of heights. Risky play may therefore be important for children's healthy development including the prevention of anxiety and broader mental health problems.

In support of this, recent research showed that children who spend more time playing adventurously have fewer symptoms of anxiety and depression and had more positive emotions during the first Covid-19 lockdown in 2020 (Dodd, Nesbit, & FitzGibbon, 2022). Furthermore, children who injured themselves falling from heights during middle childhood were *less* likely to be scared of heights at age 18 (Poulton et al., 1998). Where schools have been able to increase children's adventurous play, a number of benefits for children's mental health and their social and emotional development are noted (see below). In relation to wider health outcomes, a review conducted in 2015 found positive effects of risky play on physical activity as well as social interaction and social competence (Brussoni et al., 2015). The outcomes of this 2015 review informed the publication of an international position statement on outdoor active play in children aged 3–12 years [30]. This states that 'Access to active play in nature and outdoors—with its risks—is essential for healthy child development' (Tremblay et al., 2015, p. 1).

Why do we need to be thinking about risky play in schools?

For many children, school provides their only opportunity for outdoor, active play with their peers. The average age that a child growing up in Britain is allowed out to play without adult supervision is approximately 11 years. This has changed rapidly within the space of a generation, with parents going out to play when they were children at approximately age 9 (Dodd et al., 2021). This restricts children's opportunities for active play with their friends and their independence. After school, children most often go straight home and the proportion playing with friends after school has also declined over the past 15–20 years. Furthermore, natural environments facilitate adventurous play but children are spending less time playing in nature than previous generations; with 13% of British children playing in the natural environment for less than 1 hour a month (Dodd et al., 2021). These changes mean that school playtimes are becoming increasingly important for providing children with opportunity for all types of play, including risky play.

Despite theory and research indicating that risky play is important for children's health and development, it is often prevented or restricted in schools due to a cycle of risk-averse decision-making (Jerebene et al., 2022). Importantly though, unstructured play is relatively low risk relative to sports, which are actively supported in schools, with an estimated incidence rate of injury per 1000 h of 0.15–0.17 for play compared to 0.20–0.67 for sport (Nauta et al., 2015). When children are given space for free, unstructured play they take risks but display strategies for preventing serious injury (Christensen & Mikkelsen, 2008). In fact, children recognise that major injuries communicate carelessness and clumsiness (Green, 1997).

What happens when schools support risky play?

There are examples from the UK and internationally of schools offering outstanding play opportunities, which include opportunity for children to engage in risky play. A now famous example is the Swanson School in New Zealand, which became known as 'the school without rules'. Their approach to play is to encourage free play during breaktimes by minimising the influence of adults and in their own words they 'stopped saying no' as long as children did not hurt someone else and or damage property. They allowed children to use previously 'off-limits' areas of the playground and introduced loose parts such as car tyres, wood and pipes, letting children do whatever they wanted with them. The school describes the outcome as 'more engaged, happy kids, who are less bored and more ready to learn after recess. There is less bullying, less conflict and less accidents in the playground' (McLachlan, 2014, p. 6).

A number of play programmes exist that support schools to improve their play offering and increase risky play opportunities at school. For example, PlayBoard Northern Ireland has developed and lead the Taking Outdoor Play Seriously (TOPS) programme (see https://www.playboard.org/what-we-do/tops-taking-outdoor-play-seriously/ for more information). TOPS supports schools to change their environment and culture to better facilitate outdoor, unstructured play. It is delivered over the space of a year and schools are encouraged to put play at the core of their ethos. TOPS includes staff training, play audits, work with pupils and engagement with parents/carers to enable schools to embed high-quality, diverse play opportunities. Schools open up spaces where children have previously not been allowed (e.g., fields) and introduce loose parts, often recycled materials.

> **Box 6.2 Feedback from school staff involved in the TOPS programme**
>
> - *'Almost every day I was hearing "best day ever"!!'*
> - *'Staff saw behaviours changing with pupils. Staff saw the children much more settled back in formal learning. They were happier and excited'*
> - *'There are so many benefits to this programme. The negative behaviours outside are almost non-existent now. Children aren't bored or fighting over resources as there are plenty to go around and a variety which caters to their interests'.*
> - *'I don't think the children will ever let us go back to the way was before and I am very glad because not only does it make them happy but it makes staff have a more joyful day too'.*
>
> Provided by PlayBoard Northern Ireland with permission to reproduce.

Outdoor Play and Learning (OPAL) also offer a playtime programme, which takes a similar approach to improve the quality of play in UK primary schools. Schools that have successfully transformed their playtimes by working with OPAL report that they get more teaching time because children return to the classroom happier and settle faster, that behaviour during playtime improves and that children enjoy playtime more (Lester, Jones, & Russell, 2011). Similarly, Lavrysen et al. (2017) provided an intensive package of risky-play activities (e.g., play with height and speed) to two classes of young children; teachers reported improvements in self-esteem, conflict sensitivity and concentration.

What helps and what hinders schools that want to introduce risky play?

Research with school staff and parents highlights a range of factors that support schools to provide risky play opportunities and a range of factors that can act as barriers (e.g., Nesbit et al., 2021). It is clear that successful change to play in schools happens when school staff are committed and believe in the importance and benefits of risky play. Staff working in schools also recognise the vital role of harnessing parent support. The parents we spoke to during our research were generally able to recognise the benefits of adventurous play for their child and held positive views about risky play in schools. They did also express some concerns as well as some misperceptions about risky play that would need to be addressed for changes to be successfully supported by parents. For example, parents may believe that risky play is only acceptable under strict supervision or with supervisors have specific expertise or training.

We also know from our research that schools are concerned about external judgements (often related to health and safety) as well as the perceived professional and legal repercussions schools may face in the event of child injury. There is also uncertainty and anxiety surrounding risky play and perceptions of children as unable to judge risk and initiate play. Other considerations include a lack of prioritisation of play in schools, often attributed to increased pressures to meet educational targets, as well as perceived lack of government and financial support for risky play. Whilst it is not possible to address all of these issues easily, many can be handled through appropriate training and communication. Below we outline our recommendations regarding steps to take to improve playtimes and offer more opportunities for risky play in school.

How to support more opportunities for risky play in schools

For schools to provide better opportunities for risky play and more diverse, rich play experiences more generally, we need to address the barriers that research has highlighted and harness the support that may already be there. As outlined above, a range of different programmes exist that support schools to improve children's play experiences. These programmes often provide intensive support to schools alongside a wealth of training based on extensive experience. The programmes have many things in common that align with our own work in schools and the evidence regarding factors that help and hinder the implementation of changes to play. In the section that follows, we provide an overview of the core elements that we believe need to be addressed and included for successful change to play provision in schools.

Keep in mind that change management is a process. Schools should have autonomy to implement changes in a way that works for them and on a timescale that works for them. The following should not therefore be read as a set of rigid 'ingredients' but rather flexible guidance on what are likely to be key elements in creating successful change.

Develop a shared vision and shared values

The aim is to develop shared values, where the benefits of play, including risky play, are understood and valued by everyone in the school. Alongside that, schools should aim to develop a vision of how play can benefit their children and what they want their play offering to look like.

A good place to start is where this chapter started; get the staff team to think about their own experiences of play. Try to get them to think about and discuss what development and learning opportunities those personal play experiences created. These can vary enormously and can cover the physical, emotional and social health of the children engaged in play. For example, if a participant in such as session suggests 'Jumping off a log' as an activity they enjoyed, we can then extrapolate the learning which takes place:

A. Developing strength and co-ordination through proprioception.
B. Developing the ability to manage thrilling emotions, to moderate anxiety or excitement.
C. Learning to make judgements for themselves about how high is too high, how risky is too risky.

To help get staff engaged and to encourage reflection, it can be helpful to ask staff to use the Play Types Toolkit created by Play Scotland (available via the Play Scotland website) to consider the breadth of play on offer in school. The toolkit lists a wide range of different types of play. Simply send staff out with the toolkit list to observe what play types are on display at breaktime and then ask them to feedback. Are there some types of play that dominate? Are there types of play they didn't see at all? If there are, why might that be, and could something be changed to provide opportunities for that type of play?

When working on shared values and vision, engaging with children is crucial. Children are in the strongest position to observe and report where opportunities or problems exist. Children are also excellent advocates for diverse play experiences and will undoubtedly offer some creative examples of types of play they would like to do but can't do currently in school. Keep in mind that children will have different play preferences and play might change across age groups so talk to a wide range of children to ensure that everyone's voice is heard.

Write a school policy on play

Schools have a multitude of policy already, and while we hesitate to suggest that more policies are developed, it is clear that resources and practice often follow such statements. A Play Policy is the formal summary of the vision and values you have just developed. It is therefore of real importance that every school has a play policy, within which the value of free play, risky play, breaktime and play within learning can all be highlighted. As with all policies this should be backed up by support from the senior leadership team and school governors.

Determine and put in place appropriate processes

Once there is a clear policy valuing play, including opportunity for risky play, we need to ensure that strong processes are in place. A significant challenge to supporting children to take appropriate risks in their play whilst at school is that the typical risk management system used in schools has been developed from a workplace perspective and therefore it uses a 'risk deficit model', where all risks should be reduced to as close to zero as possible. To apply this in a play or learning context doesn't make sense because some risk is inherent and, as we have outlined above, likely to be important for healthy development. Ideally therefore a balance of risk and challenge on the one hand and risk management on the other is required.

Within the relevant legal frameworks (Health and Safety at Work Act 1974, Occupiers Liability Acts 1957 and 1984), the duty of care schools have is encased in a notion of 'reasonableness'. Building on this, the Health and Safety Executive have made clear policy statements and support a balanced approach to risk management in children's play, where benefits are considered alongside risks. This approach is known as risk benefit assessment (RBA) and provides an alternative to traditional risk management. RBA is recommended in best practice guidance across England, Scotland, Wales and Northern Ireland. A common way of implementing this without creating huge amounts of work is to add a benefit section on as an addition to existing risk assessments.

We strongly recommend that schools move towards an RBA approach but until RBAs have been conducted you will need to work within existing risk management processes that your school has in place. All schools and nurseries will have a risk management process, which might be determined by the Local Authority, Academy or Group management, Headteacher or Head of Setting. You need to be aware of your current risk management processes and paperwork (often these are connected to an Outdoor Learning or Excursions policy if you have trouble finding them). Any changes that are made to the play space or to risk assessments, including the introduction of RBAs must be approved by the appropriate person, likely the Headteacher or their delegated person.

Working with colleagues around risk management often requires a culture change and a personal understanding of the benefits and national guidance on best practice. As outlined above, research tells us that school staff are understandably concerned about their duty of care and about what parents expect when they send their children to school, so they need to be reassured that the approach taken by the school aligns with best practice and legal guidelines.

Box 6.3 National guidance on risky play

- In their document 'Children's Play and Leisure—promoting a balanced approach' the Health and Safety Executive provide a clear steer regarding play safety. They state that *'Play is great for children's well-being and development. When planning and providing play opportunities, the goal is not to eliminate risk, but to weigh up the risks and benefits. No child will learn about risk if they are wrapped in cotton wool'*. Following this reasoning they recommend that risks and benefits should be weighed up when designing and providing play opportunities and activities.
- Play Wales, Play Scotland, Play England and PlayBoard Northern Ireland all support the use of RBA. These organisations are all members of the UK Play Safety Forum, whose webpages (https://playsafetyforum.wordpress.com/resources/) include links to all relevant policy and materials.
- Dr Tim Gill has written extensively about children's risky play. His book *'No Fear: Growing up in a Risk Averse Society'* is an excellent resource and available (for free at the time of writing) on his website (rethinkingchildhood.com).

Work with parents and staff to gain support and engagement

As the research described above explains, an important element of introducing risky play is seeking parent support. Strong communication with parents is key so that they understand what is happening and why. When you talk to parents ensure that you communicate uncertainty. It isn't true that all play is 100% safe and you can't guarantee there won't be any injuries but in our research and our practice we have found that parents are mostly willing to accept risks if they understand what the benefits are in return. It can be helpful to invite parents to join a play session once you have things up and running so they can see the benefits for themselves.

It is also vital to communicate clearly with school staff about decisions being made. This includes all school staff, from senior leaders to cleaners and caretakers, teachers, support staff and lunchtime supervisors; everyone needs to be on board and supportive. With staff, particularly those with direct responsibility for supervising play, we need to communicate about the uncertainty carefully. Staff have different personal values around risk-taking, and those on the 'front line' with regard to safeguarding and duty of care may have concerns about what happens when the bumps and scuffs start happening. Their concerns are very real and should be respected, even though it is likely that some of the concern around litigation and liability is based more on rumour than fact. The following activity can be useful for working with staff and parents.

Activity

Think about sports day, an event that typically takes place at least annually at almost all schools in the UK. Pupils, parents and staff all encourage children to run faster, jump further and extend themselves to their limit. Competitors risk a fall and public failure yet jointly as a community we accept the physical, social and emotional risks faced. In fact, even the most protective of parents tend to understand and appreciate the joint enterprise that is sports day.

This example of sports day illustrates a few things:

First, it shows that parents are willing to not only accept risks but they also can be encouraging of risk-taking in the right context where there are benefits to be had. It shows that as adults around children we can all agree on an acceptable level of risk. Should a fall happen, we understand that it is acceptable legally, socially and morally, that does not require extensive paperwork nor an apologetic approach.

Second, sports day also illustrates how a positive culture and shared vision and understanding around risk can give staff confidence. While some of this confidence is given through a shared view of the risks and benefits, some is down to a process that does not hold an individual culpable because they are working within policy that stems from shared judgements (the RBA outlined above).

Staff training around risk management is a vital foundation of their confidence. This training needs to be at the level at which they are working, much risk management training is aimed at adventurous activities or very high risk, not routine and expected play. You can of course put on your own collaborative training around risk, perhaps partner up with another local setting or seek advice from schools that already offer risky play opportunities. There are also a number of organisations that offer this type of support.

Staff should also have confidence that when they are working within the confines of an RBA and their standard operating procedures then they are supported by the senior leadership team, governors and everyone else in a managerial position. They should be reassured to know that no educator or teacher has been prosecuted or litigated against if they are working to the policies and process provided.

Start to make changes

Each setting should decide what their first steps will be to facilitate risky play. This should come after the processes above are in place.

Small changes are a good place to start. These may be obvious things, often banned by the adults. Examples could include allowing children to jump off higher things, going up a slide, being out in wetter and muddier conditions, using green and natural space even if it means muddy shoes and also using tools and obstacle courses.

Conversations are vital here for those supervising play, both in the moment and subsequently. These can be professional conversations along the lines of 'What are you seeing and should we respond in some way and if so, how?'. Simply speaking with colleagues in an inquisitive and honest way can reap dividends in exploring what activities we could step back from intervening in, and which may need adult intervention.

The conversations can also be between adults and children, and between children themselves. These conversations can be used to check in on both how the child is feeling, and what their perceptions of the risk are. It is important here to allow children to develop their own risk management skills, and to be less influenced by the adults' perceptions as skills and confidence grow.

Staff will have to decide when to step in and when to step back. Again, this is best done in conversation with a colleague, and best done after both of you take a pause to consider 'what happens if I do or I don't intervene here?'. The judgement here goes back to our RBA process; RBAs should be applied dynamically, with risk always considered in the context of potential benefit.

Make more significant changes

More significant changes in risky play provision can be driven by the children and staff; as their positive beliefs and commitment to risky play are confirmed then more changes can be introduced. We should not 'force' through more risky play until staff and children are ready and demonstrate competence and confidence.

As the play becomes more risky, either in likelihood or severity, there will need to be changes to practicalities. For example, you may position a staff member next to a popular climbing tree and have a marker of 'maximum climbing height' which moves up or down depending on the children's tree climbing skill and risk judgement. You may decide to introduce bikes or scooters to small groups of children at a time, or in a confined area, until skills improve and staff observe children's competence improving. Managing these changes again comes back to professional conversations and awareness, ensuring that you are talking about risk and challenge regularly.

Monitor and review

As children and staff grow more confident, and become more skilled in making good risk judgements, ensure that two things happen:

First, make sure that other stakeholders (parents, local community, governors etc.) are made aware of the changes that have been made. When communicating, it is useful to frame the changes through the lens of the benefits. Nice ways of doing this include using display boards and sharing child's learning journals and invitations to 'stay and play' sessions. At stay-and-play sessions the staff team can share the school's vision and values with regard risky play, the children's competence, and how there is a process in place to observe and facilitate appropriate risks.

Second, ensure that there is a feedback loop. Should there be a concern, a suggested improvement, a near miss or an incident, there should be a clear process for staff to communicate with senior leaders. This feedback loop should allow staff to share their perceptions of risk as well as any anxiety or uncertainty that they feel so that concerns can be discussed in a supportive, objective way. Any learning that comes through this process should feed back into policies and processes, including risk assessments and staff training. The aim of the feedback loop is to learn, to improve and to inform policies and practice. It is not to hold individual staff to account.

Final considerations are that any new members of staff joining the school will need appropriate training and induction, and new children and families who join the school will need to be informed about the school's approach to play. Furthermore, alongside this regular feedback loop, it is best practice to revisit RBAs' policies and processes, staff training and induction procedures on at least a yearly basis. These can often be included in a Staff Training Day.

Conclusion

- Risky play is a normal part of childhood but children's opportunities for risk and adventure in their play are declining.
- Adequate opportunities for risky play are linked to a range of positive physical and mental health outcomes for children.

- Schools generally take a risk-averse approach that restricts children's play but there are many examples of schools that actively support risky play. These schools not only demonstrate that it can be done, but they also report a range of benefits for children and school staff.
- Changing playtimes for the better will require a shared vision and understanding across all members of the school community. Doing the groundwork to ensure this shared commitment is crucial to successfully embedding long-term change.
- Taking a risk-benefit approach where risks are weighed up against the benefits for children aligns with current policy guidance and will provide a richer, more diverse play environment for children.
- Facilitating risky play, like so much in play and learning, is an ongoing process of continuous improvement. Being aware of this, and having a supportive culture and simple, robust processes is the key to children accessing a richer, more exciting and diverse set of play experiences.

References

Brussoni, M., Gibbons, R., Gray, C., Ishikawa, T., Sandseter, E. B., Bienenstock, A., Chabot, G., Fuselli, P., Herrington, S., Janssen, I., Pickett, W., Power, M., Stanger, N., Sampson, M., & Tremblay, M. S. (2015). What is the relationship between risky outdoor play and health in children? A systematic review. *International Journal of Environmental Research and Public Health*, *12*(6), 6423–6454.
   Reviews the evidence that was available until the end of 2013 regarding associations between risky play and children's health broadly defined.

Christensen, P., & Mikkelsen, M. R. (2008). Jumping off and being careful: children's strategies of risk management in everyday life. *Sociology of Health & Illness*, *30*(1), 112–130.
   Paper describes how children manage risk in their everyday life and demonstrates that children know that it is important to manage risk and that they don't want to get hurt.

Dodd, H. F., & Lester, K. J. (2021). Adventurous play as a mechanism for reducing risk for childhood anxiety: A conceptual model. *Clinical Child and Family Psychology Review*, *24*(1), 164–181.
   Paper describing why risky/adventurous play might offer a protective role preventing the development of anxiety. This paper is quite detailed and provides relevant background before drawing on anxiety research to propose a conceptual model.

Dodd, H. F., FitzGibbon, L., Watson, B. E., & Nesbit, R. J. (2021). Children's play and independent mobility in 2020: Results from the British Children's play survey. *International Journal of Environmental Research and Public Health*, *18*(8), 4334.
   Reports data on trends in children's play in Britain in 2020 (prior to the Covid-19 pandemic) including where children play, how much they play in different places and how adventurously they play. Provides comparisons across demographic groups.

Dodd, H. F., Nesbit, R. J., & FitzGibbon, L. (2023). Child's play: Examining the association between time spent playing and child mental health. *Child Psychiatry & Human Development*, *54*(6), 1678–1686.

Describes how children's time spent playing adventurously and outdoors relates to their mental health. Demonstrates small but consistent associations with children who spend more time playing in an adventurous way having lower anxiety and depression. Also demonstrates that this link might be stronger in children from low-income families.

Green, J. (1997). Risk and the construction of social identity: Children's talk about accidents. *Sociology of Health & Illness, 19*(4), 457–479.

Provides insight into how children think about and describe accidents. Shows that they hold negative judgements about people who hurt themselves.

Jerebine, A., Fitton-Davies, K., Lander, N., Eyre, E. L., Duncan, M. J., & Barnett, L. M. (2022). "All the fun stuff, the teachers say, 'that's dangerous!'" Hearing from children on safety and risk in active play in schools: A systematic review. *International Journal of Behavioral Nutrition and Physical Activity, 19*(1), 1–25.

Reviews what children think about risk and activity in schools. Good resource for understanding children's perspectives better.

Lavrysen, A., Bertrands, E., Leyssen, L., Smets, L., Vanderspikken, A., & De Graef, P. (2017). Risky-play at school. Facilitating risk perception and competence in young children. *European Early Childhood Education Research Journal, 25*(1), 89–105.

Paper describes a small-scale evaluation of what happens when children are given opportunity for risky play in schools.

Lester, S., Jones, O., & Russell, W. (2011). *Supporting school improvement through play: an evaluation of South Gloucestershire's Outdoor Play and Learning programme.* Available at: http://outdoorplayandlearning.org.uk/wp-content/uploads/2016/07/supporting-school-improvement-through-play-1.pdf.

Describes in more detail the OPAL programme and provides an evaluation of the programme across a number of schools.

Little, H., & Eager, D. (2010). Risk, challenge and safety: Implications for play quality and playground design. European Early Childhood Education Research Journal, 18(4), 497–513.

McLachlan, B. (2014). Project play at Swanson school. *Play and Folklore, 61*(1), 4–8.

Nauta, J., Martin-Diener, E., Martin, B. W., Van Mechelen, W., & Verhagen, E. (2015). Injury risk during different physical activity behaviours in children: A systematic review with bias assessment. *Sports Medicine, 45*(3), 327–336.

Describes the likelihood of injury for a range of activities that children may engage in. Demonstrates that unstructured play has lower injury rates than sports.

Nesbit, R. J., Bagnall, C. L., Harvey, K., & Dodd, H. F. (2021). Perceived barriers and facilitators of adventurous play in schools: A qualitative systematic review. *Children, 8*(8), 681.

Reviews what we know about what helps and what hinders schools from providing risky play experiences for the children in their care.

Poulton, R., Davies, S., Menzies, R. G., Langley, J. D., & Silva, P. A. (1998). Evidence for a non-associative model of the acquisition of a fear of heights. *Behaviour Research and Therapy, 36*(5), 537–544.

Sandseter, E. B. (2007). Categorising risky play—How can we identify risk-taking in children's play? *European Early Childhood Education Research Journal, 15*(2), 237–252.

Describes the different ways that children take risks in their play. Focus is on early childhood in particular.

Sandseter, E. B. H., & Kennair, L. E. O. (2011). 'Children's risky play from an evolutionary perspective: The anti-phobic effects of thrilling experiences'. *Evolutionary Psychology, 9*(2). https://doi.org/10.1177/147470491100900212

Describes a theory that children play in a risky way in order to learn about things they may be predisposed to fear such as heights. It is hypothesised that playing in a risky way provides exposure and prevents fears from developing.

Spinka, M., Newberry, R. C., & Bekoff, M. (2001). Mammalian play: Training for the unexpected. *The Quarterly Review of Biology, 76*(2), 141–168.

Describes the way that mammals play and what the purpose of this type of play might be in terms of preparation for future uncertainty and coping. Of interest due to obvious links with how children naturally play if given space and time to do so.

Tremblay, M. S., Gray, C., Babcock, S., Barnes, J., Costas Bradstreet, C., Carr, D., & Brussoni, M. (2015). Position statement on active outdoor play. *International Journal of Environmental Research and Public Health, 12*(6), 6475–6505.

Position statement on the evidence and need for active outdoor play throughout childhood. Written by a diverse range of stakeholders who support this position.

CHAPTER

BRAC Play Labs: designing a high-quality, low-cost model for early years

Erum Mariam, Jahanara Ahmad, and Sarah Tabassum

Introduction

What is play? This is a simple question with no easy definitions. Understanding of play and beliefs about play vary greatly across different cultures and societies and are influenced by the dominant discourses about childhood, education, and child development. However, there is broad agreement among theorists, researchers, and educators that play is important for children's development and learning. Research shows that through play, children develop skills in all areas of development: intellectual, social, emotional, and physical (UNICEF, 2018).

This chapter provides a case study of how high-quality, low-cost, play-based early childhood education programs can be designed and implemented in low-resource settings – especially in one in which most parents and teachers believe that schooling, including preschool, should focus on academics rather than play.

How do you design a curriculum that is community-led, aligned with government standards, and culturally responsive? How do you ensure that facilitators have enough knowledge and skills to implement the curriculum when they have little to no experience? How do you design high-quality spaces and play materials using minimal resources? How do you engage parents, communities, and governments in children's learning and change traditional attitudes toward play? BRAC, one of the largest non-governmental organizations in the world, has attempted to answer these questions since 2015 when it began implementing its Play Lab model.

The Play Labs are joyful, creative, and child-friendly spaces that promote children's cognitive, language, physical, and social-emotional development through a play-based approach. They are mainly for children ages three to five and have been implemented so far in Bangladesh, Uganda, and Tanzania since 2015, reaching thousands of children. The play spaces and curriculum are designed by the BRAC

DOI: 10.4324/9781003321279-8

Figure 7.1 Children enjoying themselves on a swing in a BRAC Play Lab outdoor space © BRAC IED, 2020

Institute of Educational Development (BRAC IED) at BRAC University, which is also home to the only postgraduate studies in Early Childhood Development in Bangladesh.

This chapter will focus on the implementation story in Bangladesh. It first introduces the core components of the Play Lab and the rationale which has informed its innovative approach. It then dives deeper into how the curriculum and activities are implemented, how facilitators are selected and trained, how the spaces are designed to be playful and stimulating, how the play materials are constructed, and how the community and parents are engaged. It also focuses on how to implement it within government systems. It concludes with research findings on the effectiveness of the Play Labs and presents some recommendations that will be useful for anyone implementing play-based pedagogies and approaches, especially in low-resource settings.

What is a Play Lab?

The core components of Play Labs are as follows:

- A **play-based curriculum** that is culturally relevant and designed to suit the local contexts and is aligned with the Early Learning Development Standards set by the government of each country

> ### The Inspiration Behind Play Labs
>
> The Play Lab model has been influenced by several education and early childhood development models:
>
> - The BRAC Non-Formal Primary Education (NFPE) model has provided quality primary education to millions of underprivileged children. The Play Lab model adapted the core approaches of BRAC's NFPE model – such as schools being located in close proximity to children's houses, selecting young women from the community and training them as teachers, having a child-centered curriculum and teaching-learning strategies, and engaging parents and communities in children's education.
> - The Reggio-Emilia approach places a huge emphasis on allowing children to express themselves in "one hundred languages", collaboration and team-thinking, the environment acting as a "third teacher", and parent and community engagement (Reggio Emilia Approach, n.d.).
> - The AnjiPlay approach focuses on children's open-ended, self-determined play activities and environments that maximize the child's opportunities for imagination, inquiry, and contact with natural phenomena and elements (AnjiPlay, n.d.).

- **Play Leaders** who are hired from the community and given extensive training to facilitate the activities in the curriculum
- **Child-friendly spatial design** and use of low-cost, no-cost materials
- **Parent and community engagement** in the design and implementation of the Play Labs
- A group of experts in play, child development, education, and research form a **Play Consortium** and guide the development, implementation, and evaluation of the Play Labs

> ### Key Characteristics of the Play Lab
>
> - The best interests of the child must be kept in mind at all times.
> - One Play Leader will be assigned for each Play Lab. Along with this Play Leader, two or three mothers will volunteer by rotation to help manage the children.
> - The activities will run for 2.5 hours each day, five days a week.
> - The number of children in a Play Lab will be 25–30.
> - The Play Lab will have materials appropriate for different ages and development levels.
> - Activities will allow for flexibility depending on the children's opinions, interests, and specific situations.
> - There will be different types of play, including free play, child-led play, guided play, small group play, and large group play.

- Each month will have a different theme to guide project work and other activities.
- Each Play Lab will have a management committee composed of community members and parents/guardians.
- The community will be actively involved in selecting the Play Leader and a space for the Play Lab, as well as helping during Play Lab activities.
- There will be enough space in the Play Lab for activities suited for different ages to occur simultaneously.

Figure 7.2 A child leads an activity in a BRAC Play Lab © BRAC IED, 2019

The Theoretical Underpinning of Play Labs

The experts at BRAC IED who designed the Play Lab model have been inspired by the work of several influential theorists including Jean Piaget, Lev Vygotsky, Erik Erikson, and Urie Bronfenbrenner.

- Piaget's theories about learning emphasized the need for children to explore and experiment for themselves. Piaget suggested that children use play to assimilate their everyday experiences into their existing cognitive schema (Bergen, 2015). His work guided many principles in the Play Lab curriculum and its strong emphasis on providing learning opportunities for children.

- Vygotsky emphasized the social and cultural aspects of play. He believed that play is the way children learn to represent real experiences when these experiences are not present. Play also provides the structure children need for their social and cognitive development – the scaffolding needed for them to advance (Trawick-Smith, 2017). His theories are reflected in the design of the Play Labs where scaffolding is built into the activities, the curriculum is culturally responsive, and the Play Leader-child relationship is strongly emphasized.
- Erikson believed children use play to progress through developmental stages and his theories underpin the strong emphasis on social-emotional development in the Play Lab curriculum. He focused on the importance of the "Play Age" (three to six years) during which children take on the roles of strong imaginary characters (e.g. superheroes) or of adults who are powerful in their lives. They also create block-construction "worlds" that allow them to deal with emotional and behavioral problems from the "real world" (Bergen, 2015).
- Bronfenbrenner's ecological model holds that developmental processes do not occur in a psychological vacuum but rather that individual child development is influenced by factors in the immediate environment as well as society and culture as a whole (Trawick-Smith, 2017). His work has influenced the strong emphasis on parent and community engagement in the Play Lab design and operations.

The Play Lab curriculum

The main goal of the curriculum is to support a child's holistic development and the activities have been designed with the various aspects of development (physical, social-emotional, cognitive, and language development) in mind, in alignment with the development stages of each age. The curriculum and activities reflect the age, interests, demands, and culture of the children, as well as their environment. Activities such as singing, outdoor play, arts and crafts, dramatic, and pretend play are included as they are universally effective ways to keep children engaged. Through the blend of child-led play, open-ended play, and Play Leader-facilitated activities, the curriculum enables a stimulating and meaningful experience for the early years. The curriculum is gender inclusive and places a lot of emphasis on social-emotional development and is being reviewed to address other special needs.

Developing the Play Curriculum

In Bangladesh, the Play Curriculum was developed over two years. At first, the curriculum for ages three to four was developed, then the curriculum for ages four to five. In 2015, a review of existing policies and national and international curricula took place, and national and international experts on play and ECD were engaged. A curriculum framework was developed in 2015, which was refined further in 2016 and 2017.

Local communities were engaged to identify play activities that were unique to their context, and those activities were adapted to align with the curriculum framework. Local curriculum developers worked on the curriculum and activities for cultural relevance. As part of the testing and iterating process, observations from the field and feedback from children, Play Leaders, and other stakeholders were used to refine the activities.

Weekly Schedule

Time: 2 Hours 30 Minutes

Day	Start with Fun (Greetings and Play with Songs, Stories, and Rhymes) 30 minutes	Let's Play Together (Physical, Social, and Emotional Play) 30 minutes	Free Play 40 minutes	Let's Play and Learn (Play with Pre-math, Science, and the Environment, and Art and Crafts) 30 minutes	End with a Rhyme and a Song 20 minutes
1st	Song/Rhyme	,,	,,	Play with Pre-Math	,,
2nd	Song/Rhyme	,,	,,	Play with Pre-Math	,,
3rd	Story	,,	,,	Play with Science and Environment	,,
4th	Story	,,	,,	Play with Arts and Crafts	,,
5th	Pre-Reading and Pre-Writing	,,	,,	Play with Arts and Crafts	,,

Figure 7.3 Play Lab schedule © BRAC IED, 2019

A Day at the Play Lab

As the children start arriving, the Play Leader (PL) speaks to one or two of the children to learn more about them – for instance by asking them about their experience while coming to the Play Lab. These conversations should be recorded as notes.

Once all of the children have arrived, the PL greets them and encourages them to welcome one another. Using the notes of the earlier conversations, the PL can then perhaps introduce new information such as a safety message. If any of the children want to say something, the PL will invite them to do so.

After the welcoming morning circle ends, the PL engages the children by acting out a story, reciting a rhyme, or singing a song with them. It is key that the PL does this in a manner that encourages children to actively listen and react to the key moments – through facial expressions, vocal intonation, body gestures, expressing her own thoughts, and asking the children questions.

In the next session called *Let's Play Together*, children use different toys and play materials for activities that are designed to promote physical, social, and emotional development. Below is an example of an activity that the PL can facilitate with the children.

The PL will take the children outside. A long line will be drawn with a piece of chalk or stick on the ground, with one side named "mountain" and the other "river". PL will then explain to the children what to do. The children will be standing on the line. When the PL says "river", they will jump to the side named river, and when the PL says "mountain", they will jump to the other side. Each time the children follow instructions, everyone will clap. After a while, the children can be divided into small groups and asked to conduct the game themselves. The volunteer mothers can provide support if needed. Later on in the game, the children can briefly say each time they change sides what they will do if they reach the mountain top or the riverside. This will help them stay engaged and fully immersed in the game. Besides developing their gross motor skills, this activity also helps children develop listening skills, learn to cooperate in a group and follow instructions while keeping their imagination stimulated.

Free Play is a session during which the children can play as they like. They can play with toys in different corners of the room and with anyone of their choice. The PL should encourage them to make their own choices while sharing toys with others and respecting the common space.

During the last session of the day called *Let's Play and Learn*, the children can learn from playing games that focus on pre-math, science, environment, and arts and crafts. Below is an example of an activity that the PL can facilitate with the children.

First, everyone will sit in a circle. The PL will have a basket with some blocks in it. She will then divide the children into two groups, and a volunteer mother can help support the groups. At the beginning of the game, the PL will count out four blocks loudly and pass them to four children. She will encourage the children to count with her. Then the four children will come up, one by one, and drop the blocks in the basket. The PL can then ask, "How many blocks are there in the basket?" and help them with the answer, if needed. If the children answer correctly, they should be praised and applauded. Then another child can take the blocks out of the basket, one by one, as everyone counts together. The game can be continued with a different number of blocks. Once everyone has become familiar

> with the game, an interested child can lead the game, with the support of the PL, if needed. This game is very helpful in helping children learn basic counting to ten. It also develops their fine motor skills, helps them learn to follow instructions, and develops their attention span.
>
> As the day ends in the Play Lab, everyone will stand in a circle and talk about the day. The PL will encourage the children to share their thoughts and end with a familiar song or rhyme.

Figure 7.4 Children engaged in outdoor play in a BRAC Play Lab © BRAC IED, 2021

The role of Play Leaders/facilitators

A Play Leader's knowledge, skills, attitude, and commitment are critical to the success of the Play Lab. The Play Leader's main priority is to engage the children in a variety of age-appropriate activities and ensure their well-being. Play Leaders (usually young women, ages between 18 and 35 years) are recruited from the community which enables them to quickly win over the communities' trust. These facilitators are among the most marginalized demographic, and working and being trained as Play Leaders empower their role as changemakers and provide positive role models to the community. It is essential that the Play Leader can demonstrate certain psychosocial skills to be able to engage with children of

Figure 7.5 A Play Leader engages children in a storytelling session in a BRAC Play Lab © BRAC IED, 2021

all abilities and contexts. Some of these skills include active listening, observation, showing empathy, remaining nonjudgmental, being reliable, maintaining confidentiality, staying flexible, and having a sense of humor.

Basic Duties of a Play Leader

- Guiding and expanding children's language, self-regulation, and thinking skills by engaging in exploratory talk, effective scaffolding, supporting and expanding children's learning practices through play and creativity, and engaging in productive dialog with children
- Demonstrating an understanding of early childhood development (babies, toddlers, and young children)
- Supporting peer learning (child-to-child learning)
- Facilitating child-directed play and learning
- Facilitating hands-on learning
- Supporting parents to actively engage in Play Lab activities
- Reflecting on and documenting their practices
- Continuously developing their skills
- Building children's confidence and creating a joyful experience for them
- Designing materials with children and parents while paying attention to the local environment and available resources

Because the Play Leaders are non-specialists in the field, it is necessary to provide them with thorough training to enhance their capability in providing play-based lessons and individualized care for the children. Each Play Leader receives Basic Training (including SEL training) of six days after recruitment which covers topics like how play impacts child development, the Play Lab curriculum and how to facilitate activities in different sessions, and how to communicate with children and engage parents and community members. This training is conducted using various methods like presentations, dialogs, hands-on demonstrations, and role plays by participants. To ensure the ongoing development of skills, knowledge, and abilities, Refresher Training sessions are also required. Hence, the Play Leader receives one day of Refresher Training per month.

Design of spaces and materials

Well-designed spaces can positively impact children's experiences of learning through play. When a space is designed specifically for children, their presence in that environment will be full of joy and freedom. The design of the BRAC Play

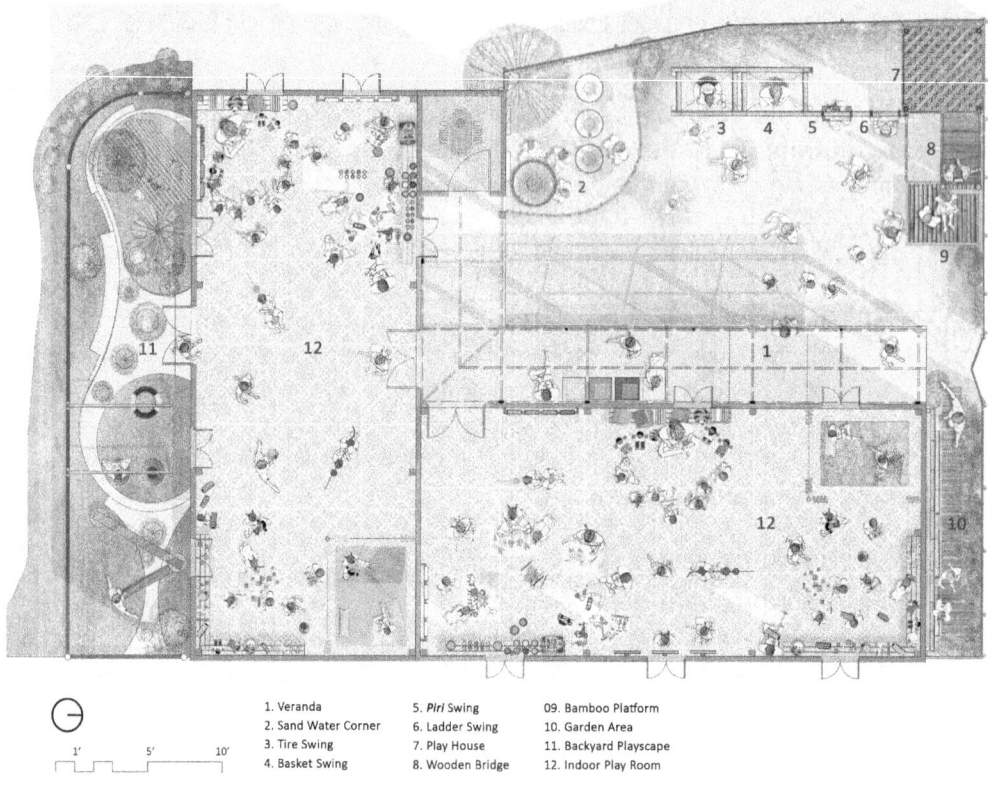

1. Veranda
2. Sand Water Corner
3. Tire Swing
4. Basket Swing
5. *Piri* Swing
6. Ladder Swing
7. Play House
8. Wooden Bridge
09. Bamboo Platform
10. Garden Area
11. Backyard Playscape
12. Indoor Play Room

Figure 7.6 Plan layout of a community-based Play Lab © BRAC IED, 2019

Labs is child-centered so that children feel safe and can decide how to shape and use their spaces with minimal support from adults.

Before the Play Labs are designed and constructed, architects and implementation staff carry out design workshops with children, families, Play Leaders, and community members where they ask them to talk about, draw, and make models of what their favorite play activities look like. Ideas generated from these workshops are used by architects as inspiration for their designs. Designs are community-led, use local resources and materials, and are adapted to local needs and environmental and cultural considerations.

The Play Labs are implemented in whatever structures are available in the community – usually a semi-permanent community-based structure made of corrugated iron sheets or in the case of government primary school (GPS) co-location, a room in the government school. Since there usually isn't a lot of space or resources, the space design is flexible to support different types of play activities, and play materials and decorations are usually made using low-cost, no-cost, and recycled materials.

There are separate corners so that many children can simultaneously engage in different kinds of play activities. These corners are as follows:

- *Shopner Bhubon* **(Dream World)** with dolls and props like cooking sets, clothing, jewelry, wooden blocks, balls, puzzles, fans, flutes, garlands, cars, used t-shirts, shoes, bags, sarees (a woman's garment, usually worn in South Asia), mirrors, ornaments, and toys made of clay

Figure 7.7 Toys made from locally sourced materials used in a BRAC Play Lab © BRAC IED, 2019

Figure 7.8 Toys made from locally sourced materials used in a BRAC Play Lab © BRAC IED, 2019

- *Ronger Bhubon* (**Art World**) with papers, pencils, crayons, and other art materials, as well as displays of children's artwork to support children's creative expression
- *Golper Bhubon* (**Story World**) with story books, masks, flashcards, and puppets where children can read and act out stories
- *Apon Bhubon* (**Own World**) with dim lighting and soft materials where children can rest and relax

Besides the four corners, the interiors of the Play Labs have open unrestricted spaces in the middle which can be used for group play activities. There are lots of windows for light and ventilation. Mats of plastic or woven from reeds are placed over the floor. The shelves around the walls are placed at children's eye level and are made of bamboo or recycled cartons. Swings and climbing cloths made from satin hang from the roof. The ceiling is painted in light colors to reflect light and make the interior space feel spacious.

Decoration materials like paper lanterns and flowers hanging on the walls are made by mothers and Play Leaders in workshops and reflect local cultural motifs. Bright colors are used to paint the interior walls, and sometimes zone-specific bright colors are used to define zones. The shoe shelves and door mats are made of recycled materials like plastic bottles. Semi-shaded verandahs act as a transition space between the interior and exterior and are equipped with natural materials

Figure 7.9 A colorful world of play – Handmade hanging decor in a BRAC Play Lab © BRAC IED, 2019

such as dry leaves and small rocks where children can play on hot or rainy days. These spaces also serve as music corners, and the floors of the verandahs are painted to create interactive surfaces for different types of games. Playful doodles are painted on the exterior walls by children, parents, and Play Leaders. Children also use their hands or leaves dipped in paint to create colorful prints or write their names using paint on the walls. Small trees and shrubs, sometimes brought by mothers from home, are planted near the Play Labs to provide greenery and ventilation. Children are encouraged to take care of the garden.

The outdoor play spaces are made in whatever outdoor spaces are found adjacent to the Play Lab structures. They are designed to promote a range of physical activities – children can climb, jump, run, duck, crawl, etc. on different textures like earth, sand, grass, and pebbles. This ensures diverse visual, tactile, and physical experiences. Intimate spaces such as tunnels and niches are created which are complementary to children's physical scale and eye level. A sand water corner, in a cool, shaded area, is demarcated by bamboo pieces, recycled plastic bottles, tires, or bricks. The design of the play equipment is multipurpose and children are encouraged to use them in lots of ways – for instance, ladder swings can be used for swinging and also climbing. The play equipment is made of bamboo, wood, tires, common household items such as *piri* (low wooden stool) and *jhuri* (traditional bamboo basket), and other low-cost, recyclable materials which are painted to protect them from rain and stabilized when being planted on the ground by using

Figure 7.10 Children playing on a wooden see-saw in a BRAC Play Lab © BRAC IED, 2019

cement or coal tar. Architects observe the unique ways children use the equipment and which ones they prefer, and this helps them to improve the existing designs and come up with new ones. The construction of the play equipment is done by local craftsmen and community members. Some common prototypes for outdoor play equipment include the following:

- Composite climbing structure made of wood
- Swings made with recycled tires and bamboo baskets
- Rope and wood ladder
- Wooden see-saw
- Rope platform
- Bamboo suspension bridge
- Bamboo tunnel

Parent and community engagement

Engagement with the Play Lab's operations builds a sense of ownership among parents and community members and helps to foster sustainability. The community's recommendations are considered when selecting sites for Play Lab centers and when recruiting Play Leaders. Parents and community members are also involved in decorating the Play Lab centers. The Play Leader is crucial in nurturing relationships with families and communities. She maintains regular communication with families –

holding meetings with them and visiting them in their homes to inform them about their children's progress and inspire them to take part in Play Lab activities. Some specific strategies for parent and community engagement are as follows:

- **Material Development Workshops:** Regular half-day long material development workshops are held where Play Leaders, caregivers, and community members develop age-appropriate, culturally relevant play materials and center decoration materials using low-cost, no-cost, locally available materials like coconut shells, leaves, pebbles, clay, straw, jute, bamboo, plastic bottles, cotton balls, socks, and pieces of clothing. Parents and community members themselves provide a lot of these materials.
- **Volunteerism:** The Play Leader is assisted by two or three mothers who volunteer by rotation to help manage the children.
- **Center Management Committees:** Each Play Lab has a management committee whose 11 members comprise parents, Play Leaders, and community people. They assist in Play Lab operations – ensuring daily operations and parent meetings run smoothly, supporting the Play Leader with her responsibilities, encouraging mothers and children to attend the Play Labs, collecting play and decoration materials, encouraging parents to pay fees on time, and holding discussions to settle any disputes.
- **Parent Meetings and Parenting Education:** Parent meetings are held to increase awareness among them about the importance of play for child development and to help change traditional mindsets and attitudes toward child-rearing. Through regular meetings, parents feel a sense of ownership toward their children's learning and cooperate to ensure that Play Labs run smoothly. Meetings are conducted in local dialects and run in a participatory manner giving all parents a chance to speak. Play Leaders also conduct sessions to teach parents about how to promote their own physical and mental well-being and how to develop closer bonds with their children. Parents are shown different play-based learning activities they can do at home with their children. Open sharing sessions are also held where mothers are given space to speak about whatever they want.

BRAC Play Labs in government primary schools

Over the last few years, pre-primary enrollment improved greatly in Bangladesh through a combination of public and non-state providers, though there were notable disparities in access across socio-economic groups and geographic areas (World Bank, 2020). The COVID-19 pandemic also caused huge disruptions in access. The national government-approved curriculum for pre-primary education is mostly academic in approach and is implemented in GPSs for one year for children ages five to six.

There are plans to revise the curriculum and expand government access to pre-primary education for children ages four to five. Many NGOs and private sector providers offer pre-primary education with customized early years learning curricula. The government has recently partnered with NGOs such as BRAC to promote play-centered pre-primary education in several pilot schools. Therefore, BRAC co-located Play Labs on GPS premises to help insert play-based learning into the curriculum and pedagogy of pre-primary education in Bangladesh and in doing so make its approach more scalable and sustainable. Currently, BRAC is part of the national technical committee to revise the pre-primary curriculum.

The GPS co-located Play Labs enroll children ages four to five for one year. Afterward, they attend government-run pre-primary classes in the same GPS from ages five to six. The curriculum in the co-located Play Labs is the same as for the community-based Play Labs and has been designed to seamlessly feed into the current government-approved pre-primary curriculum. Instructions are given in the local dialects. One session has 30 children on average and is facilitated by one Play Leader with the help of two Mother Volunteers. Sessions run six days a week and take place in pre-primary classrooms within the GPS. There are some important considerations when operating within government systems:

- *Capacity building of GPS teachers is important to transfer knowledge of play pedagogy into government systems.* Play Leaders are given foundational training on early childhood development, play-based learning, and how to implement the Play Lab curriculum. This same training is also provided to one teacher from the GPS, who is usually the head teacher or the pre-primary teacher in that school. Schools select the teacher who will receive the training, and all teachers have the chance to observe Play Labs whenever they want. GPS teachers may also volunteer to help facilitate sessions in the Play Labs if the Play Leader is not available.
- *The design has to be flexible.* The curriculum and pedagogies are fixed, but the timings of sessions differ from GPS to GPS depending on the availability of the pre-primary classrooms. There also has to be some flexibility in the spatial design. As Play Labs are implemented in the same space as GPS pre-primary classes, the decor has to be adjusted to the existing setup. Toys, books, and other materials necessary for the activities in the curriculum are provided, and GPS pre-primary students are also allowed to play with these materials. There is more flexibility in outdoor playground design though in some cases the space available to construct playgrounds may not always be ideal. Usually, school playgrounds have beautiful trees and a variety of niches where play equipment can be constructed. All GPS students have access to the built playgrounds, leading to increased attendance among GPS students.
- *There needs to be a good rapport between government stakeholders at all levels.* After getting approval from central government authorities to implement Play Labs, it is necessary to engage in discussions with government officials at district and sub-district levels to get their buy-in and engage them in school selection and implementation of the Play Labs. Regular discussions also need to be held with government officials at all levels to advocate with them the importance of play-based learning. At the school level, Play Leaders become

part of the teacher family – they maintain regular contact with GPS teachers about the operations of the Play Labs, which helps play-based pedagogy be more readily acceptable to school authorities.

- ***Strong community engagement is crucial.*** GPS Play Labs engages parents, caregivers, and community members to decorate the learning spaces. Play Leaders have regular contact with parents, and mothers volunteer to help facilitate the sessions. Monthly parent meetings are held where the importance of play and pre-primary education is discussed. Families get together in material development workshops to make play materials using low-cost, no-cost, and recyclable materials. These initiatives make parents feel delighted to be part of their children's learning and they value play as a learning tool.

Learning from evidence

Monitoring data that looks at the day-to-day activities of the Play Lab implementation such as children's attendance records and how facilitators implement the curriculum is used to improve the Play Lab implementation. The monitoring tools include observation checklists to measure the quality of interactions between the Play Leaders and the children, the environmental quality, and how faithful the program implementation is to its stated objectives. Monitoring officers collect

Figure 7.11 Curiosity leads to discovery – A child playing with blocks in a BRAC Play Lab © BRAC IED, 2019

these data regularly and share them with program staff, who use them to inform program revisions.

A study conducted by researchers at the University of Cambridge and Columbia University from 2018 to 2019 that assessed the impact of the Play Labs in Bangladesh showed that:

- The benefits of the Play Lab experience for children were extensively and consistently evident across all four of the measures of development used. For instance, the Ages and Stages Questionnaire-Third (ASQ-3) measures children's communication, gross motor, fine motor, problem-solving, and personal-social skills. For each measure, the Play Lab children outperformed the control group children, at moderate levels in year one and dramatically in year two, resulting in very dramatic differences between the two groups over the intervention's course. Children who scored below average at the baseline were able to catch up to their peers over their two years in the Play Labs, indicating the Play Labs' ability to level the playing field so all children enter primary school with the skills they need to learn and succeed.
- The Play Labs also improved both Play Leader and parents' knowledge, attitudes, and practices around ECD and play-based learning, demonstrating the ability of the Play Labs to build a quality ECD workforce and equip parents with the skills to support their children's development.

Key takeaways

- **Context and culture are crucial.** Play looks different in different places. Incorporating local play and culture makes learning more joyful and fosters belonging. Therefore, play activities in the curriculum must be defined for the local cultural context.
- **Communities and families are critical champions of play.** Insights gained from working with children and their families add richness to the content and curriculum, improving implementation. Engaging with both mothers and fathers is crucial, and building their skills as well as the communities' skills in play and early childhood creates enabling environments for children's learning to continue at home, leading to better long-term impact.
- **The facilitator-child relationship is crucial for learning.** Young children's positive interactions with facilitators strengthen all aspects of their development, and Play Leaders are trained to promote children's social-emotional development and to create a warm, nurturing, and playful bond with all children.

- **Integration of psychosocial support mechanisms for children and families in learning interventions improves developmental outcomes.** Inspired by its work with refugee children in the Rohingya camps and during the COVID-19 pandemic, BRAC IED has started integrating para-counselors (young women who are trained to provide basic psychosocial support to children and caregivers under the guidance of psychologists) in the everyday workings of the Play Labs.
- **Spatial design is important for child development.** BRAC IED went the extra mile to ensure that the design of all spaces, both indoors and outdoors, is child-friendly and joyful. The designs and play materials were constructed using low-cost, no-cost, and recyclable materials highlighting that child-friendly designs do not have to be expensive to build.
- **Concentrate on quality improvement and learning from evidence.** It is important to work with different experts and gain feedback from stakeholders to find ways to iterate to improve children's learning experiences.

References

AnjiPlay. (n.d.) http://www.anjiplay.com/
    Provides details of the AnjiPlay approach, a philosophy and approach to early education developed for public early childhood programs of Anji County, Zhejian Province, China.

Bergen, D.L. (2015). Psychological Approaches to the Study of Play. *American Journal of Play*, 8, 101–128.
    A survey of research on the psychological approaches to play and comparison to researchers from other disciplines, such as philosophy, ethology, anthropology, linguistics, and education, who have also studied play.

BRAC. (2021). *Spatial Design Guidance BRAC Play Lab Project Bangladesh.* https://go.bracusa.org/playbook
    The PlayBook is a toolkit designed to share the Play Lab approach and learning with governments, professionals, and advocates involved in promoting early childhood development. The *Spatial Design Guidance* which describes design considerations when constructing and implementing Play Labs in Bangladesh will be useful to people interested in learning from, adapting and contextualizing Play Labs to their own communities.

BRAC Institute of Educational Development. (2019a, June). *Basic Training Manual Play Lab.* https://go.bracusa.org/playbook
    The PlayBook is a toolkit designed to share the Play Lab approach and learning with governments, professionals, and advocates involved in promoting early childhood development. The *Basic Training Manual* which goes into detail about the training provided to facilitators in Bangladesh will be useful to people interested in learning from, adapting and contextualizing Play Labs to their own communities.

BRAC Institute of Educational Development. (2019b, June). *Let's Play and Have Fun: Curriculum for Three to Five-Year-Old Children*. https://go.bracusa.org/playbook

> The PlayBook is a toolkit designed to share the Play Lab approach and learning with governments, professionals, and advocates involved in promoting early childhood development. *Let's Play and Have Fun: Curriculum for Three to Five-Year-Old Children* is a curriculum guide that describes in detail the principles and operations of Play Labs in Bangladesh and all the various activities that are conducted in sessions and will be useful to people interested in learning from, adapting and contextualizing Play Labs to their own communities.

BRAC USA. (2021, December 07). *Study: Play-Based Early Childhood Development Initiative in Bangladesh Ensures All Children Are Developmentally Equipped to Benefit from School*. https://bracusa.org/study-play-based-early-childhood-development-initiative-in-bangladesh-ensures-all-children-are-equally-developmentally-equipped-to-benefit-from-school/

> This is a research brief which describes the details of the evaluation of the Play Lab project in Bangladesh carried out by researchers from Cambridge University and Columbia University.

Reggio Children. (n.d.). https://www.reggiochildren.it/en/

> Provides details on the Reggio Emilia approach, an influential educational philosophy and pedagogy.

Trawick-Smith, J. (2017). *Early Childhood Development: A Multicultural Perspective* (7th ed.). Pearson Education Inc.

> The book examines the physical, social, emotional, linguistic, and intellectual characteristics of children from birth through age eight. Within each development domain, it considers the typical and atypical development of children of diverse cultures, abilities, socioeconomic backgrounds, and gender identities.

UNICEF. (2018, October). *Learning through Play: Strengthening Learning through Play in Early Childhood Education Programmes*. https://www.unicef.org/sites/default/files/2018-12/UNICEF-Lego-Foundation-Learning-through-Play.pdf

> The brief describes the nature of pre-primary services within the broader concept of early learning and proposes a systems perspective in advocating for child-centered pedagogy and playful programs with suggested strategies.

World Bank. (2020). *The Landscape of Early Childhood Education in Bangladesh*. https://documents1.worldbank.org/curated/en/720311583471084983/pdf/The-Landscape-of-Early-Childhood-Education-in-Bangladesh.pdf

> This report reviews the landscape of the ECE system in Bangladesh, focusing on the key aspects related to the provision of ECE services such as access and equity, quality, governance and management, and financing.

CHAPTER

Developing playful mathematical thinking in Ghanaian early primary classrooms through the use of the game "Achi"

Esinam Ami Avornyo and Edith Afari Mensah

Learning about numbers and developing mathematical understanding in early primary years are vital because this knowledge serves as a foundational stage to later learning. Research suggests that developing children's mathematical understanding can be most effectively supported through the adoption of active playful approaches (e.g. Parks, 2015; Vogt et al., 2018). An important enabling factor for this type of approach is creating a "playful" learning environment with supportive materials and resources (Parker & Thomsen, 2019). However, in Ghana and other African contexts, despite a policy level emphasis on active learning in mathematics education, teachers often continue to rely on "passive" teaching styles due to lack of appropriate resources and training. There is a need, therefore, to find ways of supporting the development of children's mathematical skills through affordable resources and accessible training for teachers.

Research suggests that board games can serve as low-cost, educationally rich resources for exploring mathematical concepts in classrooms (Powell & Temple, 2001). *Achi*, a board game that originates in Ghana, offers teachers an opportunity to present mathematical ideas that are of considerable relevance in the curriculum and create a playful and meaningful context in which children can develop mathematical concepts and positive attitude towards mathematics. This chapter introduces the *Achi* game and how to integrate and redesign it to support mathematical concepts in early primary education and has relevance for Ghana and other resource-constrained educational contexts. Before we focus on the use of *Achi* in classrooms, we will look briefly at the Ghanaian educational context and how the emphasis on play-based learning has been framed within official policy.

The Ghanaian Standards Based Curriculum

In 2010, the Government of Ghana developed a 10-year Education Strategic Plan (2010–2020) aimed at providing access to good-quality, child-friendly universal basic education, by improving opportunities for all children in the first cycle of education at kindergarten, primary and junior high school levels. While the government had made impressive progress towards access and enrolment over the years, the quality of educational provision was a huge policy challenge. For instance, teaching and learning emphasised rote memorisation, with little room for children's active engagement in their own learning (Avornyo, 2018). A review of the curriculum, specifically at the early childhood level, showed that teachers' reliance on rote teaching was reinforced by the teacher-directed examples in the teacher-learner activities section of the curriculum (Avornyo, 2018). With the government's continuous commitment to improve quality, a new curriculum, the Standards Based Curriculum was introduced in 2019, and implementation began in the 2020 academic year. While maintaining some key aspects of the previous curriculum, the Standards Based Curriculum emphasises the importance of the acquisition of skills in the 4Rs – **R**eading, w**R**iting, a**R**ithmetic and c**R**eativity. In addition, the Standards Based Curriculum sets out core competencies and standards that children are to achieve and demonstrate as they progress through the curriculum. The focus on core competencies is premised on the recognition that children do not only need academic knowledge but also life skills in order to function effectively in a globalised world. To this end, regardless of the learning or subject areas, the Standards Based Curriculum highlights the need for primary children to develop the following competencies:

- critical thinking and problem solving
- creativity and innovation
- communication and collaboration
- cultural identity and global citizenship
- personal development and leadership

Children in Ghana can be enrolled in primary school from the age of 6. In the Standards Based Curriculum, mathematical learning for primary children is divided into two levels: lower primary (for children aged 6–8) and upper primary (for children aged 9–11). At both levels, the curriculum focuses on number sense development, algebraic knowledge, understanding of geometry and measurement as well as basic data analysis, with increasing levels of difficulty. In terms of instructional practices, the curriculum indicates that teachers should act as facilitators and support children's development of the various mathematical components through the use of learner-centred pedagogical approaches that draw on creative and hands-on activities, emphasising the importance of scaffolding, the use of questioning techniques that promote deep learning and integrating both formative and summative assessments.

Implications of the curriculum policy for practice

The curriculum's reference to the use of creative hands-on activities and the teacher's role as a facilitator demonstrate its support for children's active involvement in the teaching and learning of mathematical concepts. While this is a critical shift from rote teaching to facilitating learning, successful implementation depends on a range of factors, including teachers' own knowledge and skills, learner factors, physical learning environment and material resources (Parker & Thomsen, 2019). However, in this chapter we will be drawing particular attention to the physical environment and resources within the Ghanaian primary education context.

To maximise opportunities for children's engagement in active learning, the design of the classroom is critical. Classrooms need to be intentionally designed so that children can engage with learning materials and with their peers. In addition, teachers need to have access to materials and resources that can foster children's development of mathematical concepts in an active and playful way (Parker & Thomsen, 2019). However, within the Ghanaian educational landscape, learning environments generally lack these enabling features. In particular, primary classrooms, especially those in public schools, remain overcrowded with class sizes of above 50 and often with desks that are difficult to move, and teachers lack material resources beyond textbooks (Wolf & Avornyo, 2023). The absence of these resources significantly undermines efforts to improve mathematics education through the active and playful approaches described at policy level. Overcoming these obstacles necessitates the use of viable strategies that allow the introduction of low-cost, hands-on activities that are relevant for Ghanaian classrooms and for similarly resource-constrained contexts.

Board games and mathematical concept development

Playing games begins at an early age when children become interested in social forms of play that are based on following rules. Apart from contributing to children's understanding of rules, "the main developmental contribution of playing games derives from their social nature" (Whitebread et al., 2012, p. 24). Research suggests that playing games with peers and adults enables children to acquire a range of social skills, including self-restraint, turn taking and working collaboratively as a group. In reviewing Piaget's work on games, Devries (2006) argued that through game play, children learn autonomous feelings of obligation by choosing to play and to follow rules. Besides helping children to develop social skills, games have been associated with children's acquisition of mathematical knowledge and thinking. For instance, in their work with children in the USA, Ramani and Siegler (2008) found that playing board games improved children's ability to count, identify numbers, make comparison and complete number line task. Research in Hong Kong showed similar results, with playing board game being linked to children's performance on numerical skills such as making comparison and computation (Wang & Hung, 2010).

The power of board games in teaching and learning of mathematics lies in the fact that children are naturally attracted to and motivated by games. However, mathematical educators and researchers have noted that for games to offer valuable mathematical learning, they need to possess certain essential characteristics. In particular, Gough (1999) argues that the following characteristics are integral to an educationally rich game:

- competitiveness with two or more players taking turns to achieve a winning situation of some kind
- having choice about how to move throughout the game
- interaction between players so that one player's move affects the other

Generally, although board games with such characteristics (e.g. chess) are known to support children's mathematical understanding, researchers interested in multicultural mathematics (e.g. Bayeck, 2018) have provided a wealth of creative and educationally rich cultural games that can be used to support mathematics learning at school and also help children interact with aspects of different cultures. Powell and Temple (2001) emphasised that board games are important cultural instrument and that when children play these games, "They establish intellectual frameworks that enable them to further construct and comprehend complex mathematical ideas, strategies and theories" (p. 369).

Traditional board games in mathematics teaching and learning

Multicultural mathematics researchers have demonstrated that different cultural or traditional games contain mathematical values that can help promote the teaching and learning of mathematics. And introducing cultural games in classrooms and schools can serve as an important medium for helping children understand that mathematical knowledge can be found in various cultural products, including language, dances, songs and artefacts, which can lead to improved attitudes towards mathematics. African cultural games embody different mathematical concepts, including "Boolean logic, counting, simple addition, one-to-one correspondence and theoretical probabilities" (Chahine, 2020). Moreover, these games are believed to provide an effective space for the development of high order cognitive and lifelong skills such as decision-making, critical thinking and problem solving (Bayeck, 2018; Powell & Temple, 2001). The potency of these culturally derived mathematics games lies in the fact that they are entrenched in the contexts in which they arise (Chahine, 2020). So, when children play mathematics games from their culture or explore the games of a different culture, they familiarise themselves with their culture or develop a sense of their participation in a globalised community.

In Ghana, one of these games is *Achi*, a board game that provides opportunities for children to build and extend strategic thinking. Although *Achi* may have originated from Ghana, it is played widely by people in Africa and other parts of the world. In the past, *Achi* was played by marking a game board on the ground and using small sticks and stones as game pieces. Currently, the game is available commercially from a number of sources and mail-order catalogues but can easily be made using, for example, a piece of cardboard. The use of low-cost materials makes this game an inexpensive but valuable resource for playfully supporting children's learning.

Achi game and playing rules

In its original form, *Achi* is an alignment game played on a three-by-three grid, which creates nine spaces in total. It is designed by first drawing a square and then connecting the corners and middle of each side of the square (see Figure 8.1). To play *Achi*, two players are required, and each player needs to have four game pieces, which can be bottle caps or counters in two different colours – one colour for each player. The objective of *Achi* is to be the first player with three of their game pieces aligned in a row either horizontally, diagonally or vertically.

The board is empty in the beginning and the players decide who plays first. The game goes through two main phases. The first is the *drop phase* during which players take turns placing a piece on the board game one at a time on any of the nine spaces where the lines intersect. At this phase, none of the pieces can be moved until each player's four game pieces have been placed on the board. If none of the players have three pieces aligned in a row after all the eight game pieces have been dropped, then the game enters its second stage, the *move phase*. During this phase, the players take turns moving pieces along a line to an empty space and players are not allowed to jump over another piece. Players keep taking turns until a player achieves three in a row. Then the game starts again, with the losing player taking the first turn.

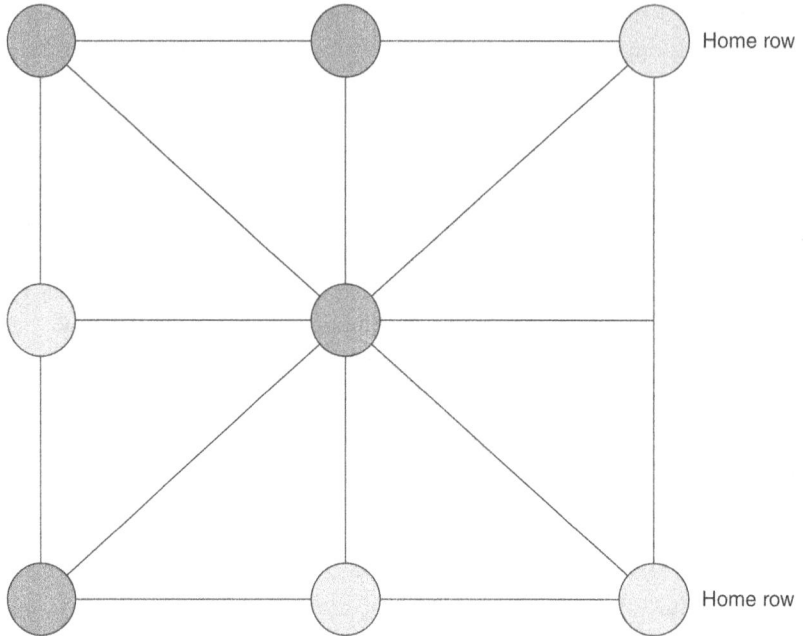

Figure 8.1 Achi game in its original form. The circular game pieces (light and dark) from two different players are shown.

Redesigning Achi for mathematics teaching and learning in Ghanaian classrooms

Children can benefit from the basic form of the game because it offers an opportunity for stimulating their thinking abilities. But once they understand and become familiar with the rules of the game, there are possibilities for redesigning it to include elements that explicitly introduce them to mathematical concepts. To illustrate the classroom potential of the game, we present an adapted version of the game played with children in primary two (see Box below). The primary two mathematics lessons focused on number addition, and each of the nine spaces had a question (see Figure 8.2). The game was played following the original rules, but the first player with a row of 3 initially sums up the questions in each space and then adds the three to get a final answer. It is important to note that the children's initial experience with playing the game was quite short, with some players winning at the *drop phase* of the game. With experience, however, they were able to learn to consider drop options that prevented the opponent from winning in the first phase.

These variations of the game can be used to teach other mathematical operations and numbers. In addition, teachers can work together with pupils to brainstorm

Developing playful mathematical thinking

Playing Achi game in a primary two classroom (private school)

In a primary two classroom, children were introduced to the game. In the beginning, the children were introduced to the game in its original form and curious about what the game involved as they were not familiar with it. The teacher explained the cultural nature of the game and how it was played. With a class size of 18, the children were put into small groups of 3, with six players for a game. Three copies of the game were designed to allow each group to interact with it. Each group was asked to select one colour of bottle caps as game pieces.

The teacher had conversations about the game rules, including an understanding of the official rules, as well as social rules such as how many turns one learner in the group can have before giving the opportunity to others. There was also an introduction to mathematical vocabulary, through asking children to identify the various shapes in the game and vertical, horizontal and diagonal lines. After the children had developed a foundational understanding of the game, they were given the opportunity to play.

The following day, the game was re-introduced to the class, but it was redesigned linking the class mathematics learning focused on number addition. The teacher and children had conversations about the redesigned game and what the object was. The children immediately noticed that the game had numbers, the addition and equal to symbols. The biggest challenge at this point was ensuring the children understood the variation of the rules requiring the addition of the numbers in the nine spaces and providing a final answer. To address this challenge, the game was played a number of times as a whole class. The teacher played with small group of children while the rest watched the game. The children were then given the opportunity to play amongst themselves. They documented their answers for each win on a sheet of paper. After everyone has had a turn, a whole class discussion was had to determine whether the sum of each question from the winning rows was correct or not. This gave room to correct any wrong answers.

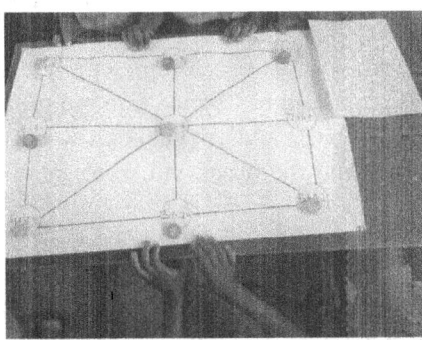 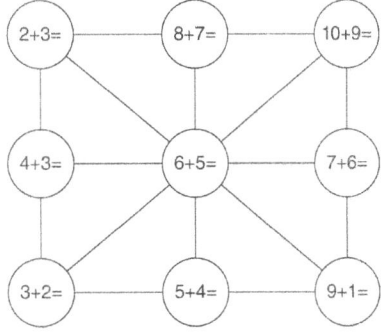

Figure 8.2 Redesigned *Achi* game for addition

new rules for the game to make it more challenging and interesting. Possible variations of the rules include the following:

- Centre to win – in order to win, the row of 3 must include the centre space
- Vertical or horizontal rows to win – in order to win, only vertical or horizontal rows of 3 are allowed. Alternatively, only diagonal rows of 3 can constitute a win
- Playing with only three pieces but in order to win, the row of 3 must include the centre space
- Using three pieces each, players begin the game with their pieces already lined up on the horizontal rows closest to them, that is, their "home rows" (see Figure 8.1). A row of three pieces on the player's home row does not constitute a win.

Tips for enhancing children's participation in the game

To provide more opportunities for children to develop their playing skills and participation, teachers could incorporate some of the following strategies:

- Introduce the game to the class by explaining its origin and how it was played in the past. It is important to emphasise the role of the game in preserving cultural or traditional practices.
- Introduce children to the game in its original form (see Figure 8.1). Ask them to take turns to draw the game either on the writing board or on sheets of paper. Guide them to identify the different shapes embedded in the game, for example rectangles, triangles and squares.
- The teacher can take turns to play the game with at least two children. This gives an opportunity to teach the rules, model how the game is played and repeat the instructions a number of times.
- Using random bits of information, such as months or days of birth, assign children to groups. Depending on the class size, number of children in a group for a game can range from four to ten, with half each representing each side of players. For example, a class of 80 pupils can be divided into ten teams, creating eight teams in total. When playing, five children will constitute the team that plays with one game piece colour and the other will represent the team that plays with the other colour.
- Allow one child at a time to play a turn for their team. To keep children engaged, encourage them to make suggestions to the player representing them. After two or three rounds of play for a child in a team, members of the team should alternate until every member of the team gets a turn.

- As the children play the game, the teacher is encouraged to move around the classroom to observe and check how the groups are doing as well as offer assistance where needed.
- An important aspect of the game is for the children to answer the mathematical question presented in the three spaces in a row horizontally, vertically or diagonally. To ensure they complete this aspect of the game, they should write the answers in their jotter or on a sheet of paper. Alternatively, teachers can incorporate this into their normal class exercise, allowing pupils to answer the questions in their exercise books.

Post-game reflections

Reflection is considered a basic process of teaching and learning that helps teachers to critically evaluate their own practice situations in order to maximise learning opportunities for their children and to ensure they learn more effectively (Finlay, 2008). Reflective practice has several benefits for teachers and their children. For example, by reflecting on their teaching, teachers can identify challenges that children have encountered, find new strategies to address these challenges and experiment with new approaches. While a number of models of reflection have been proposed in different fields of practice, Gibbs' (1988) model offers some useful basic questions that can help facilitate teacher reflection in relation to the *Achi* game. Gibbs' model is a six-stage cyclical framework that gives teachers room to describe the classroom experience through to conclusions and consider actions for future events (see Figure 8.3). Using this model, teachers can identify their strengths in relation to facilitating children's engagement with the game, areas of the game that require more attention and clarification as well as actions they will take to enhance children's interest and participation. While keeping a reflective journal will help teachers continuously review the mathematical ideas and concepts children learn through the game and support them to make maximum progress, teachers can also draw on a learner dialogue approach that allows children to play an active part in the reflection process.

Stage 1 – Description. This dimension encourages the teacher to outline the experience. This should be a factual account of what happened in the classroom. Some helpful questions to consider are as follows: "What happened?" "What did you and the pupils do?" "What did you want to happen?" "What was the outcome?"

Stage 2 – Feelings. In this section, teachers should explore any feelings and thoughts they had whilst facilitating children's engagement in the game. It is important that teachers are honest with their thoughts and emotions, even if these are

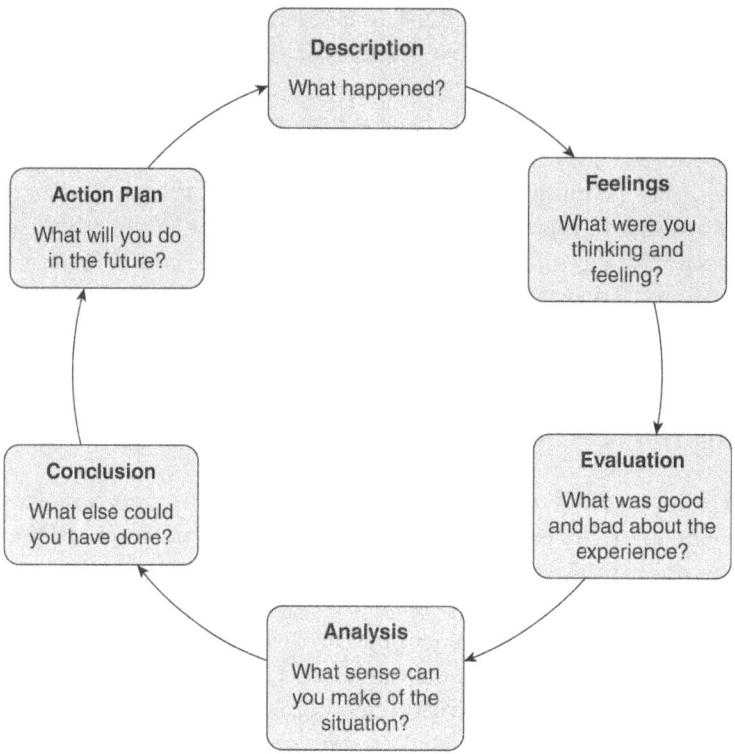

Figure 8.3 Gibbs' reflection model (1988)

negative. Questions to consider include the following: "How did you feel at the time the children were playing the game?" "What did you think when the children were playing the game?" "How do you think the children felt whilst playing the game?"

Stage 3 – Evaluation. In the evaluation dimension, teachers have the opportunity to objectively evaluate what worked and what didn't work in the game process. Consider both the positive and negative things that led to children being interested in playing the game or not. This will help identify areas that need development and clarification. Questions to consider include the following: "What went well with the game?" "What did not go well?" "What questions did you use to probe children's engagement and understanding?" "Which questions were most successful in encouraging children's participation and mathematical thinking?"

Stage 4 – Analysis. At this stage, teachers should consider what may have helped children's participation in the game or hindered it. Target different aspects of the game play (e.g. the rules, pupils' turn taking, completing mathematics questions) that went well and what went less well and make efforts to explain why. It can be useful to make reference to relevant literature/research or consider the children's reactions to the game or feedback to make sense of the experience. For example, if the children report challenges with turn taking, teachers could consider how to ensure effective turn taking within a team.

Stage 5 – Conclusion. In the conclusion section, the teacher brings the ideas together and identifies actions that can be taken to improve on the facilitation of the game. In particular, the teacher should consider answering the question, "is there anything I or the children would do differently when playing the game?"

Stage 6 – Action Plan. In the final stage, the teacher summarises all the previous components of the cycle and creates a plan for the next game experience. In this plan, the teacher needs to identify what aspects of the game they will reinforce and what they will do differently to overcome any barriers. To do this effectively, the teacher may need to identify, for example, relevant sources of information or children who could help in the process.

Playing *Achi* and the Ghanaian curriculum requirements

In addition to offering mathematical learning opportunities by helping children develop their understanding of mathematical concepts in number sense and aspects of geometry, the game offers connections with the broad aims and competencies of the Ghanaian curriculum and can help teachers to meet those requirements:

- Recognise that mathematics permeates the world around us and appreciate the usefulness, power and beauty of mathematics – *The physical structure of Achi and the rules reveal the lives of the inventors, introduce students to the beautiful relationship between mathematics and culture and how mathematics ideas are embedded in cultural artefacts.*
- Enjoy mathematics and develop patience and persistence when solving problems – *The game poses a problem for children to solve, and through patience and persistence, they develop winning strategies.*
- Understand and be able to use the language, symbols and notation of mathematics – *Several variations of the game can be designed using different mathematical operational symbols. This offers an opportunity for children to practise, use mathematical language and solve mathematical questions in a playful manner.*
- Develop mathematical curiosity, critical thinking and reasoning when solving problems – *The Achi game can provide motivation for learning. As children play, they gain and develop their spatial sense and reasoning in order to discover effective drop and move strategies based on the patterns they observe.*
- Develop communication and collaboration – *Playing the game in groups or teams is a valuable way of teaching children to work together and communicate with team members.*
- Cultural identity and global citizenship – *The game not only introduces children to the historical and cultural lives of Ghanaians but knowing that this game is played widely in other parts of the world can develop children's awareness of a globalised community, where idea from one culture transcends to others.*

Conclusion

While many mathematical skills and concepts need to be explicitly taught, mathematics education for early primary children is predicated on opportunities for playful, active and engaging interactions with teachers and peers. And including playful activities can reduce children's mathematical anxiety and foster their development of positive attitudes towards mathematics. One important way to do this is through the use of cultural board games. Culturally relevant board games from one's own culture or those played in other cultures may not only give a sense of excitement or fun but also enhance children's motivation and support their development of mathematical understanding. This chapter highlighted the inclusion of *Achi* game into mathematics instructions and how it offers support for children's learning of cultural history and mathematics in non-traditional ways that emphasise their active involvement. This low-cost and easy to make game can serve an important role in making teaching and learning of mathematics interesting and fun. Capitalising on the variations of the game and rules, teachers can develop children's mathematical ideas whilst also supporting their development of important life skills.

Although children can benefit from the cultural and mathematical values of *Achi*, it can serve as a starting point for children and teachers to explore other cultural games that can be used to support playful learning of mathematical concepts. A classic example is *Mancala*, a mathematical-rich board game played throughout most of Africa and other parts of the world under many different names and versions, including the simple two-row versions from Ghana (*Oware*), Nigeria (*Ayo* and *Okwe*) and Ivory Coast (*Awélé*) as well as the complex four-row versions from Uganda (*Omweso*) and South Africa (*Moruba*). Another cultural board game is *Pachisi*, a cross and circle game from India that can be played by two or four players. Adapting these games can provide meaningful and playful contexts conducive for fostering children's successes in mathematics and also towards achieving curricular goals and objectives.

References

Avornyo, E. A. (2018). *Investigating play and learning in the Ghanaian early years classroom: A Mixed Methods Study* (Doctoral dissertation, University of Cambridge).

Bayeck, R. Y. (2018). A review of five African board games: Is there any educational potential? *Cambridge Journal of Education, 48*(5), 533–552.

Chahine, I. C. (2020). Towards African humanity: Re-mythogolising Ubuntu through reflections on the ethnomathematics of African cultures. *Critical Studies in Teaching and Learning (CriSTaL), 8*(2), 95–111.

DeVries, R. (2006). Games with rules. In D. P. Fromberg, & D. Bergen (Eds.), *Play from birth to twelve: Contexts, perspectives, and meanings* (2nd ed., pp. 119–125). New York: Routledge.

Finlay, L. (2008). *Reflecting on 'Reflective practice'* (Practice-Based Professional Learning Paper 52 January). Retrieved from https://oro.open.ac.uk/68945/.

Gibbs, G. (1988). *Learning by doing: A guide to teaching and learning methods.* Oxford: Further Education Unit, Oxford Polytechnic.

Gough, J. (1999). Playing mathematical games: When is a game not a game? *Australian Primary Mathematics Classroom, 4*(2), 12–15.

Parker, R., & Thomsen, B. S. (2019). *Learning through play at school: A study of playful integrated pedagogies that foster children's holistic skills development in the primary school classroom.* Billund: LEGO Foundation.

Parks, A. N. (2015). *Exploring mathematics through play in the early childhood classroom.* New York, USA: Teachers College Press.

Powell, A., & Temple, O. (2001). Seeding ethnomathematics with oware: Sankofa. *Teaching Children Mathematics, 7*(6), 369–375.

Ramani, G. B., & Siegler, R. S. (2008). Promoting broad and stable improvements in low-income children's numerical knowledge through playing number board games. *Child Development, 79*(2), 375–394.

Vogt, F. H., Stebler, B., Rechsteiner, R. K., & Urech, C. (2018). Learning through play–pedagogy and learning outcomes in early childhood mathematics. *European Early Childhood Education Research Journal, 26,* 4–589.

Wang, Z., & Hung, L. M. (2010). Kindergarten children's number sense development through board games. *International Journal of Learning, 17*(8), 19–31.

Whitebread, D., Basilio, M., Kuvalja, M., & Verma, M. (2012). *The importance of play.* Brussels: Toy Industries of Europe.

Wolf, S., & Avornyo, E. A. (2023). Cultural considerations in defining classroom quality: Ghanaian Preschool teachers' agreements and disagreements with standards-based instruments. *Comparative Education Review, 67*(1), 188–210.

CHAPTER

Becoming a playful school

Idah Khan O'Neill and Bo Stjerne Thomsen

Introduction

Play and school are often seen as contradictions. Play originates from individual exploration, freedom, and imagination, whereas school tends to represent a societal obligation to equip students with already defined knowledge and understandings. For centuries, schools have been the main mechanism in which society passes on accumulated knowledge, skills, and values to the next generation. However, the original definition of school derives from the Greek, scholé, meaning "leisure" as a space to figure things out and think. When we look up popular definitions of play, it is often seen as an activity for enjoyment and recreation, rather than serious or for a practical purpose. However, we would like to suggest that perhaps there is not such a big difference between the original definition of school and being playful. When children learn through play, the teacher mediates the individual motivations and contexts of children with the societal, community, and parent expectations, while equipping children with the mindset and skills to be creative, engaged, and lifelong learners.

Informed by the science of playful learning and practical examples from the International School of Billund in Denmark, the approach of a pedagogy of play (PoP) illustrates how play and learning can mutually inform and benefit each other. In a world that is much more uncertain, and where children grow up not only to navigate an increasing amount of knowledge but also to adapt to changing circumstances, play can offer opportunities for children to experience a more empowered role. The main mechanism in which young children learn happens through play (Yogman et al., 2018), and we are now coming to a point where the learning sciences and the science of play intersect to emphasize that this relationship needs to continue throughout childhood.

Children learn through play when they are actively engaged in things they enjoy and can test and try out strategies that are meaningful to them, often in social interactions with others (Zosh et al., 2018). If one accepts this definition as a consolidated view of playful learning experiences, research suggests that play already exists within school contexts, although it looks rather different. Many contemporary pedagogical approaches, such as project- and problem-based learning, inquiry, collaborative and experiential forms of learning, originate from similar principles and result in students achieving outcomes that represent a combination of knowledge acquisition, a broad range of holistic skills, and a strong motivation for lifelong learning (Parker, Thomsen & Berry, 2022).

There are many opportunities for schools to be playful without jeopardizing the depth of understanding and deep thoughtful processes; however, the culture of a school may not necessarily be conducive to being a playful environment. The PoP centers around a few key principles, including a strong focus on playful coaching for teachers, a shared set of indicators for quality, and the deliberate integration of community spaces as part of curriculum and pedagogy. In this chapter, we offer an example from the International School of Billund in Billund, Denmark, which introduces three innovative ideas for becoming a playful school. These ideas have emerged from focused research studies involving researchers and practitioners over the past five to seven years, and it offers a new set of tools with which to navigate the paradoxes of play and learning.

The playing ground in Billund, Denmark

Billund is a fast-growing town in Southern Denmark. As a municipality, it has ambitions to become the Children's Capital. It strives to be the "best place in the world for children and families with children and be a knowledge center for children's play and learning" (Billund Municipality, n.d., para 1). In an effort to realize this goal, the International School of Billund (ISB) was set up to serve a growing number of both local and expatriate families moving into the area. Since opening its doors in August 2013, ISB has set out two ambitious goals:

- to demonstrate the power of playful learning in a real-world setting
- to make Billund—the Capital of Children—an even more attractive place to live, both for Danish and international families.

Opening with just over 60 students in kindergarten and primary, today, ISB has now over 450 students, ages 3–16, across kindergarten, primary and middle school. About a quarter of students are Danish, with the rest representing over 50 countries.

ISB's playful curriculum is built upon the rigorous educational framework of the International Baccalaureate (IB). The IB offers a continuum of international education through four educational programs: the Primary Years Programme (PYP), Middle Years Programme (MYP), Diploma Programme (DP), and Career-related Programme (CP), to students aged 3–19 (International Baccalaureate Organisation, 2023). ISB offers the PYP for students aged 3–11 years old and the

MYP for the 11–16 years old. Both programs strive to equip students with a solid and transferable foundation of academic skills, and it focuses on inquiry-driven and holistic learning, which aligns well with ISB's playful ambitions.

> *Mission of ISB: By placing PLAY at the heart of education, ISB stimulates every child's natural desire to LEARN.*
>
> *Vision of ISB: To cultivate a community of lifelong learners who will create a better world with courage, compassion, and curiosity.*

In 2015, ISB extended its commitment to place play at the heart of education, when they entered into a partnership with the Harvard Graduate School of Education's research group, Project Zero (PZ), to develop a PoP. Originally PZ emerged from the field of arts education, but over the past 50 years, it has explored a wide range of topics embracing education, intelligence, creativity, and assessment.

The partnership has enabled an active research-practice collaboration, through which the ISB school and leadership have supported an exchange of ideas and pedagogical reflections with a research community. The school has gradually expanded this with other kinds of research-practice partnerships, including the development of a Creator Space with Tufts University, the integration of Robotics with LEGO Education, and MIT, alongside a series of international publications, conferences, and workshops.

The purpose of pedagogy of play

The positive effect of play on children's intellectual, social, emotional, and physical development has already been well-documented. Here, we offer the perspective that bringing more play into the institutions tasked with nurturing these skills is essential. In other words, the why of playful learning has been covered and is deeply grounded in both the science and practice of developing knowledge and skills.

Through the PoP, staff at ISB are exploring how to put the ideas of learning through play into action, and understanding how educators can set up the conditions for playful learning to thrive. This project has afforded the learning community the opportunity to question traditional schooling norms and suggest provocative ideas that challenge and push us to reimagine the way we teach and learn.

PoP aims to help educators in the school align practices so they are all rowing in the same direction based on a shared understanding of when and how play can support learning. At ISB we begin by developing a research approach that we are calling "playful participatory research." The approach builds on action research models in which educators collaboratively and critically identify questions and develop and document emerging hypotheses.

We take inspiration from the field of play research, where students' interests and initiative are at the core of an experience, but it requires a particular mechanism to be able to scaffold that interest into a formal school environment.

This approach requires a particular mindset and we have identified at least three key ideas that support that movement:

- Teachers need the support of a set of **indicators of playful learning**, which act as a shared language and a formative assessment tool. We ask whether it is possible for teachers to say "yes" more often to student initiative and build a culture around these practices without compromising curriculum goals and standards.
- Schools need to expand professional development with **playful coaching** techniques, which give teachers tools to document and reflect on student learning. We wonder if administrators can support teachers in building the confidence to ask questions and explore the paradoxes of playing vs. learning.
- The learning environment needs to **expand into the community**, where a broader set of resources can be used for the curriculum. We explore where a school can utilize the outdoors and communities for learning by engaging in resource-sharing.

Let us expand on some of the ideas behind these examples and becoming a playful school.

Develop indicators of playful learning

Together with the PZ team, teachers at ISB have developed a tool called the indicators of playful learning which enables educators to plan for, assess, and reflect on playful teaching and learning. The development of these indicators has been informed by research as well as teachers' practices (Whitebread et al., 2012; Vygotsky & Cole, 1978; Marbina, Church & Tayler, 2011; Darling-Hammond, 2006; Weisberg et al., 2016). In *A Pedagogy of Play: Supporting Playful Learning in Classrooms and Schools*, Mardell et al. (2023, p. 48) highlight that "playful learning is universal yet shaped by culture." Therefore, it is important to understand what playful learning looks like and feels like in a particular setting.

Many examples have come from student experiences (as we will be illustrating in the examples later on), along with teacher and student interviews, teacher surveys, documentation of moments in school (e.g., video and photographs from classrooms and transcripts of conversations among children and teachers), and classroom observations, which supply data about what playful learning looks like in classrooms.

While the articulation of these indicators will continue to be an evolving process, what is emerging is a model of playful learning with indicators in three overlapping categories: choice, wonder, and delight. These categories aim to describe the quality of learners' experiences as they build understanding, knowledge, and skill. Because playful learning includes both subjective and objective dimensions, the indicators represent psychological states as well as observable behaviors. When all three categories are "in play," represented by the intersection of the circle in the middle, playful learning is most likely occurring (see Figure 9.1).

Playful learning experiences do not always have to come from the teacher. As educators look to target curriculum goals and standards, understanding the strengths, knowledge, and interests of learners is a vital part of making learning relevant. Taking playful learning seriously can sometimes mean tipping the balance of responsibility for learning toward learners. This involves looking for opportunities to turn things over to students and support them in this process. It requires flexibility and a willingness to modify teaching plans.

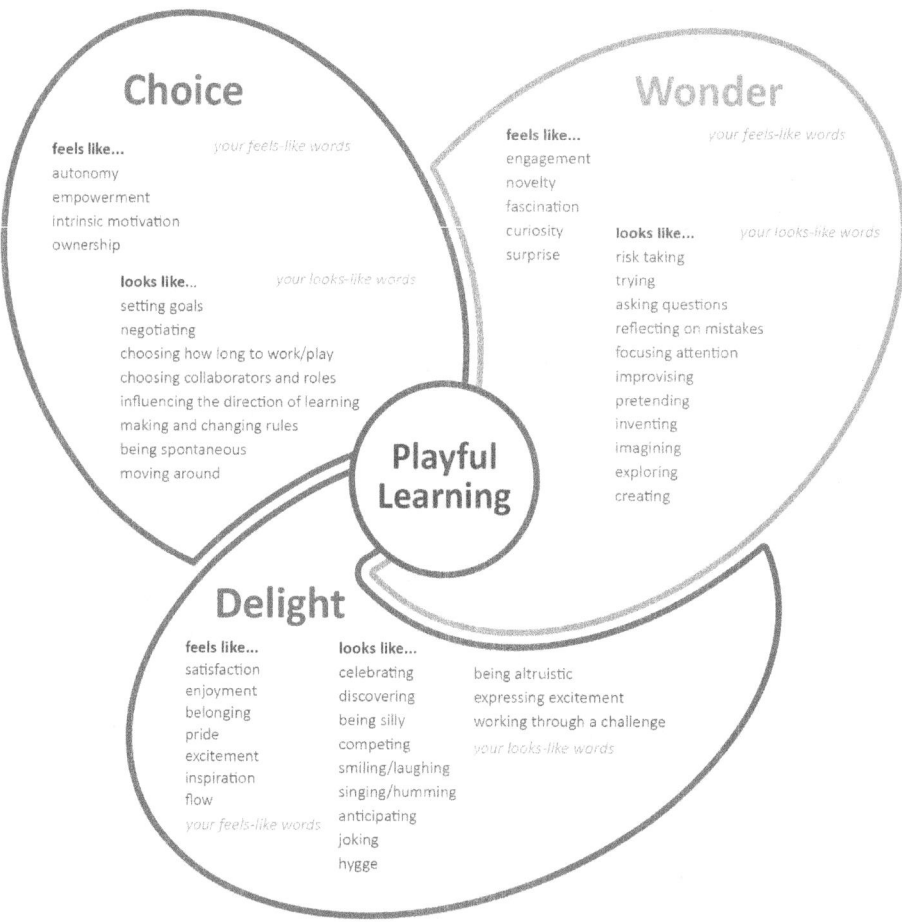

Figure 9.1 Model of playful learning

For the playful learner, choice includes a sense of autonomy, empowerment, ownership, and intrinsic motivation. Learners may experience these feelings individually or as part of a group. Collectively making choices, and the accompanying sense of being part of something bigger than oneself, can enhance feelings of empowerment and ownership. To an observer, learners demonstrating choice are setting goals, developing and sharing ideas, making and changing rules, and negotiating challenges. They are also likely to be choosing collaborators and roles, how long to work or play, and when to move around.

Here we open with a first example from the school:

Jamie (name has been changed), a 5-year-old kindergartner, has recently developed an interest in making paper planes. "Hey! Can I show you how to make the best airplane?", he asked his teacher, Maria. "I can also teach you how to make other types too," he added. Maria's desk, jackets, and bags were filled with paper planes from Jamie.

Maria took up Jamie's offer to teach her how to make the best airplane and asked if he would teach it to the whole class. Jamie took on the role of a teacher very seriously, as he pondered on which type of airplane he should teach to the class. He began making different prototypes before settling on one model that the class would learn.

The next day, Jamie came to class with a stack of A4 paper that he brought from home. He announced that the paper we have in school is of a different quality and will not be good enough for the paper plane. Now armed with the right paper, Jamie gathered his classmates in a circle and began taking the class step by step in the paper plane making process. He displayed great patience in repeating his instructions and waiting for everyone to complete the step before moving to another.

Once everyone had completed their paper planes, Jamie took the class to a long corridor to try them out. Feedback from his classmates included, "This is fun! We should do it again!". "I don't like making paper planes but I like throwing them!"

Maria saw the opportunity to use these paper planes for their math lessons in measurement, making connections to words from their phonics sessions and weaving it into their unit of inquiry on transportation.

In the airplane activity, Jamie had great influence on the direction of the learning. The indicator of "choice" illustrated how we considered the different airplane models and materials for the lesson he was going to teach. The reality for children (and often adults) is that they rarely have complete choice. As we shall see, tensions between children's interests and adult learning goals can arise in schools. What is perhaps most important about the experience of choice is that children feel autonomy and ownership and that they feel they have opportunities to do what they want to do.

The indicator of "wonder" opens up the world of curiosity, novelty, surprise, and challenge, which can engage and fascinate the learner. To an observer, a sense of wonder involves improvising or exploring, creating or inventing, pretending or imagining, and taking risks or learning from trial and error. Wonder can emerge from any situation, from the ordinary to the extraordinary. A sense of wonder might be experienced through play with materials, ideas, perspectives, music, symbols, words, languages, stories, movement, or other modes of expression.

Being asked to teach the class was certainly a new challenge for Jamie. Wanting to do a good job, he practiced and created many different paper plane prototypes before deciding on the best one to use in the lesson. Jamie also tinkered with various types of paper and found the right one to use was the type he had at home.

Similarly for Maria, it meant letting go of her teacher position in class, a bit of risk taking and being open to tweaking the course of learning, based on student interest.

The indicator of "delight" includes satisfaction, enjoyment, belonging, pride, excitement, inspiration, and flow. Learners who feel delighted may find themselves working through a challenge beyond their given space and time. Their attention may be focused. Delight may also be experienced through playful competition, celebration, or engaging in an altruistic act.

Feedback from the class indicated a sense of enjoyment particularly in seeing their paper planes take flight. But for Jamie, a great sense of pride and satisfaction was evident when all his lesson plans fell into place. The space to share his knowledge and inspire his classmates and teacher to extend the playful learning experiences in other subject areas made the learning process meaningful.

The indicators should not be seen as binary constructs. One might experience choice, wonder, or delight to a stronger or lesser degree, depending on the setting, the activity, and one's personality. A learner might feel extremely delighted running outside on the playground and have a more subdued sense of delight when listening to a story. These experiences of delight might be qualitatively different from each other, but both are experiences of delight, nonetheless. When learners experience choice, this does not necessarily mean that teachers are uninvolved in the activity. In fact, here, we can note that some teacher moves can empower learners to lead their own learning. Creating the conditions in which playful learning flourishes is influenced not only by educators in the classroom but also by larger forces that shape the context.

The indicators of playful learning tool have become a language that grounds what playful learning looks like and feels like at ISB. This tool is key to the culture-building of the school, as it strives to develop a PoP. This in turn helps the learning community to articulate playful learning practices and encourage them and we ask the following: How can teachers say "yes" more often to students' initiatives without the worry of compromising curriculum goals and standards?

Expand on playful coaching as a professional development model

Playful learning has a complex subjective nature. What is playful learning for one is not necessarily playful learning for another. This is made all the more complex by the cultural and pedagogical beliefs and values of educators. The ways in which we understand the nature of playful learning, the adult's role in supporting it, and

SEE	THINK	WONDER
(What do you notice?)	(What does it make you think about? What connections can you make?)	(What are you curious about?)

Figure 9.2 See-Think-Wonder is a favorite tool that teacher researchers often use when they are analyzing data (documentations)

its place in school are heavily influenced by culture. We can scaffold a culture of curiosity by teachers using questions to better understand the learners' viewpoints and leveraging that to propel the next phase of learning. Asking questions has been a cornerstone of great coaching. Similar to teaching, the best coaches reflect on questions to ask, but it is not just the questions themselves—it is about asking the right question at the right time in the right way.

The PoP project employs a research paradigm best described as playful participatory research (PPR). Knowledge construction in a playful participatory approach is a democratic process in which the whole school community (e.g., teachers, children, administrators, families) act as co-researchers (in varying roles and situations), engaging in both the consumption and production of knowledge. Teachers-researchers document children's learning in the classroom and share this documentation with their colleagues, who participate in interpreting and synthesizing the research (see Figure 9.2).

Brian, a grade 3 teacher, shared a video of one of his students, John, making a wand using clay. He noted that the student had no interest in any class assignments and often busied himself with his own projects. John's challenges included navigating relationships, moderating emotions, and following the rules established by his peers and teachers.

Brian is doing research on how can play improve feelings of inclusion for students with barriers to learning.

A group of fellow teacher researchers gather to watch the 2-minute video. When the clip ended, the group began listing the things they saw. "I see a creative child engaged in a task" said one of the teachers. "I see John is comfortable working on his own," said another. The group then moves on to naming the things they are thinking about. One teacher noted, "I think it is healthy to provide a space for students to do what they want and not what the teacher demands of them." This thought provoked another teacher to comment: "I think there is time and place to do what you like. Perhaps John should be allowed to do the wands only after he has completed the class assignments. That could work as a motivation for him to engage in whole class activities." This notion brought about some wonders from the other teacher researchers in the group. "But if we use his interest as a reward for learning, I wonder if you would kill the joy of learning by making it a chore and not an enjoyable task." The spiral nature of this conversation led to another idea, "I wonder if you could let John continue with his interest and projects but keeping the curricular learning goals. So, John is still developing the concepts and skills his peers are learning, but on his own terms."

Later that week, Brian proposed an idea to John. He asked him if he wanted to put up a Harry Potter wand exhibition for his classmates. Enthralled by this idea, John spent the next few days prepping for his exhibition. He made more wands and took time to set up his exhibition space. John's classmates were very impressed by his presentation and John was in his element. Through this project, John worked on his math, language, and communication skills.

As for Brian, the study group offers him a safe space to explore pedagogical perspectives and further develop his skills as a playful teacher. If we want a school that is playful for children, then there is a need for a playful learning environment—one that is engaging, joyful, creative, and satisfying—for the teachers. In playful participatory research, teachers act as agents of play and playfulness. They "play with" their role as teachers, using the classroom environment, materials, and curriculum to test out new ideas for playful learning.

In our globalized world, where educators from different backgrounds are working side by side, achieving consensus about play's role in school is an immense challenge. Yet, without a unified view of the role of play in learning and what it looks like, educators may be working at cross-purposes and contributing to further confusion.

Grounding perspective-taking discussions using the See-Think-Wonder tool enabled the language to be open with an element of curiosity. No one in the study group is telling Brian what to do but rather offering non-judgmental perspectives about the documentation he has shared. There is no rule book for a teacher to read to become a playful teacher. In valuing the parallels between student learning and adult learning, schools need to acknowledge and support the diverse nature of playful learning. If a playful teacher is expected to cater to the needs of a diverse group of students, then professional development (learning) for teachers would also need to consider the diversity of the teaching body.

At ISB, as we enter the next phase of PoP and look at articulating sound, playful, teaching practices, we are looking to develop a playful coaching model based on study group learning experiences (such as questioning using See-Think-Wonder) to help support teachers to become intentionally playful in their practice. Asking questions has proved to be an artform that playful coaches need to be competent in. Having a playful coach that teachers can turn to for support can transform the way we look at the investment schools make in professional development (learning).

A question schools wanting to implement playful learning need to consider is the following: How can administrators support teachers in building the confidence to ask questions?

Utilize community spaces in the curriculum

Making room for playful learning in schools can be difficult. Natural tensions exist between playful learning and the way teaching and learning are currently structured in most schools. As we have seen above, educators often differ in how they value playful learning practices and their understandings of the nature of play, because what is playful to one learner may not be experienced as playful by another. To those who view play as a central pathway for learning, resources such as time, space, and materials can seem in short supply.

Alice took a group of middle schoolers for a walk around the local sculpture park. They were led to a sculpture of a giant yellow head.

She asked the students to walk around the sculpture and then to stand either in front or behind the sculpted head. Once divided into two groups, students were tasked to discuss among themselves why they chose to stand on their particular side. This provided the opportunity for students to examine the sculpture before making their own choice of where they would like to stand. So instead of the teacher dividing the group up into two, here the students made an informed decision about how they are grouped. Now that they are in a group of their choice, students can begin to engage in a smaller group discussion which creates an opportunity for students to discuss and justify their choice to their peers. This exercise is helpful in knowledge construction and offers a fertile ground for the next stage of the lesson.

Following this, students sketched what they saw, paying particular attention to texture and shadow. In the arts, the concept of aesthetics is perceived differently around the world and across cultures. Aesthetics does not only address the rules and principles of beauty but should also include cultural perspectives and perception through the senses. This lesson is designed for students to explore the ways in which we discover and express ideas, feelings, nature, culture, beliefs, and values; the ways in which we reflect on, extend, and enjoy our creativity; our appreciation of the aesthetic.

Alice deliberately chose to bring the students out of the classroom for this activity. Our digitized world may offer access to boundless information on the internet. But if we limit knowledge construction within the walls of the school, we run the risk of losing connection to our surroundings and community. The ability to touch, see, and feel the sculpture gave students first-hand and a three-dimensional connection to the subject they were studying.

As a next step, the students used a small pad of Post-it notes to write adjectives which described their response to the sculpture and stuck them to the part of the sculpture they considered most applicable. These adjectives could refer to the physical appearance of the piece or the students' emotional response to the work.

Provoked by the words written, Alice led the students into a discussion of how appearance affects how we perceive people in society and how individuals may have completely different perspectives. Do we perceive the sculpture as appealing or repulsive? This and a lot more questions arose opening up the space for rich discussions in this language arts lesson.

Alice brought her learners into the "what if" space of learning, where students explore, create, invent, generate new ideas, and take different perspectives. Expanding the peripheral view of learning spaces beyond the classroom walls has enabled the community spaces to be a part of the curriculum.

Recognizing the need to make learning meaningful for learners, educators often look for opportunities for real-life applications in their curriculum planning, but what if we flip this around?

A school is not playful because it is highly resourced. The sustainability of a playful school is dependent on the community it is set in. So, while it may have access to a park, a building, a community center, a river, or a mountain, the question we might like to consider is as follows: How can a school utilize the outdoors and community spaces as powerful experiences for learning by engaging in resource-sharing?—it makes playful learning applicable in all contexts.

Future considerations

Becoming a playful school offers a range of benefits to the school, community, teachers, and students. Not only does it create a stronger focus on the overall well-being, positive engagement, and school culture, but it also offers students an opportunity to learn how to think, not what to think.

There is growing interest for schools around the world to become more playful. However, there are still questions not yet asked about the future role of teachers to anchor pedagogy in a more dynamic interplay between individuals and society.

While this might not be a definitive model for a playful school, it offers us the space to consider further questions and the intentional moves schools could take in order to become a playful school.

Schools that intend to bring together the knowledge, skills, and positive engagement could consider these four elements as part of creating culture of playful learning:

- How can the school adapt student interest to curriculum goals?
- In which way can outdoors and community spaces be used as resources for learning?
- How to shift assessment to indicators of playful learning?
- What are the ways to inform teachers of professional development with playful coaching?

We argue that schools need to become more playful to equip students with the knowledge and skills for a changing world, which also relies on teachers and school leaders to adopt a more playful mindset. This in turn will also help mobilize

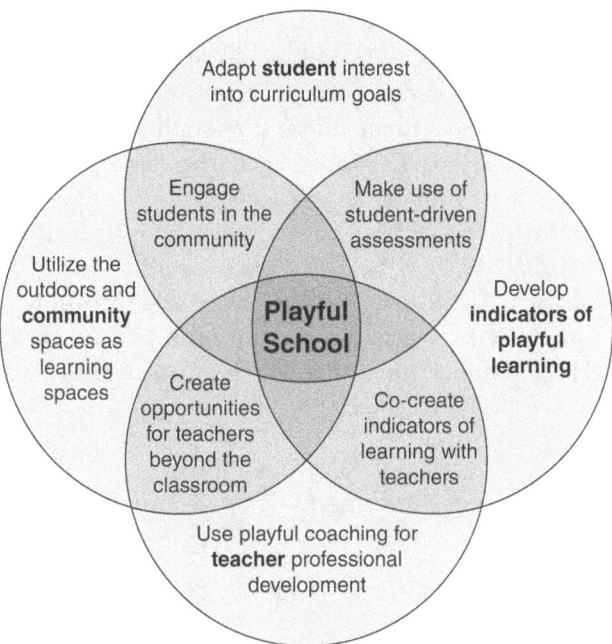

Figure 9.3 Playful school diagram

more excitement around the teaching profession and align the purpose of school as an institution with the surrounding needs of the community.

We propose that schools need to raise these questions across the environment and culture and see them as interlinked with the traditional aims of education and outcomes, as illustrated with the factors in Figure 9.3.

But arguably, these components will be limited by the level of support from the leadership team of the school. Prioritizing time for teachers to discuss and plan for playful teaching signals how play is valued at the school. Playful teaching is a whole school mindset that everyone needs to have in order to be successful. Naturally, schools will also need to check if playful teaching is aligned with the school's mission and vision. Schools cannot progress if there is no shared understanding of the ultimate goal within its learning community. The school's caretaker, teachers, students, leadership team, board members, and parents need to be onboard to realize the opportunity.

Often, we see educational models placing students at the center, supported by various stakeholders of the learning community. But the most direct and key enablers in the educational system are essentially the teachers. In the same way, we are pushed to rethink the educational landscape to adopt a more playful approach to teaching and learning, how are we then rethinking teacher professional development opportunities? Are teachers equipped to handle student-driven assessments, community-aligned curriculum, opportunities beyond the classroom and to co-create indicators of quality? In today's global and diverse classrooms, teachers are expected to cater to students' various needs. Similarly, schools need to look at relevant professional development to support their teaching staff and understand that one size does not necessarily fit all; therefore, professional development needs to offer teachers support and options beyond webinars, conferences, and workshops. Instructional coaching has proved to have a positive impact in student learning (Knight, 2019), but there is a lack of research on coaching for playful teachers. A call for a playful coaching model can help support teachers and schools to systemize playful teaching in a more personal and sustainable way. If playful teaching enables playful learning, then we need to address how we are preparing future teachers for playful teaching.

REFERENCES

Darling-Hammond, L. (2006). Constructing 21st-century teacher education. *Journal of teacher education*, 57(3), 300–314.

International Baccalaureate Organisation. (2023). Programmes. https://www.ibo.org/programmes/

Knight, J. (2019). Instructional coaching for implementing visible learning: A model for translating research into practice. *Education sciences*, 9(2), 101.

Marbina, L., Church, A., & Tayler, C. (2011). *Victorian Early Years Learning and Development Framework: Evidence Paper: Practice Principle 6: Integrated Teaching and Learning Approaches*. Parkville: University of Melbourne.

Mardell, B., Ryan, J., Krechevsky, M., Baker, M., Schulz, T. S., & LiuConstant, Y. (2023). *A Pedagogy of Play: Supporting Playful Learning in Classrooms and Schools*. Cambridge, MA: Project Zero.

Parker, R., Thomsen, B. S., & Berry, A. (2022, February). Learning through play at school–A framework for policy and practice. In *Frontiers in Education* (Vol. 7, p. 751801). Frontiers Media SA.

Vygotsky, L. S., & Cole, M. (1978). *Mind in Society: Development of Higher Psychological Processes*. Cambridge, USA: Harvard University Press. pp. 92–104

Weisberg, D. S., Hirsh-Pasek, K., Golinkoff, R. M., Kittredge, A. K., & Klahr, D. (2016). Guided play: Principles and practices. *Current directions in psychological science*, 25(3), pp. 177–182.

Whitebread, D., Basilio, M., Kuvalja, M., & Verma, M. (2012). *The Importance of Play*. Belgium: Toy Industries of Europe.

Yogman, M., Garner, A., Hutchinson, J., Hirsh-Pasek, K., & Golinkoff, R. M. Committee on Psychosocial Aspects of Child and Family Health, & Council on Communications and Media (2018). The power of play: A pediatric role in enhancing development in young children. *Pediatrics*, 142(3), pp. 1–17.

Zosh, J. M., Hirsh-Pasek, K., Hopkins, E. J., Jensen, H., Liu, C., Neale, D., … & Whitebread, D. (2018). Accessing the inaccessible: Redefining play as a spectrum. *Frontiers in psychology*, 9, 1124.

CHAPTER

Playful school leadership: being serious about leadership playfully

James Biddulph and Neil Gibrid

Introduction

In this chapter, we explore the potential benefits and challenges of expanding our understanding of school leadership in terms of play, weaving James' experiences as a playful leader with Neil's work as an academic researcher interested in school leadership. We start with an auto-ethnographic description of a moment in James' school, where he is the Executive Headteacher, that brought about reflections on the nature of playful leadership. We then consider a different school leadership needed for a new world order, building on Neil's work on adult and organisational psychology, linking with research into school culture and values-led leadership. We end by drawing together our ideas to explore the experience of playful leadership from the example of a project in the school. Throughout we aim to bring to life these ideas through presenting practical examples to illustrate playfulness in leadership. We argue that playfulness in leadership is a quality that is much needed; as leaders help navigate the grey, murky waters of complexity in schools, and the experiences of children and adults within them, colourful – celebrating diversities of thought, belief, identity, attitude and creativities.

Before this, we ought to introduce ourselves. Neil is an experienced practitioner in education and a multidisciplinary academic researcher. His PhD, and subsequent research, explores complexity, adult developmental psychology and leadership to advance our understanding of how headteachers comprehend and respond to their roles and responsibilities. James is a school leader, having danced a choreography of academic research and practitioner expertise since he qualified as a teacher in 2001. His experiences working in East London, in the United Kingdom, brought greater enthusiasm to be creative which in turn led to a positive frustration to ask questions about his own practice and how schools work. Through these experiences James began to seek ways to excite, disrupt and engage communities into becoming more playful. His PhD focused on creative learning within which play was discovered. We are both advocates for new thinking about leadership. We are positive that playfulness in leadership has the potential to inspire new solutions to old questions and moreover to ignite new questions to respond to the challenges during the 21st century.

'Let's have a carnival' – a moment of play

What follows is an auto-ethnographic description of a moment in one school in Cambridge, United Kingdom, where play is embedded into the curriculum design and where playful leadership is enacted. This example acts as a starting point to explore what playful leadership may entail. The voices are of some of the teachers who were in the meetings with James (one of the authors of this chapter). James collated them and then asked for feedback about this representation of the moment. It is a 'remembering' and narrated vignette.

This is what happened. The teaching team met with the Executive Headteacher, as we always do once a week. It was mid-winter and our Executive Headteacher came to school proclaiming that we should have a carnival.

"How many children will be involved and where will we do it?" we asked.

All 600 children and nursery – let's take the learning to the community. Let's unlock and open up our school…we need unlocking experiences.

Where will the funds come from?

They'll come.

How do we squeeze it in the curriculum and the timetable?

"We can work out the details…think differently…how do we link and connect and create meaningful journeys in a transdisciplinary way?" he answered.

And let's make it a science meets the arts event, bringing creativities alive – embodied, danced, sung, laughed out loud together! It should be a week of new pedagogic approaches and disruption. How about every child makes a costume or hat based on the science they are learning…to show their new knowledge in creative ways? How about getting the secondary school to bring their samba band? We want everyone on their balconies waving at us.

It is now mid-summer 2022, and a heatwave has arrived. Our Executive Headteacher and Director of Inclusion come to school dressed as a dragonfly and bumblebee. At 2.30 pm, all 600 children and 60 members of the team, dressed in bright costumes, led by the secondary school band, danced their way through the local streets. People on balconies waved. A moment of play and creativities is being led by some playful leaders (Figure 10.1).

What does this moment reveal about a possible 'playful' leadership? How does this repositioning of the Executive Headteacher impact the wider community's understanding of play in primary education? And how could a new playfulness in education leadership result in reimagining hopeful, more sustainable and transformative approaches to enabling every child to have the very best start in life? We

Figure 10.1 Three educators dressed in bright costumes dancing in the school carnival

return to these questions later in the chapter. Next, we move on to explore the nature of school leadership in what seems to be a new world order following the COVID-19 pandemic.

School leadership in a new world order: finding the grey area

In this section, we aim to unpack what is meant by *school* leadership. We will start with a brief definition of leadership, arguing that a key focus for school leadership is how leaders come to comprehend and act on the wide array of important responsibilities within their role. However, these responsibilities are exceptionally complex, and it is within them that the 'grey area' of school leadership exists – spaces of uncertainty that arise during each day in a school. Recent research exploring adult developmental psychology and educational leadership points towards just how challenging the handling and comprehending of this 'grey area' are. It is from this platform that we invite you to consider why the concept of play could provide the environment and challenge required to help school leaders navigate the grey murky waters of their organisations and move towards a more colourful palette.

Leadership is widely recognised as the process of influence. Many definitions of leadership do not dispute this; instead, they have different foci on the sorts of influencing activities that leadership entails. For example, some versions of distributed leadership (for example, Spillane and Diamond, 2007) argue for the spread of responsibility across the organisation. Instructional leadership scholars propose that the primary influencing activity of school leaders is centred on educational endeavours – the classroom, teaching and so forth (Hallinger, Gümüş and Bellibaş, 2020). Finally, transformational leadership adherents suggest that leaders' actions in relation to the '4 I's' – idealised influence, inspirational motivation, intellectual stimulation and individual consideration (Northouse, 2016) – are the primary drivers for influence within a leader's toolkit. Whilst the mechanisms of leadership differ within these approaches, influence remains the common factor.

Here, we argue that the responsibilities of a school leader serve as a vital focal point for understanding school leadership practice. Connolly, James and Fertig (2019) were the first to recognise that when school leaders act in relation to their responsibilities, they are influencing the organisation and are therefore leading. We support this argument for two reasons. First, in the simplest terms, school leaders have many responsibilities, and these are all critical to the successful running of a school. Barker and Rees (2020), undertaking interviews and reviews of Office for Standards in Education, Children's Services and Sills (Ofsted) reports across multiple settings, demonstrated that school leaders have an extremely wide set of responsibilities within their portfolio – from financial management to curriculum, safeguarding to health and safety. How a school leader acts in relation to this broad portfolio of responsibilities can have a colossal effect – the decisions a school leader makes can shape the life chances of individuals (Liebowitz and Porter, 2019), families and communities for generations to come. Therefore, when a school leader acts in relation to their responsibilities, there is a large potential for influence and for this influence to shape the lives of many young people, their families and their futures. However, when we examine the types of responsibilities that school leaders face and the contexts in which they service, we can begin to unpack why school leadership can be so challenging and 'grey' – why more problems arise and why the complexity of school organisations means that there is no clear-cut way or strategy to resolve all these issues.

Complexity is synonymous with school leadership. Hawkins and James (2018) summarise complexity in schools through the acronym C.E.L.L.S – complex, evolving, loosely linked systems.

Complex: Complexity theory has been used to describe ecosystems, organisations, financial markets and more (Lewin, 2000). What complexity theory does is lay down some principles for how organisations work. These include a high number of interactions which can occur across a large number of variables within a system; that the appearance of stability is achieved through small challenges elsewhere; that the system is more than the sum of its parts; that new variables within can emerge from the interaction between other variables; and that cause and effect are non-linear.

Evolving: How are schools constantly evolving? First, the high degree of interaction leads to the emergence of new properties or variables within a system. New components or parts of the system change how the system operates. Subsequently, the system is never standing still and takes on different shapes according to these interactions. Therefore, the system can be said to be evolving due to internal interactions forcing changes. In addition, complex systems adapt in response to changes within the environment — these adaptations are intended to help ensure the relevance of the organisation going forward, and unsuccessful adaptation will mean the organisation can become less relevant.

Loosely linked systems: A school is a series of different units, or systems, e.g., a teaching staff system and a student system. These systems are distinct from each other — the teaching staff system will have different variables and dependencies when compared to that of the student system. However, they are interconnected, in that they interact and therefore affect each other. Changes in one system can lead to consequences for other systems.

The consequences of considering a school as a complex system often resonate with the day-to-day assumptions that school leaders have about their organisations. Complexity explains the following:

- Why it can be so hard to determine cause and effect?
- Why it is sometimes difficult to determine what is happening and why different people understand situations in different ways?
- Why best laid plans (usually) end up very little like a plan initially conceived?
- Why people present such a challenge — they interact a lot with others and across hierarchical norms. Hence, they facilitate complexity?

Schools are therefore complex — but how does this organisational complexity affect leaders? Rittel and Webber (1973) described the types of problems that leaders face as having the following features:

- 'Wicked problems' are essentially unique. As such, individuals involved in the problems can hold different, yet valid perceptions of the problem. The word 'wicked' in the United Kingdom has a number of meanings: the first is in being 'bad', and the second is more colloquial referring to something that is amazing or incredible. This double meaning — contradictory — suggests different ways of viewing the problems faced.
- Applying a solution to a wicked problem is challenging. First, there is no solution which can be universally agreed to be the 'correct' solution. Second, because the problem is unique, you cannot transplant solutions from other similar problems and expect a predictable or comparable outcome. Finally, it is not possible to test the possible solution to the wicked problem in advance.
- The wicked problem is likely to have emerged from another problem.
- There is a No Stopping Rule. Essentially, this means that the problem can continue after there has been an attempt to apply the solution to the problem.

So far, we have argued that a considerable part of how we influence, or lead, in schools is facing the complexity of their organisation and the wickedness inherent to the responsibilities within their roles.

The challenge with these problems is that they place a considerable demand on how adults are expected to process and subsequently act. Jane Loevinger (1976; Hy and Loevinger, 1996) was an eminent American psychologist who explored the stages by which adults come to comprehend circumstances and situations which are challenging, complex or 'wicked'. Her work entitled 'Adult Ego Development' established eight stages of development which adults can move through throughout their lives. Within each stage, the capacity to comprehend and perceive different orders of complexity grows.

Gilbride, James and Carr (2021; Forthcoming) were the first to explore whether or not school principals of different stages interacted and responded to complexity and wicked problems in different ways. Fundamental differences were established between headteachers in the three most common stages (as seen in Table 10.1) typically found in adults:

As in Loevinger's original work, Gilbride, James and Carr (2021) recognised that it was only in the later Stage 3/Individualist stages that the components of wicked problems/complex environments were recognised in how they comprehended and responded to their responsibilities:

Rittel and Webber (1973) suggest that wicked problems are hard to define, have multiple explanations and have no stopping rule; that the problem might be a consequence of another problem. The solutions to the wicked problems are not right or wrong; there is no test for the solution suggested, and all the attempts to solve the problem might have consequences which are irreversible and not forgettable; indeed, the problem may be seen as unique to the context and will not have an obvious solution. The individualist stage response to these wicked problems includes the following:

- Identifying the need for a wide lens on the problem.
- Recognising how the problem is entangled with other problems.
- Making attempts to comprehend the history of the incident.
- Making attempts to understand potential consequences of action.
- Proactively seeking 'grey' information that could make the situation less vague – insights and opinions.
- Collaborating to build solution – did not impose a solution but would look to build one through collaboration and dialogue. Therefore, a recognition that the solution is too complex for an individual to operate on their own.
- Recognising the need to understand beyond the incident.
- Recognising that the incident will have consequences that need to be monitored, i.e., there is no test, there are consequences and not necessarily right or wrong.
- Providing support beyond the immediate situation – the need for fine-tuning with no clear solution.
- Using policy as a guide but not as a firm rule
- Recognising the unique nature of the problem – look to understand the history of the incident inductively; build an understanding and solution in co-construction with those around them, as opposed to a centrally imposed solution.

Table 10.1 Summary of different stages of adult ego development and school leadership practice

Data theme	Stage of adult ego development		
	Self-aware/Stage 1	Conscientious/Stage 2	Individualist/Stage 3
The sense-making process	An emphasis on collecting 'hard evidence' about the incident. An emphasis on individual sense-making. An immediate and rapid response. A desire to respond according to the relevant policy.	The collection of hard evidence and explanations. Predominantly individual sense-making using a limited range of possible explanations. Close attention to detail in responding to the incident. A desire to provide support to those involved in the incident. Low dependency on policy.	Seeking hard evidence, reasons, insights and intuitive judgements of others. Allowing understanding to emerge. Co-construction of understanding with others. Involvement of a range of others. Understanding the perspective of others. Reflecting and taking time to reflect. Seeking connections beyond the critical incident. The provision of support and feedback. Seeking to promote staff development through the incident. Seeking to ensure widespread understanding. Reliance on policy not a data theme.
Feelings and the sense-making process	Not a theme in the data	A need to minimise feelings and their expression as emotions. A need to know the affective state of others involved in the critical incident.	Feelings are a central aspect of the critical incident. An empathetic approach. Provision of opportunities for those involved to express their feelings about the incident. Seeking to ensure the effective well-being of those involved.
The involvement of others in the sense-making process	Others were: providers of information; an audience for the expression of feelings.	Others were: trusted advisers; an audience for off-loading feelings; a source of validation.	Others were: co-constructors of a shared understanding; providers of guidance on who to involve; sounding boards; expected to be involved.
How others experience the principals	As solution/outcome focussed; as a significant source of influence	As having particular qualities or traits; as taking a logical, rational approach in responding to a critical incident; as highly emotive choosing the appropriate moment to express their feelings.	As having a deep and significant effect on those they worked with; able to identify the issues that others cannot see.

Source: Taken from Gilbride, James and Carr (2021).

Features of Wicked Problems Alongside Definition of Individualist Stage of Adult Ego Development (Adapted from Carr, Gilbride and James, 2017).

Thus far, we have established two key points:

1. It is the later stages of adult ego development where headteachers can work with the complexity inherent to the responsibilities of school. It is in these later stages that school leaders are more likely to comfortably handle situations which can be ambiguous; grey; without any guarantee of right or wrong or predictability.
2. Indeed, it is clear that the earlier stages' approach to grey ambiguity is to either see the situation as black or white and unambiguous or to actively work to control their exposure to the complexity of the situation.

Why do school leaders need to work within ambiguity? How did James manage the ambiguity of the creative arts week and the resulting public manifestation of his playful leadership? By treating their responsibilities as concrete, school leaders risk missing the full comprehension of the problems with which they are faced. For example, if the school leader fails to recognise the situation as ambiguous, they might be more inclined to apply firm solutions without any safeguards or willingness to revisit in the light of evidence. They might not seek out the opinions and perspectives of a broad range of individuals and instead continue to make sense of the situation on their own. Or, as we have seen in the school leaders in Stage 2, they may apply approaches which contain ambiguity. Put another way, the actions they undertake might be less appropriate than if the ambiguous nature of their circumstances were fully embraced. All this matters because the responsibilities that school leaders have are broad, important and critical way in which they directly and indirectly influence and, therefore, lead.

However, because embracing ambiguity is associated with later, rarer stages, it means most school leaders will require support and help to embrace the ambiguity and wider complexity within their responsibilities. Several authors (Kegan and Lahey, 2009; Day et al, 2014; Drago-Severson and Blum-DeStefano, 2014; Gilbride, James and Carr, 2021) have recognised that certain conditions need to be met for adults to begin to explore the complexity and their own stage development. These features include:

Disruptive experiences: Disruptive, or dis-equilibrating, experiences are different enough from an individual's day-to-day experience to promote an internal conflict. These conflicts can force individuals to reconsider their underlying approach and, consequently, advance in their stage of AED (Manners and Durkin, 2000; Manners, Durkin and Nesdale, 2004). These might occur as individual events or events that occur over a period of time which can be brought together to help individuals reconsider their internal sensemaking model.

Supportive holding environments: A supportive holding environment is considered to be both safe and uncomfortable (Kahn, 2001). Such an environment is usually created within a network of peers. Having your internal sense-making models challenged by a disruptive experience is both emotive and cognitively challenging: emotive, because of anxiety of uncertainty, cognitively challenging and the sensemaking tools at your disposal are struggling to meet the needs of the problem and, without support, we can resist such efforts for change (Baron and Cayer, 2011).

This is where we believe play can help: play provides a holding environment and a low-stakes situation whereby school leaders can take risks and practice and face up to disruption and challenge. By leveraging play, school leaders could embrace greater degrees of ambiguity and complexity whilst also helping them to make better day-to-day decisions for their communities. The following section will outline what play can look like in a school leaders' practice, and how the concept of play can facilitate the adults in these roles to come to terms with complexity and ambiguity.

Playful leadership

From a social-cultural perspective, humans are naturally playful (Huizinga, 2016). Play is a unique quality of activity that is different from ordinary life:

> play [is] a special form of activity, as a 'significant form', as a social function…if we find play is based on the manipulation of certain images, on a certain 'imagination' of reality (i.e. its conversion into images), then our main concern will be to grasp the value and significance of these images and their 'imagination'.
> *(Huizinga, 2016: 4)*

It is also the direct opposite of seriousness. Or is it? If you watch a child immersed in play, one can see the complete concentration, the suspension of reality, the convinced imaginings of new realities, the possibilities of thinking and the fully engaged embodiment in the play. Play is serious business. A child doesn't play with sand, they construct new cities. A child doesn't pretend to be a superhero, they are saving the planet. As well as being seriously important and yet also not serious, play also involves laughter. But play is not foolish or necessarily light-hearted. Consider ways in which the best teams revolve around high-quality relationships and clarity of roles and expectations. In these teams, laughter is present as a cultural way of being that connects and forms the notion of the team but does not detract from the seriousness of the work required. Building from Huizinga's 'play as culture' theory, 'all play is voluntary activity' because, 'play to order is no longer play: it could at best be but a forcible imitation of it. By this quality of freedom alone, play marks itself off from the course of the natural process' (p. 7). If it cannot be 'ordered', how do leaders inspire a playful approach to the challenges in their contexts?

Miguel Sicart (2014) moves beyond the cultural definition provided by Huizinga. He suggests that play is contextual, that it involves understanding the 'rules of the game' as well as thinking, manipulating, changing and adapting the rules. He explains that play is a dynamic movement from creation to destruction and vice versa. In this way, play is carnivalesque – the freedom from an institutionalised world that brings a different quality to the experience of living. For example, a playful leadership requires reimagining the conventional institutional rules of the game to find better solutions and bolder ideas. Sicart's view is that play is disruptive. A powerful guide, on our journey to understand what a playful leadership might entail, is in the view that 'play is like a language – a way of being in the world, of making sense of it' (p. 18). Moreover, that it takes place, 'in a context as a balance between creation and destruction, between adherence to a structure and the pleasures of destruction. Playing is freedom' (Sicart, 2014: 18). James' vignette is an example of disruptive action of school life and the school days to give space, temporal, physical and symbolic, for new ideas which arise from playfulness in the school community.

One well-documented example of possible playful leadership in action is in the *Learning without Limits* study (Hart et al, 2004) and subsequent *Creating Learning without Limits* (Swann et al, 2012) research project. Realising that principled action and leadership can enable inclusive learning for *all* children and teachers, the principles identified in the qualities of leadership were as follows:

- Trust
- Co-agency
- An ethic of 'everybody'

Creating Learning without Limits (Swann et al, 2012) identified seven key leadership dispositions for building an inclusive culture of challenge and success. In particular, the emphasis on dispositions that led to greater professional agency and learning were desired (Swann et al, 2012: 88). In Figure 10.2, the rainbow

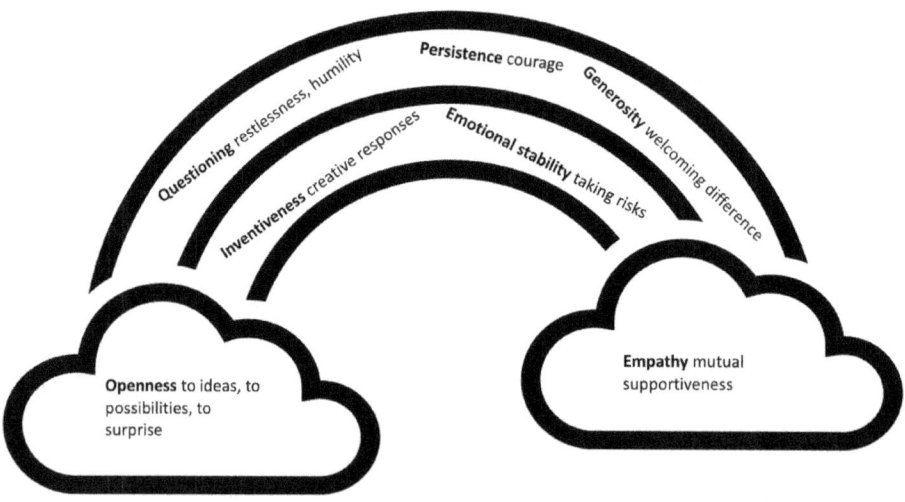

Figure 10.2 A rainbow depiction of the opportunities of *Creating Learning without Limits*

metaphor is used; that playfulness in leadership can transcend the grey murkiness and standard responses to the many challenges within schools.

These qualities are not dissimilar to those involved in creative learning. The notion of an *enabling space* (Biddulph and Burnard, 2021) that fostered *possibility thinking* (Burnard, Kelly and Biddulph, 2010, 2016) forms the necessary principles of trust, courage to take risks in learning and teaching and in seeing teachers as intellectuals who enquire and research their practice. The University of Cambridge Primary School (UCPS) culture was such that *'releasing the imagination and celebrating the art of the possible'* was embedded and became their strapline. Creativities and imagination are synonymous with playfulness, it could be argued (Biddulph and Burnard, 2021). Bringing together definitions of creative learning to consider how playful leadership and the learning inspired by a playful/creative approach could be identified. For example, 'Imaginative activity fashioned so as to produce outcomes that are both original and of value' (NACCCE, 1999: 29) or 'Significant imaginative achievement as evidenced in the creation of new knowledge as determined by the imaginative insight of the person or persons responsible and judged by appropriate observers to be both original and of value as situated in different domain contexts' (Craft et al, 2007: 76). What do these definitions mean in relation to playful leadership? Where is the original response, of value for the context in which it is created? School leaders must know their schools and people well to support an expansion of the possibilities of creative learning. For example, the literature references creative learning as accepting uncertainties, as the fertile ground in which new ideas are sowed:

- 'Creative learning is simply any learning that develops the capacity to be creative. It equips young people with the knowledge and skills they need to succeed in today's world, nurturing ways of thinking and working that encourage imagination, independence, tolerance of ambiguity and risk, openness, the raising of aspirations' (in Galton, 2008)
- 'When educators talk about creative learning, they generally mean teaching that allows students to use their imaginations, have ideas, generate multiple possible solutions to problems, communicate in a variety of media and in general "think outside the box"' (Sefton-Green et al, 2011: 2)

Both Burnard (2016) and later Biddulph (2022) emphasise the co-construction of ideas – that creative endeavours involve the collaboration of people, a socially constructed activity: especially important is the notion that creative learning is a mediated activity in which imaginative achievement and the development of knowledge have a crucial role. Creative learning involves participation and is developed in relationships with people engaged in collaborative activities in which they develop their thoughts together (Burnard, 2018).

If we return to the carnival moment that started this chapter, the playfulness that arose was not mandated by the Executive Headteacher. Rather, it was modelled in the uncertainties, the curiosity, the confidence in successful outcomes and the imaginative possibilities-thinking. The sense of being in a space of uncertainty – of not knowing – was present in the example, and indeed James' reflection shows an internal struggle about the decisions he had made and his sense of role and positionality. However, it is also true that the impact of such an approach remains unknown. Playfulness does not translate to quick changes in practice; it is not a scientific approach and is perhaps not easily measured.

> ### Reflection from James' journal
>
> The reception children (five-year-olds) decided that a dragonfly was shiny and so I needed glitter in my beard. They came to my office, nervously and like imps, creeping around the door frame and shouting, 'you need glitter, Dragonfly!' They then, with their class teacher, added it to my beard, laughing and excited at this disruption of roles. Sometime later, when we were about to start, I had a moment of doubt, the ego rising. What would people think? Surely this isn't the role of an Executive Headteacher. The parents need to have trust in the school leadership and here am I about to dance around. This isn't the Dr Biddulph they see suited and with tie each day. This is not what they need from me. This is a new costume. Is it one step too far? Does this type of repositioning give confidence in the community? What is the message I am giving? Too late. I have purple glitter on my face. Here goes.

Conversely, Elena Natale found strength in the immersive experience, both professional and educational, and was strengthened by James' playful modelling and repositioning. At the time, Elena was the coordinator of the carnival project and reflected on the experience of preparing the massed-school event,

> ### Reflection: Elena Natale the arts curriculum leader
>
> When I think of inspiring and playful leadership, the image of James dressed in purple, bright carnival costumes, dancing, singing and creating art on his hands and knees springs to mind. I think of the professional development staff meetings spent creating a professional community through song and dance, the metaphors used, the examples of practice and the moments of reflection.
>
> Immersed in the reality of the school, James acts as the caring driver leading the bus on amazing adventures to wonderful places. In my years teaching at UCPS, I developed my leadership skills through productive

dialogue with James and moments where a project came up and I said yes to it. This was the case for whole school creative art projects that at first I never thought I could organise given the scale of these events. What made me have that 'yes-I-can-do-it-attitude' was the certainty that I would be supported and could always ask for help or advice but at the same time that I was trusted to achieve what had been agreed.

Playful leadership is one open to change, where risks are taken and where there is no fear of failure. It is a leadership that is aware of the needs of children, staff and the community and that starts from the prime objective of caring for children and their learning. It is also founded on knowledge, grounded in classroom practice and based on experiences with children, families and the school community. It is a leadership that has a ripple effect and inspires others.

The dancing bumblebee, Aimee Durning, also reflected on the experience of working with James on this event. She brings forward the idea of possibility thinking and asks the question 'what if?'

Aimee Durning, Director of Inclusion's reflection on the carnival and leadership

'Come on! Come on... are you coming?' I was stood on the mound dressed as a Bumblebee, tapping my feet and clapping my hands to the beats of the Samba Band.

'Coming where?' I asked.

'To the front of the procession, to dance the route of course', he said.

To dance the route, to the beat of the Samba Band, followed by 600 children! How joyful, I thought to myself. Everyone was here, everyone was included. This community event, albeit educational and creative, was an unusual event. Unusual in the sense that the Executive Headteacher dressed as a dragonfly, followed by a bumblebee, followed by a Dream Catcher on a Friday afternoon in July. Together we danced the streets and entertained the crowds. It isn't about the dance or dressing up though.

Skipping, jumping and adding in plenty of samba side steps, I knew my numerous Zumba sessions would one day come in handy but never had I imagined it would be at my school's carnival. Laughing and joking and guiding the children along the way, we lead the children on a memorable merry dance.

> This event did not feel alien to me because this wasn't the first time that I had been taken out of my comfort zone. Or asked to do something different from the educational norm. For years now, Anna Craft's words, 'What if…..' had become the mantra of what we did under the playful leadership of James Biddulph. He made us alive in asking more, better, bolder questions:
>
> What if……
>   We imagine we are in a West End Show (we did)
> What if…..
>   We are all fairies in the forest (we did)
> What if….
>   We were recording artists composing a song (we did)
> What if……
>   We found ourselves trapped in a workhouse empathising with Oliver Twist (we did)
>
> How lucky I am that all these opportunities opened up our playfulness through the disruptive professional learning we engaged in. Imagination ignited, I wonder what our next, *What if…..* will be?

Her sense of place-making is evidenced here: *how lucky I am*, an emotive response to the event and was unusual because she and all the staff were being asked to be/think/act differently from their typical positions. The repositioning of adults is also remembered as the modelling of new open ways of being given value.

Indeed, another external voice brought different insights into the playfulness being modelled by James and his team. Jane Wheeler, a music leader who was involved in the carnival science project, also reflected on the leadership qualities:

Jane Wheeler's reflection: Music-Artist-Teacher who took part in the carnival project

I was thinking about the journey of James from the time when I worked with him in London. James always had and continues to have a way of being one of the group, a learner alongside, an enquirer and adventurer, while calmly bringing his expertise to the table. He somehow goes on the journey with all participants, while dropping into the mix his incredible knowledge of recent and past research, of books and resources to seek out. I have always enjoyed collaborating with James, as much for all of the above reasons as for his sense of fun. He takes 'excellence' very seriously and yet remains playful, and open to other participants' ideas, or challenges, whether from children or adults. I learn from him every time we work together, yet he still manages to make me feel like the expert in the room. The carnival was a perfect example of this serious playfulness.

Jane identifies the centrality of collaboration, of modelling learning, of being excellent and open to ideas and challenges, all balanced with a light-hearted playfulness.

Another voice: one grandparent emailed the school to explain their view of the event and of the time their child had spent at the school. In the email, there is a reflection about the positionality of the headteacher:

> ### Email from grandparent of child at UCPS
>
> Finally, I have to say how I have witnessed your dedication to the children and your staff. I have seen how your confidence has grown over the years and how you lead by example. To watch you lead the carnival procession around Eddington last week was such a joy. From the many adults I have spoken with, they have all said the same thing 'this wouldn't have happened in my school'. I wonder how many heads would participate so enthusiastically today. Given time the children will comprehend how fortunate they are. I explained to Sandra that my primary school headteacher, Miss Fielding, was at least 100 years old and her leadership skills involved instilling fear and humiliation in the children. I am sure that when Sandra is an adult and talks about her primary school education, it will be with positive memories, thanks to UPCS. (I think she will also put you in a different age bracket!)
>
> (Email received from a grandparent: 21 July 2022 16:14)

In these different voices, from parent to teacher, school leader to musician, the qualities of playful leadership (Figure 10.3) could be considered as:

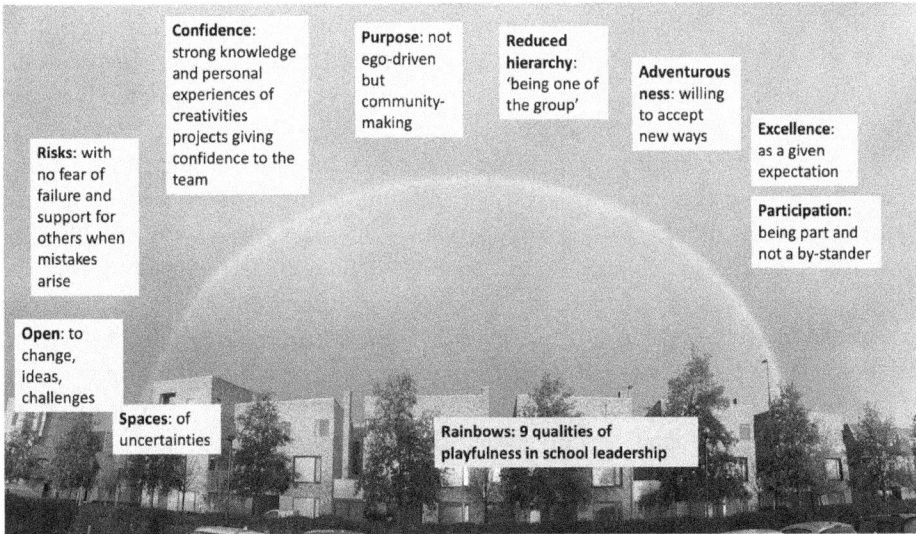

Figure 10.3 9 qualities of playfulness in school leadership

The image is a view from the UCPS, looking out into the community, where people live, where families and children live. It reminds us of the important ongoing bridging, linking, conjoining and collaboration needed to develop qualities of learning that engage children in play. Families must understand the purpose of play in education through the playful responses made by the adults in school. But this must be within a context of seriousness – leaders in being serious about play show explicitly the impact of play on the outcomes of children academically and socially.

Playful leadership as the new school order: new rainbow areas

Throughout this chapter, we have referred to ambiguity in association with the colour 'grey'. Grey is typically used as an adjective for the unclear, such as 'grey, murky waters', or to recognise the nuance between the binary, black and white positions of right or wrong. Grey can, of course, be considered a morose colour – a patient can be described as looking 'grey' or how the weather is looking 'grey'. Grey can also refer to fog, confusion, visibility or stifling.

Is grey an appropriate choice of colour to associate with the ambiguity and complexity that come through the responsibilities that school leaders hold? On one hand, yes. As we have described, learning to lead in ambiguity and complexity is far from easy – it is like swimming through muddy waters in the fog; it requires middle-ground, diplomatic and balanced being, thinking and acting, perhaps? Ambiguity can make us feel nervous and uncertain. Indeed, as outlined in an earlier section, many adults proactively manage situations to avoid exposure to uncertainties and there is an inclination to eradicate such ambiguity. The colour grey could be argued as an appropriate colour to describe these circumstances, in part due to the effect these can have when structures and support are not in place for school leaders to comprehend and grow themselves and their organisations.

On the other hand, we believe that the concept of playful leadership enables a diversity of ideas, decisions and possibilities, as leaders learn to feel comfortable in the uncomfortableness of uncertainties; the grey becomes diffracted into a multi-coloured array of ideas – a rainbow of possibilities. Rainbows, with their palette of colours, shed light on situations revealing the diversity in ways of seeing them and possibilities for change. They can be 'seen', just like the grey murky water, yet ambiguous in both where they have emerged from and where they are going. Rainbows are associated with joy with possibility and progress. Because the concept of play provides mechanisms and approaches which facilitate individuals to conceptualise and respond to complexity, such situations become positive and progressive, in short: being serious about play enables school leaders to work through the challenges they face whilst at the same time embracing ambiguity.

Let us take an example. The challenges presented by Special Educational Needs and Disabilities (SEND) education are conceptualised as presenting wicked problems (Armstrong, 2017) and a recent survey of school leaders identified SEND as a domain most likely to present as complex (Getting Heads Together, 2021). The range of special needs in our classrooms and schools in the United Kingdom, the economic challenges of funding specialist support and the eco-social-political problems can make it difficult for leaders to determine what to do. There are multiple and valid angles around any given situation. There are no fixed solutions that can be transplanted from one context to the next, and nothing can be applied which will produce a certain, guaranteed effect. School leaders, who have responsibility for ensuring the progress and thriving of all children, could easily find these circumstances grey and feel vulnerable, especially considering the vulnerability for children. The response in this 'grey space' could be the status quo and a desire to quickly solve the problem – no matter how unsolvable. How might the features of play help in such challenging circumstances? Where are the qualities of openness and being comfortable in the uncomfortable spaces of uncertainty? Where are the risks? And linked confidences? How does the sense of purpose arise in ways that reduce the hierarchy so that there are more opportunities for participation through and in an adventurous spirit of curiosity? Linked with this rainbow image, James playfully responded with a poem, using his personal journal and expressing his own position as Executive Headteacher – it is his search for more colourful responses to the grey murkiness that could fog or cloud his thinking and the thinking and responding of his team.

A Rainbow of Diverse Uncertainties: poem for playfulness in leadership

It starts with spaces of uncertainties
A resounding **openness** to change
Creating a culture of **asking questions**
Some asked before, some more **bold**,
Modelling uncertainty and not knowing
Prompting more dialogue.

Then, when the leader shares their worries
those **risky** bits and says
What would happen if...?
How would we know when...?
What could go wrong if...?
We still **fear the failure**
Yet the **courage** to go for it anyway exists
We <u>must</u> give it a try
Model some **confidence** that life can be better
Live the social imagination
Creatives,
imaginations,
possibilities abound
and we say 'Yes'

Not a fool hardy yes
but a **confident (even in uncertainties) yes!**

The power of humans to collaborate and find out becomes
the heartbeat DNA of our school.

I am the Head
But we each have heads and ways of knowing and so
Less hierarchy but responsibilities clearly defined
Our purpose is always for the children
Drop the ego
Us and we
Not I and me
And with an **adventurous spirit**
Raise the temperature in the team explicitly,
So, more droplets of possibility rise into those murky grey clouds:
'We are going to work on big audacious hairy problems…
it is going to be tough, but we can do it together…'

And we must **join in actively**
Leaders rolling those sleeves and putting on the wings
Finding the light in the clouds
Finding the pot of gold
Crafting new stories
Share it – the ups and downs and inside outs
Bring it – that **spirit of yes-full adventuring curiosity**
alive through ways you/we/they bring life into our schools
Through **highest leadership expectations**,
modelled in **open-hearted leadership vulnerabilities**.
Move through and beyond the murky grey
Rain and sun
Wicked problems celebrate
And **dance the rainbow**.

Conclusion

In this chapter, we outlined the ambiguity and complexity with which school leaders are faced. Adult development research within educational leadership points to how such complexities are challenging for adults to work through and requires us to consider a paradigm shift in the support and practice of school leadership. The concept of play could provide the necessary prompts, structures and holding environment to enable school leaders to expose themselves to the complexity of the task at hand. Thus, the school leader has a platform to comprehend, sit with uncertainty, draw from an ethic of possibilities and engage in moments of acting. Rather than the grey murky ambiguity that can drain the spirits and leave people exhausted and overwhelmed, school leaders are more likely to experience the rainbow of progress, possibility and positivity – because they engage with a mindset that is playful. Importantly, adjusting how we communicate the stories, old and newly crafted, influences the people within teams and schools – it is a subtle modelling of playfulness that could lead to more playful, creative and imaginative solution-focused teachers and teaching assistants.

References

Armstrong, D. (2017). Wicked problems in special and inclusive education. *Journal of Research in Special Educational Needs*, 17(4), pp. 229–236.

Barker, J., & Rees, T. (2020) 2020: A new perspective for school leadership? Impact (9). Available at 2020: A new perspective for school leadership? (chartered.college). (Accessed 17 August 2023).

Baron, C., & Cayer, M. (2011). Fostering post-conventional consciousness in leaders: why and how? *Journal of Management Development*, 30(4), pp. 344–365.

Biddulph, J., 2022. Intercultural creative learning: New spaces for nurturing compassionate global citizenship. *Journal of Supranational Policies of Education*, (16), pp.13–28.

Biddulph, J., & Burnard, P. (2021). Storying the journey to new spaces of intercultural creative learning. In: P. Burnard & M. Loughrey (Eds.), (2022) *Sculpting New Creativities in Primary Education*, pp. 45–61. London: Routledge.

Burnard, P. (2016). *Musical Creativities in Practice*. Translated into Chinese. Shanghai, China: Shanghai Music Press.

Burnard, P., Kelly, E., & Biddulph, J. (2010). Mapping the creative journeying in practitioner research. In: M. Khine & I. Saleh (Eds.), *Practitioner Research: Teachers' Investigations in Classroom Teaching*, pp. 1–15. Hauppauge, NY: Nova Science Publishers.

Burnard, P., MacKinlay, E., & Powell, K. (2016). *The Routledge International Handbook of Intercultural Arts Research*. London: Routledge.

Carr, S., Gilbride, N. M., & James, C. (2017). School principals: their adult ego development stage, their sense-making capabilities and how others experience them, *American Education Research Association: Teachers Leading Education Reform: The Power and Potential of Professional Learning Communities*, 27 April–1 May 2017. San Antonio, TX.

Connolly, M., James, C., & Fertig, M. (2019). The difference between educational management and educational leadership and the importance of educational responsibility. *Educational Management Administration & Leadership*, 47(4), pp. 504–519.

Craft, A., Cremin, T., Burnard, P., & Chappell, K. (2007). Developing creative learning through possibility thinking with children aged 3–7. In: A. Craft, T. Cremin, & P. Burnard (Eds.), *Creative Learning 3–11 and How We Document It*. London: Trentham.

Day, D. V., Fleenor, J. W., Atwater, L. E., Sturm, R. E., & McKee, R. A. (2014). Advances in leader and leadership development: a review of 25 years of research and theory. *The Leadership Quarterly*, 25(1), pp. 63–82.

Drago-Severson, E., & Blum-DeStefano, J. (2014). Leadership for transformational learning: a developmental approach to supporting leaders' thinking and practice. *Journal of Research on Leadership Education*, 9(2), pp. 113–141.

Galton, M. (2008). *Creative Practitioners in Schools and Classrooms* (Final Report of the Project: The Pedagogy of Creative Practitioners in Schools). Cambridge: Creative Partnerships/Faculty of Education.

Getting Heads Together (2021). A review of the range of complex issues facing school heads across varied EU settings. Available at http://www.gettingheadstogether.eu/wp-content/uploads/2022/04/GHT-O1-A1-English.pdf

Gilbride, N., James, C., & Carr, S. (2021). School principals at different stages of adult ego development: Their sense-making capabilities and how others experience them. *Educational Management Administration & Leadership*, 49(2), pp. 234–250.

Gilbride, N., James, C., & Carr, S. (2021). School principals at different stages of adult ego development: their sense-making capabilities and how others experience them. *Educational Management Administration & Leadership*, 49(2), pp. 234–250.

Hallinger, P., Gümüş, S., & Bellibaş, M. Ş. (2020). 'Are principals instructional leaders yet?' A science map of the knowledge base on instructional leadership, 1940–2018. *Scientometrics*, 122(3), pp. 1629–1650.

Hart, S., Dixon, A., Drummon, M. J., & McIntyre, D., (Eds.) (2004). *Learning without Limits*. Maidenhead: Open University Press.

Hawkins, M., & James, C. (2018). Developing a perspective on schools as complex, evolving, loosely linking systems. *Educational Management Administration & Leadership*, 46(5), pp. 729–748.

Huizinga, J. (2016). *Homo Ludens: A Study of the Play Element in Culture*. Angelico Press.

Hy, L. X., & Loevinger, J. (1996). *Measuring Ego Development*. New York: Lawrence Erlbaum Associates, Inc.

Kahn, W. (2001). Holding environments at work. *The Journal of Applied Behavioural Science*, 37(3), pp. 260–279.

Kegan, R., & Lahey, L. L. (2009). *Immunity to Change: How to Overcome It and Unlock Potential in Yourself and Your Organization*. USA: Harvard Business Press.

Lewin, R. (2000). *Complexity: Life at the Edge of Chaos*. Chicago, IL: University of Chicago Press.

Liebowitz, D. D., & Porter, L. (2019). The effect of principal behaviors on student, teacher, and school outcomes: a systematic review and meta-analysis of the empirical literature. *Review of Educational Research*, 89(5), pp. 785–827.

Loevinger, J. (1976). *Ego Development*. San Francisco, CA: Jossey-Bass.

Manners, J., & Durkin, K. (2000). Processes involved in adult ego development: a conceptual framework. *Developmental Review*, 20(4), pp. 475–513.

Manners, J., Durkin, K., & Nesdale, A. (2004). Promoting advanced ego development among adults. *Journal of Adult Development*, 11(1), pp. 19–27.

NACCCE (1999). Nationary Advisory Committee on Creative & Cultural Education *All our furtures: Creativity, Culture & Education, London, DFEE.*

Northouse, P. G. (2016). *Leadership: Theory and Practice*. 7th ed. Los Angeles, CA: SAGE.

Rittel, H. W., & Webber, M. M. (1973). Dilemmas in a general theory of planning. *Policy Sciences*, 4(2), pp. 155–169.

Sefton-Green, J., Thomson, P., Jones, K., & Bresler, L., (Eds.) (2011). *The Routledge Handbook of Creative Learning*. Oxon: Routledge.

Sicart, M. (2014). *Play Matters*. USA: MIT Press.

Spillane, J. P., & Diamond, J. B. (Eds.) (2007). *Distributed Leadership in Practice*. New York: Teachers College, Columbia University.

Swann, M., Peacock, A., Hart, S., & Drummond, M. (2012). *Creating Learning without Limits*. Glasgow: Open University Press.

CHAPTER

Fostering playful learning in school through a Pedagogy of Play

Mara Krechevsky

> *Play is a strategy for learning, not a set of activities you need to make time for.*
> –Susan MacKay, Center for Playful Inquiry, Portland, OR, USA

> *The aim of teaching is not to produce learning, but to produce the conditions for learning.*
> –Loris Malaguzzi, Reggio Emilia, Italy

How can play support children's learning in schools? To some, bringing play into the context of school is like mixing oil and water. The main purpose of school is to learn (or—to use Malaguzzi's phrase—*to produce the conditions for learning*), while the main purpose of play is to enjoy oneself. Play is a natural part of childhood; school is a cultural contrivance. While learning and enjoyment are certainly not mutually exclusive, playful learning in schools requires navigating a series of paradoxes between the nature of school and the nature of play (Kuschner, 2012) and ongoing negotiation between adult learning goals and student-led learning. Yet supporting playful learning in schools is one way to bring the culture of childhood and the culture of schooling together. And, because what is playful for one is not necessarily playful for another, to foster playful learning in the classroom, teachers need to know what playful learning looks and feels like.

In this chapter, I provide an overview of the Pedagogy of Play (PoP) project, define key terms, and discuss why educators need a PoP—a systematic approach to the practice and study of playful learning and teaching in school. After an initial snapshot of one group of teachers' efforts to set up the conditions for playful learning, I identify six principles that provide a rationale for a PoP and three cross-cultural indicators of what playful learning in schools looks and feels like. I spend the bulk of the chapter describing five classroom practices and related strategies for teachers who want to support playful learning in their classrooms.

Too many rules on the playground

The rules on the playground at the International School of Billund (ISB) in Denmark include the following: *No going up the slide, trees are not for climbing, no digging outside of the sandbox, no throwing items over the fence.* What would happen if there were fewer rules?

This was the question posed by Marina Benavente Barbon, a member of the ISB Kindergarten Playful Environments Study Group (see Figure 11.1). Over the course of the 2016–2017 school year, Marina and her co-teacher, Carolina Ayala, experimented with replacing a list of ten playground rules with just two: (1) We take care of each other, and (2) we take care of the materials on the playground. Teachers asked the children to create and wear green "freedom bracelets" during outdoor time to remind them of the guidelines. Children rode their bicycles on parts of the playground that were usually off-limits, played ball over the fence, and picked apples from the apple tree, mostly without incident.

Marina and Carolina videotaped short clips of children's play and wrote observations to share with the study group. They posted their documentation and reflections on the study group Padlet (an online collaborative platform) to

Figure 11.1 The playful environments study group

discuss at upcoming meetings. They also shared video clips back with the children. During one study group discussion, several teachers noticed an increase in children's creativity and experimentation. Even though children were doing things not typically allowed, they were still making safe choices. Other teachers expressed concern about the adults' responsibility for children's safety.

Marina and Carolina shared their documentation with the school leadership team. The leadership team was impressed, musing out loud about the relationship between rulemaking and limit-setting and creativity. The head of school noted the key role of trust and freedom in the experiment. Marina believed that the experience enabled children to feel more powerful and competent during outdoor play and that the children were more capable of handling the responsibility than she had thought (see Baker & Benavente Barbon, 2017, for a more detailed description of this experiment). She suggested that next year, before finalizing the rules, those in charge of making the rules spend some time observing children playing and consult with the teachers first.

★★★

Marina and Carolina were teacher-researchers participating in the PoP project, a collaboration between Project Zero (PZ), a research center at the Harvard Graduate School of Education, and the Lego Foundation to reimagine learning in school. The PZ research team investigated three questions:

- Why do educators need a PoP?
- What does playful learning in schools look and feel like?
- How can educators support playful learning in the classroom?

Below, I briefly summarize the PoP project and the research team's responses to the first two questions, but I spend the majority of the chapter on the third question—unpacking classroom practices for supporting playful learning in school.

Overview of the pedagogy of play project

The goal of the PoP project was to develop a systematic and collaborative approach to the practice and study of playful learning and teaching in schools across age groups and subject areas. PoP launched its research in 2015 at ISB, later working with schools in South Africa, the US, and Colombia. Because the research team sees educators as producers of knowledge and valued contributors to research on teaching and learning (Cochran-Smith & Lytle, 1999), our research was highly collaborative in its design, data collection, and iterative analysis across the four research sites. The schools were purposively selected (Miles et al., 2014) based on their commitment to playful learning. Due to challenges related to the Covid-19 pandemic, the number of schools and methodological approaches

Table 11.1 Overview of participants and data sources

Context	Number and types of schools	Number of teachers	Grades taught	Total observations by research team	Total teacher interviews	Total school leader interviews	Total focus groups
Denmark	1 (independent)	40	Preschool to Grade 8	40	80	8	12
S. Africa	3 (2 public, 1 independent)	11	Preschool to Grade 8	92	33	8	2
US	6 (4 public, 2 independent)	22	Kindergarten to Grade 9	88	40	12	1
Colombia	5 (4 public, 1 independent)	17	Preschool to Grade 7	96	48	15	N/A

in each country varied (see Table 11.1 for an overview of participants and data sources). In Denmark, we combined ethnography with a form of action research called *Playful Participatory Research* (*PPR*), reflected in the opening vignette. In the other three countries, we used ethnographic, qualitative, and action research approaches, collecting data from semi-structured interviews with teachers, school leaders, and learners; classroom observations of learning through play; and focus groups with learners.

Definition of terms

There are many ways to define terms and concepts like play, learning, and playful learning. As a research team, we reached consensus on the below definitions.

- In the PoP research, we view *play* along a continuum, from free play (minimal guidance or support) to guided play, with purposeful adult support (Zosh et al., 2018). Weisberg et al. (2016, p. 177) define guided play as "learning experiences that combine the child-directed nature of free play with a focus on learning outcomes and adult mentorship."
- In our view, *learning* is a consequence of thinking, not just the transmission of a body of knowledge (Perkins, 1992). Learners need to think *about* and *with* the content of what they are learning.
- *Playful learning* in schools is always a negotiation between adult learning goals and student-directed learning. Rinaldi and Moss' (2004, p. 2) description of learning in the municipal preschools of Reggio Emilia, Italy, conveys what such negotiation entails:

  > *Learning is not the transmission of a defined body of knowledge… It is constructive, the subject constructing her or his own knowledge but always in democratic relationships with others and being open to different ways of seeing, since individual knowledge is always partial and provisional. From this perspective, learning is a process of constructing, testing and reconstructing theories, constantly creating new knowledge….*

- *PPR* is a relatively new form of research that engages teachers in playful activities to promote creative thinking and ideas to try out in the classroom with a playful mindset (Baker & Davila, 2018; Baker & Ryan, 2021). In *PPR*, teachers identify research questions (in this case, about play and learning) that are relevant for their practice. Teachers form study groups, test ideas in their classrooms, observe and record children's play and learning, and bring selected artifacts to the study group to collectively analyze and discuss implications both for the presenting teacher and for teaching and learning more generally (see also Cochran-Smith & Lytle, 1999, 2009; Weinbaum et al., 2004).
- The process of gathering artifacts that make thinking or learning visible can be referred to as *documentation* or *pedagogical documentation*, which we define as the practice of *observing, recording, interpreting, and sharing the processes and products of learning in different media in order to deepen learning* (Krechevsky et al., 2013). With the support of documentation, *PPR* can help teachers navigate the paradoxes or what Kuschner (2012) calls the "unremitting contradictions" that inevitably arise between the nature of play and the nature of school.

Question 1: *Why do educators need a pedagogy of play?*

The first question we addressed is why educators need a PoP. Based on a review of the literature, conversations with educators and researchers around the world, interviews with educators and students in the four research sites, and much deliberation among the PoP research team, we identified the six principles in Table 11.2 as the foundation for a PoP (Mardell et al., 2023).

A significant body of research shows that play supports children's intellectual, social, emotional, and physical development (Copple & Bredekamp, 2009; Hirsch-Pasek et al., 2009; Zosh et al., 2018). Play fosters intrinsic motivation, imagination, active engagement, and risk-taking, enhancing brain structure and function (Yogman et al., 2018; *principle 1*). However, when play *enters school*, it encounters externally determined standards and learning goals shaped by adults. This is not to say there is never room for free play in school, but rather, in school, play becomes a strategy for learning the knowledge, skills, and dispositions deemed important for becoming contributing members of society 2). At the

Table 11.2 Six principles of a Pedagogy of Play

PoP Principles
1. Play supports learning.
2. Playful learning in school involves play with a purpose.
3. Paradoxes between play and school add complexity to teaching and learning.
4. Playful learning is universal and shaped by culture.
5. Playful mindsets are central to playful learning.
6. Supportive school cultures enable playful learning to thrive.

same time, several paradoxes appear that complicate the dialogue between teaching and learning (Kuschner, 2012), for example,

- Play is timeless, with players often losing themselves in play, whereas school is timetabled.
- Play can be chaotic, messy, and noisy, whereas schools are expected to be places of order.
- Play involves taking risks, whereas schools are designed to keep children safe.
- In play, children are in charge, whereas in school, the agenda is often set by adults.

Although these paradoxes will never go away (*principle 3*), they can be fruitfully explored by educators to better understand and address them in their setting. The kindergarten teachers in the opening anecdote took on the tension around rules by systematically gathering documentation of children's activity to further investigate and navigate the paradox.

In addition, although play and playful learning are universal, they are also shaped by culture, which means each school needs to arrive at a shared understanding of what playful learning looks and feels like in its own context (*principle 4*). Children and adults also benefit from a playful mindset or disposition to frame experiences as occasions for joy, curiosity, and creativity. Designing experiences that foster such a mindset is essential to playful learning for children and adults (*principle 5*). Finally, to create a culture of playful learning for children, schools need to provide a culture of playful learning for adults, in which they can take "responsible risks," such as Marina and Carolina questioning the need for so many rules on the playground. School leaders and administrators need to foster a playful and supportive school culture for adults, just as teachers strive to create in their classrooms (*principle 6*).

Question 2: *What does playful learning in schools look and feel like?*

The fourth PoP principle – that playful learning is both universal and culturally specific – is connected to our second research question, *what does playful learning in schools look and feel like?* because what is playful to one is not necessarily playful to another. In order to know whether playful learning is taking place, one needs to look at both what playful learning *looks* like (observable behaviors) and what it *feels* like (psychological states, as reported by the learner). Based on a review of the literature on play and learning, classroom observations, and semi-structured interviews and focus groups of teachers, school leaders, and students at the different research sites, we co-developed with teachers the four sets of indicators shown in

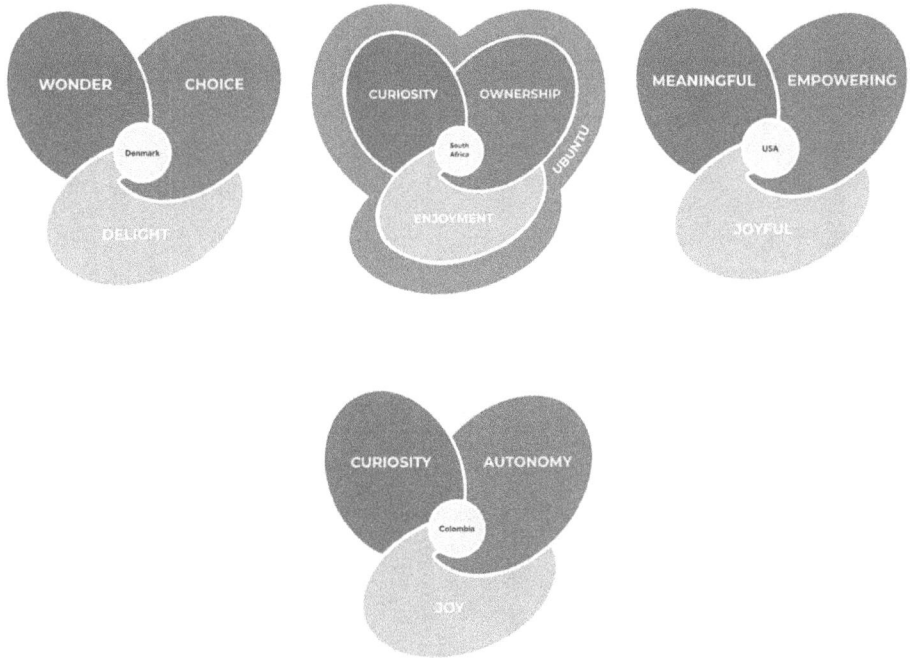

Figure 11.2 Playful learning indicators from schools in Denmark, South Africa, the US, and Colombia

Figure 11.2 (see Mardell et al., 2023 for more information; see also O'Neill and Stjerne-Thomson chapter in this book).

Playful learning is most likely to occur at the intersection of the indicators in each model, though even in the most playful of classrooms, not all indicators will be visible or felt all the time. Each indicator also has a number of *markers* that describe in greater detail what playful learning looks and feels like. For example, at ISB in Denmark, wonder *feels like* engagement, curiosity, and surprise, and it *looks like* asking questions, pretending, and inventing (see Figure 11.3). Choice *feels like* autonomy, empowerment, and ownership and it *looks like* setting goals, being spontaneous, and making and changing rules. In South Africa, the philosophy of *ubuntu* (a sense of harmony, compassion, and interconnectedness, summarized by Desmond Tutu as "a person is a person through other people") underlies all three indicators. The support of other people makes ownership, curiosity, and enjoyment possible (see Mardell et al., 2023 for a complete list of indicators and markers).

To generate cross-cultural indicators, we conducted a meta-review of the indicators and markers across the four research sites. After reanalyzing the data and getting feedback from educators involved in co-creating the first sets of indicators, we identified three cross-cultural indicators of playful learning: *Learners leading*

Indicators of Playful Learning from the International School of Billund in Denmark

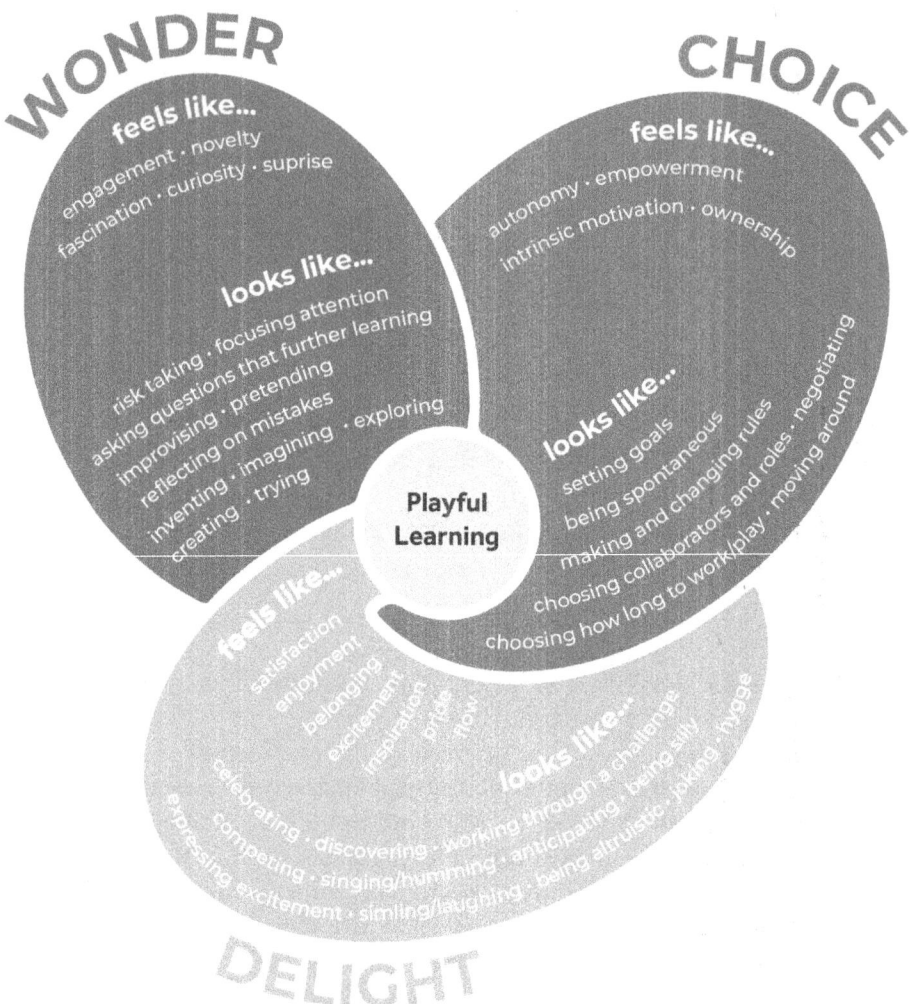

Figure 11.3 Indicators and markers of playful learning at the International School of Billund, Denmark

Source: © 2022. President and Fellows of Harvard College. The ISB indicators were developed by Pedagogy of Play at Project Zero. Inspired by research at the International School of Billund and funded by the LEGO Foundation, the work is licensed under Creative Commons Attribution-NonCommercial-ShareAlike 4.0 International.

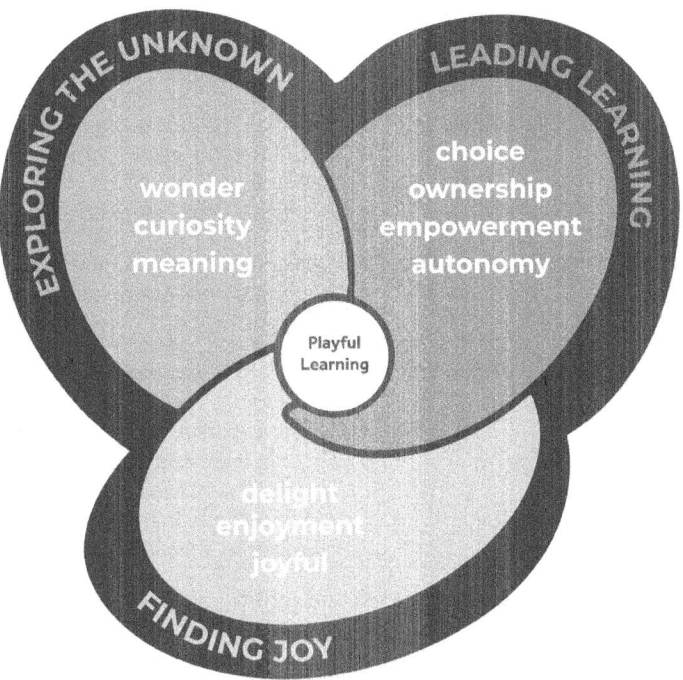

Figure 11.4 Cross-cultural indicators of playful learning

learning, exploring the unknown, and *finding joy in learning* (see Figure 11.4). We also created a *Playful Learning Indicators Research Guide* to help educators in any context develop indicators for their own setting (Mardell et al., 2023). A collective understanding of playful learning can ground conversations about incorporating a PoP in classrooms and schools and provide a shared reference point when planning for and assessing playful learning.

Question 3: *How can educators support playful learning in the classroom?*

Once educators have a shared understanding of what playful learning looks like and how to tell when it is happening, the question becomes how to support playful learning in the classroom. Based on our collaboration with educators from around the globe, our own teaching experiences, and multiple iterations of playful learning practices, we identified five classroom practices, along with related strategies and tools, that foster learning through play from preschool through middle school

Table 11.3 Playful learning classroom practices and strategies

Practices	Strategies
Empower learners to lead their own learning	■ Gel to know your learners ■ Involve learners in decision-making ■ Reflect on learning with learners
Build a culture of collaborative learning	■ Use play to build relationships ■ Facilitate purposeful conversations to build knowledge ■ Foster a culture of feedback
Promote experimentation and risk-taking	■ Design open-ended investigations ■ Encourage risk-taking as a strategy for learning
Encourage imaginative thinking	■ Share stories to engage and enhance learning ■ Use role-play and pretend scenarios ■ Provide materials and experiences that engage the senses and the body ■ Ask questions that invite curiosity and imaginative thinking
Welcome all emotions generated through play	■ Design for joy ■ Use play to explore complex issues ■ Support learners in working through frustration

(see Table 11.3). At the same time, we invite the readers of this book to "hack" the tools to best fit their own settings (see *License to Hack Cards* in Appendix). The remainder of this chapter focuses on the five practices.

Practice #1: Empower learners to lead their own learning

Empowering learners to lead their own learning entails tipping the balance of responsibility for learning toward learners. It involves both making plans and a willingness to modify plans and considering which aspects of learning might be productively turned over to students (with adult guidance). While teachers need to balance learning objectives with facilitating play with a purpose, students can often drive learning in ways that move thinking forward. In the opening anecdote, Marina and Carolina sought to empower children by reducing the number of playground rules so they could experience more choice, wonder, and delight. Children felt trusted, they required less adult supervision, and no trees or equipment were damaged during the experiment. Three strategies in particular empower learners to direct their learning: *Getting to know your learners, involving learners in decision-making*, and *reflecting on learning*. Many of the strategies come with teaching tools to support teachers in putting the ideas into practice (see Appendix).

Getting to know your learners refers to asking learners questions about their strengths, passions, and lives outside of school so teachers can design learning experiences connected to their abilities and interests. At the beginning of the school year, Liz Caffrey, a middle school math teacher in Boston (US), asks students to write her a letter about their lives and answer questions like, "As a math learner, how do you learn best? What do you do for fun? Tell me a math story from your life." Liz uses this information when choosing which current events involving math to discuss, such as sports, baking, or immigration, as well as for informing her teaching more generally.

Teachers can *involve learners in decision-making* by seeking their input into three aspects of learning: The *content* (or what they are learning), the *process* (or how they are learning), and the learning *product* (or how they show what they know). Learners can also have input into decisions such as the set-up of classroom space, norms, whom to work with, and ways to greet each other. A study group of middle school teachers at ISB decided to replace two weeks of the standard school schedule by asking students to create their own schedules. Apart from a required morning and afternoon meeting, students could choose when during the day to schedule their subjects. Teachers gave students the assignments and estimated time frames and made themselves available for support. Although the experiment got off to a rocky start, and some students found it stressful, most enjoyed choosing when, where, and with whom to work; they were eager to help each other; and they began to assume more responsibility for their learning (see Krechevsky et al., 2019).

Learning is not a linear process, and playful learning is full of serendipity and surprises. To learn through play, learners need to *reflect on learning*, which also empowers them to lead their own learning by deepening their knowledge of ideas and content and supporting their understanding of how they learn. Note that there is a difference between reflecting on playful learning and making the reflection process itself playful. Because learners differ in what they find playful, giving them a choice of format for reflection can be helpful. Marina and Carolina engage the children in reflection when they share video clips from their documentation to ground a discussion about playing with fewer rules on the playground.

Practice #2: Build a culture of collaborative learning

Feelings of playful learning are often activated and sustained by being part of a group. Playful learning is enhanced when players exchange, build on, or disagree with each other's ideas. The three indicators of ownership, curiosity, and enjoyment in South African schools are all grounded in the South African concept of *ubuntu*, which emphasizes a person's humanity through their community with other people (see Figure 11.4). Rinaldi and Moss (2004) describe learners building knowledge in democratic relationships with others, which entails constructing, testing, and reconstructing theories while remaining open to other points of view. To build a culture of collaborative learning in the classroom, three strategies are particularly useful: *Using play to build relationships, facilitating purposeful conversations to build knowledge,* and *fostering a culture of feedback*.

There are many ways to *use play to build relationships*. Relationship-building does not just happen during recess or free choice time. It also happens while learning academic content knowledge and skills. Teachers can support this relationship-building by

- putting more thought into the composition of small groups;
- asking learners to turn and talk before responding to questions posed by the teacher;
- referring learners to their peers, rather than answering a student's question themselves; and
- pausing before intervening in a conflict to see if students can work out the issue on their own.

Teachers might also want to review individual learning experiences more generally to decide whether reframing them as collaborative might deepen the quality of learning. Listening for and making visible the language of collaboration in the classroom also supports a culture of playful learning ("How do you want to start?"; "What's your idea?").

PZ has developed a set of thinking routines that are useful for *facilitating purposeful conversations to build knowledge*. The routines provide supportive structures for learners to explore, synthesize, or dig deeper into ideas (see *Selecting a Thinking Routine* in Appendix). At the Nova Pioneer Ormonde School in South Africa, rather than provide an official definition of informational texts, fifth grade teacher Firdous Ismail Korolia invites students to discuss their own definitions in small groups (see Figure 11.5). When the small groups are ready to share their definitions with the whole group, Firdous asks the students to call on each other to speak.

Figure 11.5 A small group discussing their definitions of informational texts

A lively debate about the relationship between facts and fiction ensues when one student claims that Spiderman spinning webs from his hands is a fact, even though Spiderman is a fictional character. Firdous expands the discussion further by asking students to share the debate with their families (Mardell et al., 2023).

Such conversations can be described as playful because they engage the learners' minds and emotions in a fact-finding quest for knowledge. The purpose of the conversation is not just to share what children already know but also to create new knowledge. This type of exchange also *fosters a culture of feedback* which is instrumental to supporting playful learning. Rather than serving as the primary source of knowledge, teachers encourage children to enlist the cognitive contributions and emotional support of their peers. Above all, teachers want children to experience the *desire* to communicate by providing compelling opportunities to express curiosity, wonder, and joy.

Practice #3: Promote experimentation and risk-taking

For classrooms to support playful learning for children, schools need to support playful learning for adults. Marina and Carolina take a risk by posing their question about fewer rules on the playground. When they introduce children to the idea of research, they are transparent about their wish to try something new. Evolutionary biologists believe that play evolved to provide a safe way to try out new behaviors and ideas (Bateson & Martin, 2013). Schools exist, in part, as safe places for children (and adults) to experiment, make mistakes, and learn from failure. Many of the practices and strategies for supporting learning through play require teachers to take some degree of risk (e.g., letting learners lead their learning without a predetermined outcome). *Designing open-ended investigations* and *encouraging risk-taking* are strategies that promote mindsets where children try out ideas and don't give up when the going gets hard. Marina and Carolina model this type of experimentation when they share the documentation from their experiment with the children. The children end up surprising their teachers by continuing to make safe choices—even inventing their own safety rules.

Rather than use a textbook activity on frame structures (structures with a combination of beams, columns, and slabs that can resist lateral and gravity loads), Ntombifuthi Chiloane, a natural science and technology teacher at the Esikhisini Primary School in Pretoria, South Africa, creates an open-ended investigation for her 11-year-old learners. The textbook had suggested that each student make and strength-test a triangle and two other shapes using struts made from paper. Instead, Ntombifuthi gives her class of 40 a variety of materials and challenges them to make any structure they want, as long as it is "strong." Almost all the children choose to work in small groups to make the strongest structure, with some groups more collaborative and some more competitive. The students produce a range of structures, from windmills to the human skeleton, using different methods for achieving stability. Afterward, children reflect on which structures were more or less stable and why.

Teachers like Ntombifuthi normalize risk-taking and making mistakes by celebrating them as opportunities to learn and try again and by facilitating conversation about the relationship between taking risks and learning. Such moments can also be celebrated with a special cheer or a silly dance. Sitting with and working through challenge is a critical life skill. When teachers resist the urge to solve problems for their students, they contribute to setting up a culture of experimentation and risk-taking (see *Creating a Classroom Culture of Risk-taking* in Appendix).

Practice #4: Encourage imaginative thinking

Engaging the imagination invites learners to explore, envision, invent, and take different perspectives. Strategies to support imaginative thinking in the classroom include *sharing stories to engage and enhance learning, using role-play and pretend scenarios, providing materials and experiences that engage the senses and the body,* and *asking questions that invite curiosity and imaginative thinking.*

Sharing stories and *using role-play and pretend scenarios* provide meaningful frames for learners across age groups to explore knowledge, experiences, and ideas from different perspectives. For primary classrooms, Vivian Gussin Paley's Storytelling/Story Acting is a popular approach for dictating and acting out stories (Cooper, 2009). For older students, teachers might ask that they tell a story about a time they felt like a scientist or act out a story using their new mathematical knowledge in a real-life situation. Role-play and pretend scenarios engage children's imagination while exploring different viewpoints and subject areas. PZ's perspective-taking thinking routines foster students' capacity to look beyond their own point of view to consider the thoughts, feelings, and experiences of others.

Providing materials and experiences that engage the senses and the body also encourages imaginative thinking. The children in Marina and Carolina's class became enchanted with the simple green bracelets signifying the guidelines for their new freedom. Simple and affordable materials like cardboard, paper, stones, leaves, and paperclips support learners to explore and represent ideas in new ways, making their thinking visible to themselves and others. Older students can be asked to create a model of a system they are studying or to represent a key idea in a chapter using a medium that doesn't involve language. Moving parts of the body or using chants or gestures can also make repetition and memorization engaging and fun.

Finally, *asking questions that invite curiosity and imaginative thinking* provokes wonder and curiosity. Consider the difference between asking a child, "*What are the phases of the moon?*" and "*What have you noticed about the moon?*". Questions with multiple answers or without definitive answers encourage learners to play with ideas and normalize the experience of uncertainty in life (see *Imaginative Sparks Generator* in Appendix for questions that inspire imaginative thinking). Teachers can identify what children wonder about by observing their play and interactions over time. Making questions visible on a classroom wall serves as a reminder to stay curious and seek meaning. Questions like *where do ideas come from?* and *how do stories connect us?* open up opportunities for further learning.

Practice #5: Welcome all emotions generated through play

Play produces a range of emotions from enjoyment and exhilaration to frustration and despair. Deep learning involves this same range of emotions. The neuroscientist Mary Helen Immordino-Yang (2015) says "it is literally neurobiologically impossible to think deeply about things that you don't care about." There are many ways to design learning experiences to create feelings of belonging, ownership, wonder, and pride. Different experiences will appeal to different students so offering choice can be helpful. Three strategies for welcoming and valuing a variety of emotions are *designing for joy, using play to explore complex issues*, and *supporting learners in working through frustration*.

Recommending that school should be joyful does not mean we do not take learning seriously. We do. But it is important not to confuse taking schooling seriously with removing joy and pleasure from the learning process. We lament the absence of delight in too many schools. Creating the green freedom bracelets brought Marina's kindergartners unanticipated pleasure and delight. *Designing for joy* can include posing puzzles and challenges, the use of novel materials, engaging in games or team competitions, redesigning the classroom, or asking students to do any of these. Starting class by posting a provocative image, quote, or riddle on the wall related to the topic you're teaching or transforming the classroom into a *salon* or a courtroom captures students' curiosity and imagination. When starting a unit on the rainforest, ISB middle school teacher Tue Rabenhoj dimmed the lights and played the sounds of the rainforest as students entered the room.

Play can also help children find the courage to face and explore difficult topics—even in conditions of extreme distress such as the World War II concentration camps, children still engaged in play (Solis et al., 2020). Children regularly incorporate themes of violence and terror in their play. They have the right to learn about challenging topics like climate change, war, and economic and racial inequities. But this does not mean "anything goes." Such topics can lead to feelings of sadness and anger, especially for children with a history of trauma. At the same time, play offers a way for children to experience empathy, encounter and try on different perspectives, and imagine alternative outcomes. *Using play to explore complex issues* benefits from trust and a safe space where students feel comfortable sharing their thoughts and feelings.

When learners are fully engaged in learning through play, negotiating ideas and resources with others can pose a challenge. Learning through play can generate feelings of discontent and exasperation as well as satisfaction. Yet conflict and frustration are also occasions for learning. *Supporting learners in working through frustration* can take many forms, from validating the emotions and slowing things down to encouraging listening and collaborative problem-solving. Reflecting on what just occurred is also important. The aim is not to eliminate uncomfortable feelings but to help learners stay in a productive and safe space where they can feel the emotions and still take risks to solve problems. (See *Supporting Learners with Conflict and Frustration* in Appendix.)

Concluding note

In a complex and uncertain world, a PoP holds out hope for an educational approach that prepares young people for the known and the unknown—where self-directed learning can thrive within the constraints of a school schedule, where children's interests and passions are both honored and aligned with standards-based curricula, and where responsible experimentation and healthy risk-taking take place in a stable and nurturing environment. To be clear, a PoP does not suggest that all learning must be playful, nor that all play entails significant learning, but rather, that play is a powerful strategy for learning (as Susan MacKay argues) that brings together cognitive, social, and emotional qualities that enhance learning (D. Perkins, personal communication, May 8, 2016). Or, in the words of Vea Vecchi, a veteran *atelierista* from the Reggio Emilia preschools, *"Rationality without feeling and empathy, like imagination without cognition and rationality, build up partial, incomplete human knowledge."* If we can combine rationality *with* feeling and empathy and imagination *with* cognition and rationality, we will be better equipped to participate meaningfully and productively in personal and civic life.

For more information on the PoP project, see www.pz.harvard.edu/projects/pedagogy-of-play. The site includes a free and downloadable book designed for classroom teachers and school leaders (Mardell et al., 2023). The book summarizes the PoP research, includes illustrated pictures of classroom practice, offers practices and tools that support learning through play, and contains two guides—one for developing indicators of playful learning in diverse contexts (*Playful Learning Indicators Research Guide*) and one for carrying out PPR in which educators engage in playful activities to identify questions and things to try in the classroom, supported by documentation (*PPR Guide*). The site also contains numerous papers and additional examples of classroom practice. A second website (www.pz.harvard.edu/pop-teacher-education-resources) is intended for teacher educators. It includes a detailed, free, downloadable instructor guide for a 14-week course based on the three core questions of PoP. Materials include a course syllabus along with PowerPoint slides for each session, activity cards and assignments, suggested readings, and a video library from a range of age groups and locations. There is also contact information for a worldwide network of teacher educators.

Key take-aways from the chapter

- Supporting playful learning in schools is one way to bring the culture of childhood and the culture of schooling together.
- Playful learning in schools requires navigating a series of paradoxes between the nature of school and the nature of play.
- Playful learning in schools is a negotiation between adult learning goals and student-led learning.
- To foster playful learning in schools, you need to know what playful learning looks and feels like; what is playful for one is not necessarily playful for another.
- For classrooms to support playful learning for children, schools need to support playful learning for adults.

Acknowledgements

The Pedagogy of Play Project was supported by generous grants from the Lego Foundation. I am deeply grateful to Ben Mardell and Jen Ryan for many helpful comments on a previous draft of this chapter.

References

Baker, M. and Benavente Barbon, M. (2017). *Too Many Rules on the Playground: Working the Paradox between Safety and Freedom*. Picture of Practice. Project Zero and International School of Billund.

Baker, M. and Davila, G. (2018) Inquiry Is Play: Playful Participatory Research. *Voices of Practitioners, Young Children*, 73(5), 64–71.

Baker, M. and Ryan, J. (2021): Playful provocations and playful mindsets: teacher learning and identity shifts through playful participatory research, *International Journal of Play*, DOI: 10.1080/21594937.2021.1878770. To link to this article: https://doi.org/10.1080/21594937.2021.1878770

Barnett, L. and Owens, M. (2015). Does play have to be playful? In J. Johnson, S. Eberle, T. Henricks and D. Kuschner (eds), *The Handbook of the Study of Play* (pp. 453–459). Lanham/Boulder/New York/London: Rowman & Littlefield.

Bateson, P.P.G. and Martin, P. (2013). *Play, Playfulness, Creativity and Innovation*. Cambridge; New York: Cambridge University Press.

Cochran-Smith, M. and Lytle, S. (1999) Relationships of Knowledge and Practice: Teacher Learning in Communities, *Review of Research in Education*, 24(1), 249–305.

Cochran-Smith, M. and Lytle, S. (2009) *Inquiry as Stance: Practitioner Research for the Next Generation*. New York: Teachers College Press.

Cooper, P. (2009). *The Classrooms All Young Children Need: Lessons in Teaching from Vivian Paley* Chicago: University of Chicago Press.

Copple, C. and Bredekamp, S. (2009). *Developmentally Appropriate Practice in Early Childhood Programs Serving Children from Birth through Age 8* (3rd ed.). Washington D.C.: National Association for the Education of Young Children.

Hirsh-Pasek, K., Golinkoff, R.M., Berk, L.E. and Singer, D.G. (2009). *A Mandate for Playful Learning in Preschool: Presenting the Evidence*. Oxford University Press.

Immordino-Yang, M. (2015). *Emotions, Learning, and the Brain: Exploring the Educational Implications of Affective Neuroscience*. New York: Norton.

Krechevsky, M., with Baldwin, M., Rodriguez, M., Christensen, L., Jorgensen, M., Jorgensen, O., Krishnadas, S., Overgaard, S. & Rabenhoj, T. (2019). "Frankly It's A Gamble": What Happens When Middle School Students Compose their Own Schedules? *Scottish Educational Review* 51(2), 71–89.

Krechevsky, M., Mardell, B., Rivard, M. and Wilson, D. (2013). *Visible Learners: Using Reggio-inspired Approaches in All Classrooms*, San Francisco: Jossey-Bass.

Kuschner, D. (2012). Play is Natural to Childhood but School is Not: The Problem of Integrating Play into the Curriculum, *International Journal of Play*, 1(3), 242–249.

Mardell, B., Ryan, J., Krechevsky, M., Baker, M., Schulz, S. and Liu-Constant, Y. (2023). *A Pedagogy of Play: Supporting Playful Learning in Classrooms and Schools*.

Miles, M., Huberman, M. and Saldana, J. (2014). *Qualitative Data Analysis: A Methods Sourcebook. Third Edition*. SAGE Publications.

Perkins, D. Personal communication to Jen Ryan, May 8, 2016

Perkins, D. (1992). *Smart Schools: From Training Memories to Educating Minds*. New York; Toronto: Free Press; Macmillan Canada.

Rinaldi, C. and Moss, P. (2004). "What is Reggio?" *Children in Europe: Celebrating 40 years of Reggio Emilia-the Pedagogical Thought and Practice Underlying the World-renowned Early Services in Italy*. March 2004. Scotland. Children in Scotland (p2)

Solis, L., Liu, C. and Popp, J. (2020). Learning to Cope through Play. https://cms.learningthroughplay.com/media/jqifsynb/learning-to-cope-through-play.pdf.

Weinbaum, A., Allen, D., Blythe, T. and Simon, K. (2004). *Teaching as Inquiry: Asking Hard Questions to Improve Practice and Student Achievement*. New York: Teachers College Press.

Weisberg, D., Hirsh-Pasek, K., Golinkoff, R., Kittredge, A. and Klahr, D. (2016). Guided Play: Principles and Practices. *Current Directions in Psychological Science* 25 (3): 177–82; p.177.

Yogman, M., Garner, A., Hutchinson, J., Hirsh-Pasek, K. and Golinkoff, R. (2018). American Association of Pediatrics Committee on Psychosocial Aspects of Child and Family Health, Council on Communications and Media. The Power of Play: A Pediatric Role in Enhancing Development in Young Children. *Pediatrics*; *142*(3):e20182058.

Zosh, J., Hirsh-Pasek, K., Hopkins, E. and Jensen, H. (2018). Accessing the Inaccessible: Redefining Play as a Spectrum, *Frontiers in Psychology*, *9*:1124, 1–12. doi:10.3389/fpsyg.2018.01124

Zosh, J., Hassinger-Das, B. and Laurie, M. (2022). *Learning Through Play and the Development of Holistic Skills Across Childhood*. Lego Foundation.

Appendix A Sample Tools for PoP Practices

(see Mardell et al., 2023, for the complete set of tools)

- Empower learners to lead their own learning: **License to Hack Cards**
- Build a culture of collaborative learning: **Selecting a Thinking Routine**
- Promote experimentation and risk-taking: **Creating a Classroom Culture of Risk-taking**
- Encourage imaginative thinking: **Imaginative Sparks Generator**
- Welcome all emotions generated through play: **Supporting Learners with Conflict and Frustration**

[I]t's wrong to think of play as the interruption of ordinary life. Consider instead playing as the underlying, always there, continuum of experience … Ordinary life is netted out of playing but play continually squeezes through even the smallest holes … [W]ork and other activities constantly feed on the underlying ground of playing, using the play mood for refreshment, unusual ways of turning things around, insights, breaks, openings and especially looseness.

(Schechner, 1988: 16)

Play is for children not for school

James Biddulph

Can you remember what it was like to play when you were a child? What did it feel like? What did you think, talk about, imagine, create, laugh about and embody? And when was the last time you played as an adult? What type of play? When? With whom? This book, within a series of books about research-informed practices, aims to challenge, deepen and expand our thinking about the purpose of play in schools, as a pedagogy and as a practice for children and adults.

Children often visit my office, in a school where I am Executive Headteacher. On one wet Wednesday lunchtime, three children came (drenched, laughing and confidently telling me they were wet and that it was wet play time). They stood by my radiator and asked, "what did you play in the olden days?" I asked how old they thought I was (I won't reveal their answers). But it was an interesting question. What did I play when I was their age? The first thing that came to mind is this:

> I remember cycling down the valley to the stream and fields. The only two rules my parents had were to be back by 5pm and to not come back escorted by the police. At the river (which was the boundary to an imagined world of Kingdoms and evil creatures), we collected heavy stones (which were boulders dragged by prisoners and Elephant-type animals) and created a dam to stop the flow of the mighty river (or was this a bridge or portal to the next battle scene?) My brother was Chief of the Military and I (being the older brother) was King Wizard of all the Domains and told him what to do. Adults passed alongside the river, smiling. Little did they know that we were in a bloody battle for the survival of humanity. The dam stopped the flow of the stream and soon the water was rising, overspilling onto the river pathway and trickling towards the open door of the public house restaurant. When the water was quicker flowing towards the adult diners in the pub, did our imaginations falter, as we saw the red faced landlord stomping towards the door, the river and us. We scarpered, hiding in the poppy fields, sweaty, laughing and excited that we had escaped (and beaten the evil creatures). Rule number two: do not get escorted home by the police.

In this personal reflection, the value of immersion, without adult direction or interference, seems important. As an adult I would observe this moment as 'two children playing by a stream'. However, we were never actually in the valley by a stream. Instead, we were transported to another world that was purely made, evoked through our language and embodied in the ways we splashed and fell, and pushed and grabbed one another; in the ways that we sat in silence, crafting the wall to dam the stream; or in the ways we stood back and looked at our creation. What is the playful quality and value in this moment? Why has it remained in my memory? This is one version of play and we have seen in the diverse chapters herein, the multiplicity and diversity of play enactments.

Of course, children play. But should *schools* be places of playfulness? In an educational world in which the discourse is polarised, for example that creativity and high standards are mutually exclusive, and in which one form of knowledge is reified as the key purpose and function of education, how does play become part of the waft and weave in the fabric of educational possibilities?

Of course, adults also have the propensity to play. But should *schools* be places of playfulness in professional learning and development? In Biddulph and Cariss (2021) we suggest that developing awareness of the ways educators see themselves, reflect and engage in meaningful discussion as a community allows for more playful, imaginative and creative possibilities. I have also suggested ways in which we suspend our role as expert, as educator or school leader, and to approach the life of school and education from the position of a stranger (Biddulph and Baldacchino, 2023). In so doing, there is an opportunity to look again at our practices, to consider better responses to persistent issues or to focus on different ways in which we work. Teachers do see play as essential and positive, although there is a "certain hesitation regarding play in the school world. Play during breaks was one thing, but play used in teaching was not seen as equally natural" (Sandberg and Heden, 2011: p.236). While drama, games, physical activities involve play as structured and rules based, the development of freer forms of play are less obviously intertwined in the life of UK schools. How does the teacher, from a pedagogical standpoint, try to bring play into teaching?

There is a difference in the ways child and adult enact their play, however. The authors in this book have suggested various development points to expand play in the educational experience of children in school. There is also a real tension between fostering playfulness in school in a way that does not reduce the robust standards-driven accountabilities – and this takes effort, development of systems of evaluation and assessment and, importantly, clear professional learning that deepens our collective understanding of play, of children's play, of the neuroscience of play, the social constructionist view of play, the cultural understanding of play and the diverse ways in which it is expressed and lived out in the realities of our diverse social communities. John Hattie builds an evidence-based awareness of the impact of play, suggesting that the place of play in enhancing achievement has long been cited and seems very powerful (Hattie, 2009). For younger children, play makes a difference. And the difference is likely to be related to learning about peer relationship and learning from peers in meeting and facing challenges, the consequences of deliberative practice in play and the satisfaction from deciding or becoming aware of the learning that occurs during play.

In the end, as adults, we must stop playing with children's childhoods. The Cambridge Primary Review (Alexander, 2010) suggested that primary education should enable children to "encounter and begin to explore the wealth of human experience…through the different ways through which humans make sense of their world and act upon it: intellectual, moral, spiritual, aesthetic, social, emotional and physical…" (Alexander, 2010: p.258). Furthermore, we must be playful in creating playful opportunities for children to engage in play within school, formally and informally, with and without adult intervention. Children's habitus is to play. Our role, as educators, is to consider how we engage with them with humility, curiosity, questioning and the capacity to suspend disbelief and be swept along in the various playful ways in which they naturally engage in their worlds. Play is not only for children. It is also for the adults who educate them. In modelling the capacity to occupy 'spaces of uncertainty' (Biddulph and Baldacchino, 2023), to face challenges, to consider new ways of engaging in the world, to ask bigger, better questions, to suspend what we believe to think about what might be is to engage the social imagination. Play is for schools because schools are highly intense social places – and schools that are playful could nurture more healthy, balanced, mentally robust people who can together face the challenges of an uncertain world.

References

Alexander, R. (Ed.) (2010). *Children, Their World, Their Education: Final Report and Recommendations of the Cambridge Primary Review.* London: Routledge.

Biddulph, J., & Baldacchino, J. (2023). Wilful strangers in a possible democracy. In Biddulph, J. Rolls, L. and Flutter, J. (Eds.), *Unleashing Children's Voices in New Democratic Primary Education* (p. xxxx). London: Routledge.

Biddulph, J., & Burnard, P. (2021). Storying the journey to new spaces of intercultural creative learning. In Burnard, P. & Loughery, M. (Eds.), *Sculpting New Creativities in Primary Education* (pp. 45–61). London: Routledge.

Biddulph, J. & Carris, J. (2020). Creative Ways of Learning. In Hargreaves, E. and Rolls, L. (Eds). *Reimagining professional development in schools.* Routledge.

Hattie, J. (2009) *Visible Learning: A Synthesis of Over 800 Meta-Analysis Relating to Achievement.* London: Routledge

Sandberg, A., & Heden, R. (2011). Play's importance in school. *Education 3–13, 39*(3), 317–329.

Appendix

License to Hack Cards

Inviting learners to shape the learning process

It is up to you and your learners to determine which playful learning experiences work best. The License to Hack Cards, originally developed by educators at the University College Lillebælt in Denmark, gives your learners permission to change any part of a learning experience to create increased ownership of learning. (The text on the example here translates to "You have permission to change the learning process in order to make it more meaningful or deepen learning.") Here are some ideas about how to use License to Hack Cards with learners of any age:

- Print cards on playing-card-sized paper and distribute them to your learners at the start of a learning experience. Explain that they can "play" their card at any point in the learning experience if they have an idea of how to make the learning better for themselves or for the group.
- Create a poster-sized version to hang in your classroom after introducing the idea to your learners.
- Ask your learners, "How else do you think we could use a License to Hack? What ideas do you have?" (For younger learners, first explain the idea and share examples of times you or they have "hacked.")

© 2021. President and Fellows of Harvard College. License to Hack Cards was developed by Pedagogy of Play at Project Zero. Funded by the LEGO Foundation, the work is licensed under Creative Commons Attribution-NonCommercial-ShareAlike 4.0 International.

- Reflect on the hacks. Ask students if the hack supported learning (make sure the judgment is about the hack and not the hacker).
- Keep a card for yourself too, and give yourself license to hack as you plan and teach your curriculum!

More than one way

- If the word "hack" does not feel right in your context, engage your students in considering other options, e.g., *License to Improvise, License to Suggest New Ideas, License to Adapt, License to Try Something Different, License to....* [add your own framing].
- Give a small number of cards to a group of learners for the year. Tell them they need to reach an agreement about how best to use them.
- Experiment with other ways for learners to shape the learning experience that will work best for them, such as "This card entitles me to ... work on my own right now," "...work past the end time," "...make as many mistakes as I need to," "...try and fail," "...take a 5-minute break," or "...seek help from another student or teacher...."
- Introduce families to the idea of a license to hack. Encourage them to consider how their child might hack one aspect of their home life, e.g., how chores are carried out or how furniture is organized, in order to make it more fun, fair, or functional. Like at school, adults continue to have the final say. Invite families to share what their children came up with.

Appendix

To learn more about the Pedagogy of Play project visit *http://pz.harvard.edu/projects/pedagogy-of-play*.

Selecting a Thinking Routine

A menu of routines for facilitating knowledge-building conversations

Exploring ideas

- **See-Think-Wonder:** Encourages learners to make careful and thoughtful observations and sets the stage for inquiry.
- **Think, Puzzle, Explore:** Activates prior knowledge, generates ideas and curiosity, and sets the stage for deeper inquiry.
- **Chalk Talk:** Helps learners consider ideas, questions, or problems by silently writing responses to a prompt and making connections to the responses of others.
- **Compass Points:** Helps learners explore various sides of a proposition or idea before expressing an opinion about it.
- **Question Starts:** Gives learners practice developing good questions.

Synthesizing ideas

- **Headlines:** Helps learners capture the essence of an idea, topic, discussion, or event.
- **CSI: Color-Symbol-Image:** Aids learners in distilling the essence of ideas nonverbally.
- **Generate-Sort-Connect-Elaborate:** Helps learners organize their understanding of a topic through concept mapping.
- **Connect-Extend-Challenge:** Helps learners connect new ideas to prior knowledge.
- **I used to think... Now I think...:** Assists learners in reflecting on how and why their thinking has changed.

Digging deeper

- **What Makes You Say That?:** Promotes evidence-based reasoning by asking learners to share their interpretations.
- **Circle of Viewpoints:** Facilitates exploring diverse perspectives.
- **Step In-Step Out-Step Back** (see also, **Step Inside**): Promotes developing a disposition to take social and cultural perspectives responsibly.
- **Word-Phrase-Sentence:** Helps learners capture the essence of a text.

Other

- **Think-Pair-Share:** Promotes learners' understanding through active reasoning and explanation.
- **The 3 Ys:** Encourages learners to develop intrinsic motivation to investigate a topic by uncovering its significance in different contexts.

- **Circles of Action:** Supports learners to move beyond understanding and take action.
- **Me-You-Space-Time (MYST):** Helps teachers prepare for making thinking visible.
- **Ladder of Feedback:** Supports learners in giving and receiving feedback.

Tips for Using this Tool

- You can find the routines at: http://www.pz.harvard.edu/thinking-routines.
- The routines are designed to foster students' content knowledge and thinking skills and dispositions across subjects. They can be used over and over again to help learners build knowledge as they exchange, build on, or disagree with each other's ideas.
- Your learning goals should drive the use of thinking routines, rather than the other way around.
- The routines are intended to become one of the regular ways that students go about the process of learning in the classroom, rather than "another thing to do."
- Use a small number of routines consistently, rather than multiple routines once or twice so they become part of learners' thinking patterns.
- Choosing which material to use with a thinking routine is as important as choosing which routine to use.
- Many of the routines are best carried out in a group. Even if a routine can be completed individually, it is useful to share individual responses in a small or large group.
- Routines can be carried out in person or virtually. Online, students might post thoughts in a shared online space so they can review classmates' thoughts and discuss implications.
- Most of the routines exist in both English and Spanish.
- See https://pz.harvard.edu/thinking-routines for additional routines. PZ routines include routines to explore objects and systems, works of art and music, possibilities and analogies, perspective-taking, controversies and dilemmas, and global thinking.

Notes

- These **Thinking routines** were mainly developed by Project Zero researchers.
- Chalk talk is adapted from Hilton Smith of the Foxfire Fund.
- Think-Pair-Share is adapted from: Lyman, F. T. (1981). "The Responsive Classroom Discussion: The Inclusion of All Students," in A. Anderson (Ed.), Mainstreaming Digest (pp. 109–113). College Park: University of Maryland Press.

Creating a Culture of Risk-taking

Conversations, norms, and routines that normalize risk-taking, making mistakes, and experimentation

Facilitate conversations to unpack the meaning of terms like "risk-taking" and "making mistakes."

- Ask, "What comes to mind when you think about the word [risk-taking]?"
- Record learners' responses on a large piece of paper. Afterward, ask them what they notice or wonder about.
- Revisit the page from time to time to see if new insights or questions have emerged. (See also, Cracking Open Words[1] and the Making Meaning Routine[2].)

Discuss examples to explore the relationship between risk-taking and learning.

Choose a provocative video, image, or artifact that shows humans or animals taking risks (see suggested video clips on p.2). Then facilitate an open-ended conversation about play, learning, and risk-taking, using one or more of the following prompts:

- What do you notice? Point to what makes you say that.
- Where did you see the play taking place? Where did you see learning taking place? What makes you say that?
- Does everyone agree? Who has another point of view?
- What is the connection between learning and risk-taking? Learning and play?
- What are your own experiences of taking risks? What did you learn?

Use language, routines, and rituals that encourage risk-taking and mistakes.

- In collaboration with your learners, develop classroom norms or rules that highlight risk-taking and experimentation, e.g., "*We take risks (or make mistakes) to help ourselves and others learn.*"
- Create a "mistake of the day/week" ritual, in which you and the children nominate, record, and celebrate mistakes and the learning that follows. For example, ask children at the end of each day/week, "*What was a helpful mistake you made today/this week? What did you learn?*"
- Invent playful language with children to describe unexpected or surprising moments of learning from mistakes or risk-taking, e.g., "oopsie," "beautiful mistakes," and "do-overs".

Appendix

- Ask two students to serve as "risk observers" to record notable moments of risk-taking or mistake-making to revisit with the class. Discuss when and where risk-taking and mistake-making seem to support learning.
- Start a "beautiful" or "favorite mistakes" wall, either in or outside the classroom.
- Facilitate a brainstorming session to harvest ideas about a question or problem, with a ground-rule that you cannot critique another person's idea.

Tips for Using this Tool

- Creating a culture of experimentation and risk-taking is an ongoing process.
- Model risk-taking and making mistakes in your teaching (perhaps even making mistakes on purpose!). Be transparent when trying something new or unknown. Talk through making a mistake out loud—how you feel about it, what you learned, and what you might do differently next time.
- It is perfectly normal for children and adults to experience anxiety when trying something new. Name the anxiety and reassure learners that feeling anxious shows they care about what they are attempting.
- Suggested video clips about risk-taking:

Human Risk-taking

- Choose an excerpt from this 16-minute film of children and adults deciding whether to jump off a 10-meter diving board (The New York Times; Jan. 30, 2017). Available at: https://youtu.be/5QMlIjSnt_E.
- A six-minute YouTube video of learners in an Anji Play kindergarten (China) jumping off a plank on top of an oil drum. Available at: https://youtu.be/cuksYrro7Cc (video by Anji Play; Jan. 9, 2018)
- YouTube clips from the British TV show "Educating Yorkshire," in which a student overcomes his stammer with the help of his teacher.
    - End-of-Year School Speech: https://youtu.be/aM4mDJYDgBE (video by Our Stories; Jul. 23, 2020).
    - Student and Teacher Retelling the Story: https://youtu.be/B3yuE8jFkwc (video by Our Stories; Dec. 14, 2020).

Animal Risk-taking

- A one-minute YouTube video of a crow using a bottle cap to slide down a snowy roof: https://youtu.be/3dWw9GLcOeA (video by Aleksey Vnukov; Jan. 12, 2012).
- Choose an excerpt from the 50-minute YouTube wildlife documentary, "Animals Like Us: Animal Play": https://youtu.be/WImKDJuaCmU (video by Best Documentary; May 5, 2016).
- A two-minute YouTube video of lion cubs playing in their pride: https://youtu.be/TeCkm-BEZ-8 (video by Discovery; Jun. 4, 2015).

Notes

1 **Cracking Open Words** is an Inspiring Inventiveness tool, co-developed by the Opal School (US) and Project Zero. Available at: http://www.pz.harvard.edu/resources/cracking-open-words.
2 The **Making Meaning Routine** is from the book, *The Power of Making Thinking Visible*, by Ron Ritchhart and Mark Church. Available at: https://openingpaths.org/blog/wp-content/uploads/2018/03/Making-Meaning-Routine-Ron-Ritchhart-CoT.pdf.

Appendix

Imaginative Spark Generator

Questions to inspire imaginative thinking

Open-ended questions that draw on the imagination

- Use the following Question Starts[1] to help you and your students brainstorm interesting questions about a topic:

■ Why...?	■ What are the reasons...?	■ Suppose that...?
■ What if...?	■ What is the purpose of...?	■ What if we knew...?
■ Imagine...	■ How would it be different if...?	■ What would change if...

- **Ask questions that invite children to take different perspectives,** such as, *"What would the weather report sound like from a [worm's] perspective?" "What would [the exhaust pipe] say if it could talk?"*
- **Show the class or a small group a photograph, object, or drawing, and ask them what they think it is.** Have students ask each other, in turn, "What else could it be?"[2] Afterward, ask them to reflect on what they learned about using their imaginations.
- **When studying the natural or physical environment, invite students to use their imagination;** e.g., when learning about animal habitats, ask students to create their own animal that might thrive in a particular environment. When studying transportation, ask students to design new ways they could get from home to school.

Provocations that trigger the imagination

- **Put a work of art, intriguing quote, or provocative question related to the topic you are studying on the wall** to inspire wonder in the classroom. Provide post-it notes and a pencil for students to share their thinking and wondering over time.
- **Juxtapose two items or ideas that are not typically paired.** For example, pair cut and dying flowers with a bean seed sprouting or a growing plant, or pair voting laws and sports rules. Ask students what they notice and what they imagine about possible connections.

- **Choose an object or system related to a topic you are studying** (e.g., the body, an automobile factory, or a branch of government). Ask learners to identify its parts, purposes, and the people who interact with it. Pose one or more of the following questions: "In what ways could it be made more effective? ...efficient? ...ethical? ...beautiful?" (See "Imagine If..."[3] thinking routine.)

Tips for using this tool

- Play is activated by just the right amount of novelty and surprise. Too little novelty can lead to boredom; too much can create anxiety—monitor learner engagement when posing the above questions or provocations over time. Involve learners in deciding what to repeat and vary.
- Other examples of questions that invite perspective-taking include the following: "*How might [your grandchildren] respond to this question 50 years from now?*" "*What would [the flower] look like if you were high up on a ladder?*" "*What would you ask [an author/a scientist/an artist] about their [book/theories/creations]?*"
- Brainstorm additions to the list above with your colleagues and/or students.
- If learners develop a concept or theory based on their imagination that does not reflect reality, rather than correcting them, hold them accountable to the logic or parameters of the task or question within their own description.
- Design is everywhere! Ask learners, in pairs or trios, to go on a Design Hunt[4] around the classroom, school, or neighborhood to find designed objects or systems. Ask them to photograph or sketch the object or system and share: (1) what they notice; (2) what they think the designer considered when creating the object or system; (3) how they might redesign it and why.

Notes

1 **Question Starts** is a thinking routine from Project Zero (also available in Spanish). Available at: http://www.pz.harvard.edu/resources/creative-question-starts.
2 **What Else Could It Be?** is an Inspiring Inventiveness tool, co-developed by the Opal School (US) and Project Zero. Available at: http://www.pz.harvard.edu/resources/what-else-could-it-be.
3 **"Imagine If..."** is a thinking routine developed by the Agency by Design project at Project Zero (also available in Spanish). Available at: http://www.pz.harvard.edu/resources/imagine-if.
4 **Design Hunt** was developed by the Agency by Design project at Project Zero. See http://agencybydesign.org/sites/default/files/AbD%20Design%20Hunt%20.pdf.

Appendix

Supporting Learners with Conflict and Frustration

A protocol, principles, and teaching moves to support learners in navigating conflict

A protocol for addressing conflict during play[1]

- *Validate the emotion:* "I see you are really upset. How did you feel when___?"
- *Slow things down:* "What were you trying to do? Tell me more about___." "Let's take a minute of silence for everyone to jot down their thoughts and feelings."
- *Encourage listening:* "I heard you say____." "Did you hear what__said?" "What is a question you might ask__to better understand where they're coming from?"
- *Support problem-solving:* "How can you imagine this problem being solved? What ideas do you have?" "What's another strategy you can try?"
- *Reflect on what just happened:* "What were you hoping would happen?" "What surprised you?" "Do you see ways to resolve this conflict?"

Principles to keep in mind

- Children come to school with a variety of experiences with conflict, some of which may include trauma. Responding to each child's individual needs and histories is critical. Make a habit of asking yourself, *"What is happening for this child?"* rather than *"What is wrong with this child?"*
- Remember that you are not there to take away the hard feelings but to help learners stay in a productive and safe space where they can experience difficult emotions and still take risks to solve problems. You can support this process by approaching it with a sense of curiosity and inquiry, rather than judgment.
- Strong emotions can sometimes interfere with clear thinking. Cooling off should not be a punishment, but a powerful and responsible decision for the good of everyone.
- If children seem particularly reluctant to take risks, try to figure out the source of their resistance. Is it fear? Lack of practice with persistence? Prior experiences with failure?

Possible teaching moves

- With your students, develop a set of norms for your classroom community. Consider norms such as, "It is OK to disagree" and the "24-hour rule" ("If someone says something that bothers you, you have 24 hours to decide either to talk to that person or to make your peace with the comment").

- Encourage a culture of "Do-Overs."[2] Begin by inviting children who struggle with collaboration to participate in a Do-Over—a low-risk way to reset or restart something that went wrong. Do-Overs are applicable to any kind of physical or emotional challenge—unnecessary physicality, hurtful words, miscommunications or misunderstandings, or exclusionary behavior.
- Ask students to reflect on experiences of conflict: "*What do you think happened?*" "*What did you learn?*" "*What would you like to do differently in the future?*" Invite students to share their reflections with the group so others can learn from their experience. (You can model working through frustration or conflict by sharing your own experiences, which can give learners language and strategies for coping with strong emotions.)
- Make (or ask children to make) and post a menu of children's problem-solving strategies, with visual icons created by the children. Invite children to practice a strategy in the absence of conflict. Post compelling quotes from children about conflict in the classroom.

Tips for using this tool

- When learners are genuinely engaged in their work and ideas, negotiating ideas and resources with others, learning through play can open the door to strong emotions. Yet conflict and frustration can also be opportunities for learning. Use this tool to support and encourage learners when playful learning gets hard.
- For younger learners, if you notice conflict, move closer physically, but still give them a chance to work out the problem before intervening. A quick way to make sure everyone feels heard afterward is to ask the child(ren) in distress for a signal of two thumbs up, to the side, or down, about how they're feeling.
- For older learners, peers can often be more successful than adults in helping students resolve conflict. You might create a "peacekeeper" role and enlist students in negotiating and mediating conflicts for their classmates.

Notes

1 Many of the questions and tips in the "Protocol for Addressing Conflict during Play" come from Making Friends with Conflict, a tool created by the Inspiring Agents of Change Project at Project Zero. Available at http://www.pz.harvard.edu/resources/making-friends-with-conflict.

2 Do-Overs was created by the Inspiring Agents of Change Project at Project Zero. Available at: http://www.pz.harvard.edu/resources/do-over.

Index

Note: *Italicized* and **bold** pages refer to figures and tables respectively, and page numbers followed by "n" refer to notes.

4Rs, in Standards Based Curriculum 122

ableism: in education 49–50; linked to play and assessment 51–52
Abry, T. 29
Achi game 121–122; enhancing children's participation in 128–129; Ghanaian curriculum requirement and 131; playing in primary two classroom (private school) 127; and playing rules 125, *126*; post-game reflections 129–131, *130*; redesigning 126–128, *127*
Adult Ego Development stages 152, **153**
adult *vs.* child play 186
adventurous play *see* risky play
agency 2, 18, 66–67, 78, 79, 81, 83, 156
Aimee's playful journey 10–14
ambiguity, playful leadership and 154, 162
animal risk-taking 194
AnjiPlay approach 103
apon bhubon (own world) 112
assessment 1, 12, 48, 50, 123, 145; ableism linked to play and 51–52; of children's development 21; of children's play and learning 52; risk 94, 97; school readiness 28, 31

Bangladesh: BRAC Play Labs in 3, 101–119; government primary schools BRAC Play Labs in 115–117; *see also* BRAC Play Labs
Barker, B. 30
Barker, J. 150

Bassok, D. 29
Biddulph, J. 6, 157, 185
Blaskova, L. J. 54
board games, mathematical development and 123–125
books sharing, children's 35–36
Booth, A. 30
BRAC Institute of Educational Development (BRAC IED) 101–102, *102*
BRAC Non-Formal Primary Education (NFPE) model 103
BRAC Play Labs 101–102, *102*, *104*, *108*; benefits of 118; core components of 102–103; COVID-19 pandemic and 115, 119; curriculum 105; a day in 106–108, *108*; decoration materials and 112–113, *113*; definition of 102–103; design of spaces and materials 110–114; developing curriculum 106; duties of play leaders 109–110; in government primary schools 115–117; impact of 118; implementation of *117*, 117–118; inspiration behind 103; key characteristics of 103–104; outdoor play spaces 113–114, *114*; parents and community engagement in 114–115, 117; role of play leaders/facilitators in 108–110, *109*; schedule **106**; theoretical underpinning of 104–105; toys in 111–112, *111–112*
British Children's Play Survey 88
Bronfenbrenner, U. 104–105
Brooker, L. 29
Burnard, P. 157

Cambridge Primary Review 14
Carris, J. 185
Carr, S. 152
case examples: of play 69–81, *70–71*, *74*, *76–77*, **78**, *79*, *81*; of playful leadership 158–161
Center Management Committees 115
child/children: learn through play 134–135; play 185–187; in playful learning tasks 24; with special needs and disabilities 24
child-friendly spatial design 103
children: ability to navigate friendships 30; early school adjustment 29–33; family lives 31; feeling able and enthusiastic for school 30; having supportive environments with opportunities to play 30; ideas and dialogue through role-play 82–83, **82–83**; intrinsic motivation 32; language development 35–36; mathematical learning 121–132; outdoor play 23; physical play 36; pretend play 36–37; right to play 1, 3; risky play 87–88; role-play in learning 74–78; rough-and-tumble play 36; school readiness 27–29, *31*, *32*; school readiness, poverty and inequalities in 37–38; self-regulation 36; sharing books 35–36; socio-emotional development 36–37; with speech, language and communication needs (SLCN) 54–55; voice/voices 60, 63
children's development (cognitive, socio-emotional, physical) 28, 33, 35, 67, 101, 105, 182
Children's Thoughts about School Study 29–30
Church, M. 195n2
classroom environment 23
Classroom Handbook 59
Coe, R. 83–84
collaborative learning 177–179
Colombia, indicators of playful learning at 173, *173*
Coltman, P. 6, 67
Columbia University 118
community 24, 27, 33, 40, 59, 98, 101, 111, 143–145, 148, 162, 177, 186; engagement (*see* community engagement)
community engagement 103, 114–115, 117
community spaces in curriculum 143–144
conflict during play 198–199
Connolly, M. 150
COOL (Choosing Our Own Learning) Time 18–19
COVID-19 pandemic 15; BRAC Play Labs and 115, 119
Cracking Open Words 195n1

Creating Learning without Limits *156*, 156–157
creative learning, definition of 157
creativities 4, 6, 8, 17, 147–148, 157
Crenshaw, K. 53
curiosity 83–84
curriculum: designing 6, 101; Ghanaian standards based 122–123; goals 68; implications of, in Ghanaian classrooms 123; utilizing community spaces in 143–144

Dangerous Elements 87, **87**
Dangerous Tools 87, **87**
Danniels, E. 56, 61
Davey Smith, G. 28
Davies, N. M. 28
Denmark, indicators of playful learning at 173, *173–174*; *see also* International School of Billund (Denmark)
Design Hunt 197n4
Desmond Tutu 173
DeVries, R. 124
Disappear/Get Lost 87, **88**
disruptive experiences 154
distributed leadership 149
Dockett, S. 29
Dodd, H. F. 87, 89
Do-Overs 193, 199, 199n2
Dorling, D. 28
Doyle, O. 38–39
Durning, A. 159–160

education: inclusive (*see* inclusive education); systemic racism in 53
Effective Provision of Pre-School Education (EPPE) project 37–38
Einarsdottir, J. 29
Emilia, R. 23
empowerment 139, 173
Encyclopaedia on Early Childhood Development 41
engagement 83–84
England: principles of school curriculum in 18–19; two-form entry school in 5
Erikson, E. 104–105
experience relates to children's perceptions 57–58
experiential learning 1

Fabian, H. 29
facilitation, in inclusive play-based learning 57
family 27, 30, 31, 33–34, 40, 41, 61
Favazza, P. C. 60

Fertig, M. 150
free play 87, 107
friendships 3, 24, 30, 49, 55

Ghanaian Standards Based Curriculum 122–123
Gibbs, G. 129–131; reflection model 129–131, *130*
Gibson, J. L. 54
Gilbride, N. 152
golper bhubon (story world) 112
Gough, J. 124
'grace and courtesy' approach 21
Grantham-McGregor, S. 40
Great Denham 23
Great Heights 87, **87**
group play activities, in BRAC Play Lab 111–113
guided play 18, 21, 68, 69, 78

Harrison, L. 29
Hawkins, M. 150
Helicopter Stories 23
High Speed 87, **87**
Hirsh-Pasek, K. 68
home-visiting programme 38, 40
human risk-taking 194

I CAN (children's communication charity) 61
imaginative play *see* pretend play
imaginative spark generator 196–197
imaginative thinking 196–197
"Imagine If…" 197n3
Immordino-Yang, M. 181
inclusive education 48, 51, 54, 61, 68; *see also* inclusive play-based learning
inclusive language 49–56; ableism linked to play and assessment 51–52; history of 51; and peer relationships 54–56; representation and 52–53; and well-being 53–54
inclusive play-based learning 56–58, *57*; designing 58, 59–60; experience 57–58; facilitation 57; getting help from peers in 60–61; outcomes 58; resources and readings 62–63
inequalities, in children's school readiness 37–38
Infant/Toddler Environment Rating Scale®, Revised (ITERS-R™) 59
instructional leadership 149–150
International School of Billund (Denmark) 134; indicators of playful learning at 173, *174*; playful curriculum 135–136; playing ground in 135–136; rules on playground at *168*, 168–169

intersectionality 53
Isaacs, S. 51

James, C. 150, 152
Jensen, H. 18
Jordan, P. 29

Keating, I. 29
Kennair, L. E. O. 89
knowledge-building conversations 191–192
Kuschner, D. 171–172

Ladd, G. W. 28
language 2, 33, 61, 75–76, 78, 101, 124, 131, 140, 156, 178, 193–194; comparisons *50*; development 35–36, 105; difficulties 49; inclusive (*see* inclusive language)
Latham, S. 29
Lavrysen, A. 91
learning: definition of 170; facilitator-child relationship in 118; Froebelian approaches to teaching and 21; hit-and-miss approach to 17–18; importance of play for 17; inclusive play-based 56–58, *57*; nuances and complexities of classroom 84; play-based approaches to 18; problem-based 135; project-based 135
Lees, E. 49
LEGO Foundation 4–5
Lester, K. J. 87, 89
Let's Think (Cognitive Acceleration) 21
License to Hack Cards *188*, 188–190, *190*
Lillard, A. S. 37
LoCasale-Crouch, J. 29
Loevinger, J. 151
London: play assessment tool 12; school in 5
'Look Who's Talking: Eliciting the Voices of Children from Birth to Seven' project 60

make-believe play *see* pretend play
Making Meaning Routine 195n2
Mancala (mathematical-rich board game) 132
Mantle of the Expert 23
Mardell, B. 137
Margetts, K. 29
material development workshops 115
mathematical development, board games and 123–125
mathematical learning/teaching: Achi game in 121–122; children's 121–132; redesigning Achi for 126–128, *127*
Mavers, D. 29

medical model terminology *verses* neurodiversity 50
meta-analysis 35, 42
Morris, T. T. 28
Mo Scéal (My Story) from the Irish National Council for Curriculum and Assessment 42
Moss, P. 170, 177
motivation 83–84
movements, defined 69
Murphy, K. 51
Murray, E. 29
Murray, L. 36

neurodivergent 50
neurodiverse 50
notion of an enabling space 157
Nursery World: Children's perspectives on starting school 42

O'Farrelly, C. 30
Outdoor Play and Learning (OPAL) 91
outdoor play 23, 169; children in 105, *108*; equipment 114; playground design 116

PACE (Playfulness, Acceptance, Curiosity and Empathy) approach 13
parental sensitivity 33–34
parent and community engagement 103
parent-child interactions 33–34; play in 34–37
parent-child pretend play 37
parenting programmes: Preparing for Life Programme 38–39; Reach Up early childhood programme 40–41; video-feedback intervention to promote Positive Parenting and Sensitive Discipline 39–40
parent meetings and parenting education 115
parents' view of school readiness 29
Parker, R. 56–58
pedagogical documentation 171
pedagogy 1, 2, 5–6, 116–117, 135; *see also* pedagogy of play (PoP)
pedagogy of play (PoP) 1, 2, 134, 167–181; overview of 169–171, **170**; principles of **171**, 171–172; Project Zero and 135; purpose of 136–137; tools for 184
A Pedagogy of Play: Supporting Playful Learning in Classrooms and Schools (Mardell) 137
PEDAL Research Centre: Play and the transition to school 42
peer-to-peer listening 21
Pemberton, E. 53
Perry, B. 29

Peters, S. 29
physical injury risks 88
physical play 18, 36
Piaget, J. 21, 104–105
play 185–187; as activity 67; as additional time 67–68; adults intervened in 19; adult *vs.* child 186–187; case examples of 69–81, *70–71, 74, 76–77,* **78**, *79, 81*; children choices in 23; children from LBU to 55; children's outdoor 23; conflict during 198–199; crucial element of 21; definition of 68–69, 101, 170; designing, in primary education 66–84; as discovery only 68; elements of 70; emotions generated through 181; essential ingredients of 5; examples of 69–70, *70*; five 'trails' for 19, *20*; at home 27–42; importance for learning 17; individual strategies 19, *20*; issues in 17; learning through 2, 18; misconception of 1; moments of 39; with objects and spatial reasoning 35; as only something unstructured 68; in parent-child interactions 34–37; pedagogical principles to 24–25; in primary education 48–63; quality learning through 57; and school 134–146; school leadership in 147–165; social and cultural aspects of 105; storytelling approach in 23–24; theory and research into 67; unstructured 68; view of 18
play age, importance of 105
play-based curriculum 19
play-based pedagogical approach 6
play consortium 103
play equipment, design of 113–114, *114*
playful coaching 135, 137, 140–142, 144, 146; *see also* teaching
playful enquiry 4–15
playful environments study group *168*
playful leadership 2, 147–165; ambiguity and 154, 162; case examples of 158–161; concept of 162; creative learning and *156*, 156–158; documented example of *156*, 156–157; features of 154–155; moment of play about 148–149, *149*; as new school order 162–164; qualities of *156*, 156–157; school leadership practice 149–155
playful learning: classroom practices and strategies 175–181, **176**, *178*; collaborative learning 177–179; at Colombia *173*; cross-cultural indicators of *175*; definition of 170; at Denmark 173, *173–174*; empowering learners 176–177; encouraging imaginative thinking 180; experimentation and risk-taking 179–180; future of 144–146, *145*;

indicators of 137–140, *138*; License to Hack Cards and *188*, 188–190, *190*; menu of routines for 190–192; risk-taking and 193–194; in schools 172–175; at South Africa *173*; at US *173*
playful learning activities 54
playfulness, as teaching approach 83–84
playful participatory research (PPR) 141, 170, 171
Play in Education, Development and Learning (PEDAL) Research Centre 1, 4–5, 10, 19, 42, 67
playing with objects 18
playing with rules 18
play leaders/facilitators 103; Basic Training (including SEL training) for 110; Refresher Training sessions for 110; role of 108–110, *109*
Play with Impact 87, **88**
Position statement from the Educational Transitions and Change Research Group 42
poverty, in children's school readiness 37–38
Powell, A. 124
The Power of Making Thinking Visible (Ritchhart and Church) 195n2
Preparing for Life Programme 38–39
pretend play 36–37; in toddlers and preschoolers 37
primary education: designing play in 66–84; inclusive language 49–56, *50*; mathematical understandings in 121–132; planning and implementation 58–59; play in 48–63
primary schools, risky play in 86–98
problem-based learning 135
professional development 10, 11, 18–19, 137, 140–142, 145–146, 158
project: Children's Thoughts about School Study 29–30; Effective Provision of Pre-School Education (EPPE) 37–38; *see also specific projects*
project-based learning approach 23, 135
Project Zero Harvard Graduate School of Education 136, 169, *174*, 194, 195n1, 197n1–2, 199n1–2
Protocol for Addressing Conflict during Play 198, 199n1
Pyle, A. 56, 61

QR code 23

Ramani, G. B. 124
Ramchandani, P. 10
Ramey, C. T. 28
Ramey, S. L. 28

randomised controlled trial 29–30, 38–39, 42
Reach Up early childhood programme 40–41
Rees, T. 150
Refresher Training sessions 110
Reggio-Emilia approach 103
Relationship Education, Relationships and Sex Education, and Health Education (RSHE) 55
representation and inclusive practice 52–53
richness of play 3
Rinaldi, C. 170, 177
risk assessment 94, 97
risk benefit assessment (RBA) 94
risk-taking: animal 194; human 194; playful learning and 193–194
risky play: categories of 87–88, **87–88**; changes in 96–97; definition of 86–87, 86–88, **87–88**; facilitating 96; happenings of school supporting 90–91; importance of 88–89; monitor and review 97; national guidance on 94; opportunities for, in schools 92–97; phobia and 89; in primary schools 86–98; processes in 93–94; research at schools for 91–92; in schools 89–90; schools policy on 93; seeking parent and staff support in 95–96; shared vision and shared values in 92–93
Ritchhart, R. 195n2
Rittel, H. W. 151–152
Roberts, J. 29
role-play 18; children's ideas and dialogue through 82–83, **82–83**
ronger bhubon (art world) 112
rough-and-tumble play 36, 87, **87**

Sandseter, E. B. 87–89
scaffolding play 13
school(s): happenings of, supporting risky play 90–91; and play 134–146; risky play in 89–90
school 360 values *22*
school leader: responsibilities of 150–151; types of problems faced by 151–154; wicked problem and 151–154; *see also* school leadership
school leadership: 4 I's 150; complexity theory 150–151; definitions of 149–150; in play 147–165; qualities of playfulness in *161*, 161–162; wickedness and 151–154
school readiness: assessments 31; children's 27–29, *31*, *32*; poverty and inequalities in children's 37–38; resources for 41–42; role of families in 33–38; teachers and parents' views of 29
See-Think-Wonder tool *141*, 141–142

sense of self-efficacy 32
shopner bhubon (dream world) 111
Sicart, M. 155–156
Siegler, R. S. 124
Smith, J. A. 40
Smith, P. K. 68–69
social construction 21
social interactivity 70
socialisation development 13
Social Learning and Collaboration in Schools: Learning to Thrive through Play 11
social relationships 5
South Africa, indicators of playful learning at 173, *173*, 178–179
spaces for play 4, 24, 30, 59, 90, 101, 110–111, 113
spatial design for child development 119
special educational needs and disabilities (SEND) 49, 51, 162–163
Spinka, M. 89
stay-and-play sessions 97
STEAM lessons (STEM) 8
storytelling approach, in play 23–24
Storytelling Schools 23
supportive holding environment 154–155
symbolic play 18
systematic review 34, 38, 42
systemic racism in education 53

Taking Outdoor Play Seriously (TOPS) programme 90, 91
Tanzania 101
Tatlow-Golden, M. 30
teacher(s): interactions with children 21; view of school readiness 29; *see also* teaching
teacher-child relationship 33
teaching: about behaviours to children 21; 'grace and courtesy' approach in 21; literacy 23–24; mathematics 124–125; of oracy 21; as professional development model 140–142, *141*
teaching approach, playfulness as 83–84

team games 14
Temple, O. 124
TRAIL (Teachers Reflecting on Agency in Learning) materials 19
transformational leadership 150

Uganda 101
UK: learning through play in 2, 5; playful learning opportunities in 6
United Nations' World Conference on Special Education Needs in Salamanca (1994) 51
United States, indicators of playful learning at 173, *173*
University of Cambridge Primary School (UCPS) 1, 4, 6, 157; case study 11–14; culture 157; curriculum design 6–8, *7*; educators at 8; guiding principles 6–7; playful enquiry 6–7, *9*; research to practice 10
A University's Challenge, Cambridge's Primary School for the Nation (Gronn and Biddulph) 6
unremitting contradictions 171
unstructured play 68

Vicarious Risk 87, **88**
video-feedback intervention to promote Positive Parenting and Sensitive Discipline (VIPP-SD) 39–40
Voice 21 (national oracy charity) 21
Vollstedt, R. 68–69
volunteerism 115
Vygotsky, L. S. 21, 104–105

Wall, K. 60
Webber, M. M. 151–152
Weisberg, D. 170
What Else Could It Be? 197n2
Wheeler, J. 160
Whitebread, D. 6, 67
White, R. 69
wicked problem, school leader and 151–154
Wright, S. 59

205

For Product Safety Concerns and Information please contact our EU representative GPSR@taylorandfrancis.com
Taylor & Francis Verlag GmbH, Kaufingerstraße 24, 80331 München, Germany

www.ingramcontent.com/pod-product-compliance
Lightning Source LLC
Chambersburg PA
CBHW060300240426

43661CB00060B/2847